The International in Security, Security in the International

International Relations continues to come under fire for its relative absence of international perspectives. In this exciting new volume, Pinar Bilgin encourages readers to consider both why and how 'non-core' geo-cultural sites allow us to think differently about key aspects of global politics.

Seeking to further debates surrounding thinking beyond the 'West'/'non-West' divide, this book analyses how scholarship on, and conceptions of, the international outside core contexts are tied up with peripheral actors' search for security. Accordingly, Bilgin looks at core/periphery dynamics not only in terms of the production of knowledge in the production of IR scholarship, or material threats, but also peripheral actors' conceptions of the international in terms of 'standard of civilisation' and their more contemporary guises, which she terms as 'hierarchy in anarchical society'. The first three chapters provide a critical overview of the limits of 'our' theorising about IR and security, as well as a discussion on the track record of critical approaches to IR and security in addressing those limits. The following three chapters offer one way of addressing the limits of 'our' theorising about IR and security: by inquiring into the international in security, security in the international. Each of these chapters makes a theoretical point and explores this in a spotlight section that further illustrates the point to aid student learning.

A genuinely innovative contribution to this rapidly emerging field within IR, this book is essential reading for students and scholars of Critical Security, International Relations Theory and Global IR.

Pinar Bilgin is Professor of International Relations at Bilkent University, Turkey. She is the author of *Regional Security in the Middle East: A Critical Perspective* (Routledge, 2005) and co-editor of the *Routledge Handbook of International Political Sociology* (2017).

Worlding Beyond the West

Series Editors:
Arlene B. Tickner, *Universidad de los Andes, Bogotá*, **Ole Wæver**, *University of Copenhagen, Denmark*, **David Blaney**, *Macalester College, USA* and **Inanna Hamati-Ataya**, *Aberystwyth University, UK*

Historically, the International Relations (IR) discipline has established its boundaries, issues, and theories based upon Western experience and traditions of thought. This series explores the role of geocultural factors, institutions, and academic practices in creating the concepts, epistemologies, and methodologies through which IR knowledge is produced. This entails identifying alternatives for thinking about the "international" that are more in tune with local concerns and traditions outside the West. But it also implies provincializing Western IR and empirically studying the practice of producing IR knowledge at multiple sites within the so-called 'West'.

1. International Relations Scholarship Around the World
Edited by Arlene B. Tickner and Ole Wæver

2. Thinking the International Differently
Edited by Arlene B. Tickner and David L. Blaney

3. International Relations in France
Writing between Discipline and State
Henrik Breitenbauch

4. Claiming the International
Edited by Arlene B. Tickner and David L. Blaney

5. Border Thinking on the edges of the West
Crossing Over the Hellespont
Andrew Davison

6. Worlding Brazil
Intellectuals, Identity and Security
Laura Lima

7. International Relations and American Dominance
A Diverse Discipline
Helen Turton

8. Global Indigenous Politics
A Subtle Revolution
Sheryl Lightfoot

9. Constructing a Chinese School of International Relations
Ongoing Debates and Sociological Realities
Edited by Yongjin Zhang and Teng-Chi Chang

10. The International in Security, Security in the International
Pinar Bilgin

The International in Security, Security in the International

Pinar Bilgin

LONDON AND NEW YORK

First published 2017
by Routledge
2 Park Square, Milton Park, Abingdon, Oxon OX14 4RN

and by Routledge
711 Third Avenue, New York, NY 10017

Routledge is an imprint of the Taylor & Francis Group, an informa business

© 2017 Pinar Bilgin

The right of Pinar Bilgin to be identified as author of this work has been
asserted by him/her in accordance with sections 77 and 78 of the Copyright,
Designs and Patents Act 1988.

All rights reserved. No part of this book may be reprinted or reproduced or
utilised in any form or by any electronic, mechanical, or other means, now
known or hereafter invented, including photocopying and recording, or in
any information storage or retrieval system, without permission in writing
from the publishers.

Trademark notice: Product or corporate names may be trademarks or registered
trademarks, and are used only for identification and explanation without
intent to infringe.

British Library Cataloguing in Publication Data
A catalogue record for this book is available from the British Library

Library of Congress Cataloging in Publication Data
Names: Bilgin, Pinar, 1971- author.
Title: The international in security, security in the international /
Pinar Bilgin.
Description: New York, NY : Routledge, 2016. | Series: Worlding beyond
the west | Includes bibliographical references and index.
Identifiers: LCCN 2016003348| ISBN 9781138925311 (hardback) |
ISBN 9781315683812 (ebook) | ISBN 9781138925328 (pbk.)
Subjects: LCSH: International relations--Philosophy. | Security,
International--Philosophy. | East and West--Philosophy.
Classification: LCC JZ1305 .B55 2016 | DDC 355/.0330001--dc23
LC record available at https://lccn.loc.gov/2016003348

ISBN: 978-1-138-92531-1 (hbk)
ISBN: 978-1-138-92532-8 (pbk)
ISBN: 978-1-31568-381-2 (ebk)

Typeset in Bembo
by Taylor & Francis Books

Contents

Acknowledgement		vi
	Introduction	1
1	Limits of theorising about IR and security	16
2	Critical theorising about IR and security	41
3	How to access others' conceptions of the international	84
4	Inquiring into security in the international	106
5	Inquiring into the international in security	128
6	Civilisation, dialogue, in/security	159
	Conclusion	176
Index		185

Acknowledgement

I would like to thank the following people and institutions: Ole Wæver, Arlene Tickner and David Blaney for nurturing this book from the very beginning; Bilkent University for granting a much needed study leave; Department of War Studies at King's College London for providing me an institutional home; Vivienne Jabri for her generous mentorship; Claudia Aradau, Didier Bigo and Peter Busch for their gracious welcome and support during my study leave in London where most of this book was written; Anna Agathangelou, İlker Aytürk, Tarak Barkawi, Zeynep Gülşah Çapan, Siba Grovogui, Monica Herz, L.H.M. Ling, Mustapha Kamal Pasha and Karen Smith for reading and commenting on all or parts of the manuscript; Thomas Diez, Karin Fierke and Gunther Hellman for inviting me to present my research and receive valuable feedback; Centre for the Resolution of International Conflict (CRIC) at the University of Copenhagen, and Centre for Contemporary Middle East Studies at the University of Southern Denmark for providing intellectual sanctuary during the critical writing-up period; Turkish Academy of Sciences for a GEBİP fellowship, Metin Heper and İlhan Tekeli for mentorship; Ken Booth for introducing me to critical security studies and teaching me how to remain a student even after I had students of my own; and my family for their constant support.

If I remain sceptical about the 'Western'/'non-Western' binary in organising our thinking about the international, blame it on my formation: As a student of IR from Ankara, it took my Ph.D. training in Aberystwyth and encounters with inspiring IR scholars from all around the world at annual meetings of the International Studies Association at various North American locales, to begin to question my 'standard' training in IR, and learn to be curious about 'different' ways of thinking about the international and security.

27 December 2015, Ankara

Introduction

This book seeks to respond to two questions that are interlinked. The first question has kept students of International Relations (IR) busy for a long time:[1] *How to think about security in a world characterised by a multiplicity of inequalities and differences.* Those who sought to reach beyond the limits of our existing theorising about IR and security in responding to this question turned to study IR scholarship in other parts of the world to see what alternatives were on offer. Their findings gave rise to another question: *How is it that IR scholarship in other parts of the world does not reflect the kind of 'difference' found in texts and contexts outside IR and/or North America and Western Europe, but adopts the 'standard' concepts and theories of the field, notwithstanding their well-known limits?*

In the attempt to respond to these questions, I build on the contributions of critical security studies (defined broadly)[2] and draw upon the insights of post-colonial studies[3] to suggest that we inquire into *the international in security, and security in the international.* By inquiring into 'the international in security', I mean reflecting on others' conceptions of the international as we study security. Inquiring into 'security in the international' entails worlding IR to recognise how others' insecurities, which are experienced in a world that is already worlded, have shaped (and have been shaped by) their approaches to the international. By 'others', I mean those who are 'perched on the bottom rung' of world politics (Enloe, 1997) – i.e. those who happen not to be located on or near the top of hierarchies in world politics, enjoying unequal power and influence in shaping various dynamics, including their own portrayal in world politics.

The international, as 'a distinct location of politics' (Jabri, 2013: 2) is the subject matter of IR. Yet, some of its critics consider the academic field of IR as 'an obstacle to a recognition and exploration of [the international], rather than a guide to it' (Seth, 2013: 29, also see Paolini, 1999, Grovogui, 2006). This is mainly because mainstream approaches to IR and security have remained oblivious to the particularity of IR's conception of the international as 'anarchy', and overlooked others' experiences with 'hierarchy' (but see Donnelly, 2006, Wendt and Friedheim, 2009). While inequalities tied up with differences are constitutive of the international, this is not always spelled out in our theorising on IR and security (but see Pasha and Murphy, 2002). IR rests

2   *Introduction*

on a particular conception of the international as a realm of sovereign states enjoying some forms of equality, with little reflection on underlying inequalities, forms of inclusion and exclusion (Walker, 2002).

In those instances when mainstream approaches engage with hierarchy, observed Robert Vitalis (2005: 164), they explain it as a 'natural order among states, where "the strong do what they will, the weak do what they must"'. John Hobson (2014: 559) concurred, noting that mainstream approaches rest upon unacknowledged and under-analysed inequalities between states that are 'derived from various *a priori* Eurocentric-hierarchic conceptions of the "standard of civilisation"'. Relegating one's contemporaries to the past by temporalising difference and spatialising time as such (Fabian, 1983, Paolini, 1999, Hindess, 2007), has had significant implications for shaping the way 'we' understand world politics, 'ourselves' and 'others', with asymmetrical implications for those who happen to be located near the 'bottom rung' (Enloe, 1997) of world hierarchies. Thinking about security in a world characterised by a multiplicity of inequalities and differences entails some way of accessing others' conceptions of the international as shaped by their experiences with hierarchies of world politics.

Accessing others' conceptions of the international has turned out to be a challenging task for students of world politics. Those who looked at IR studies in other parts of the world were thwarted in their efforts as they found that IR scholarship outside North America and Western Europe seems to be shaped by 'similar' concepts and categories as mainstream approaches to IR. As documented in the first volume of the 'Worlding Beyond the West' series (of which this book is a part) (Tickner and Wæver, 2009a), surveys of IR studies in other parts of the world have shown that IR scholarship outside North America and Western Europe is structured around the so-called 'standard' concepts and categories of IR. For instance, a particularly statist and military-focused conception of 'security' prevails in IR scholarship in various parts of the world (Bilgin, 2012, Tickner and Herz, 2012, Zhang, 2007). Such findings are unanticipated given the well-known limits of the concept of 'security', as discussed by students of critical security studies and the global South.[4] These findings are also disheartening to those who seek to incorporate others' conceptions of the international into the study of security in a world characterised by a multiplicity of inequalities and differences.

What I suggest here is that, rather than explaining away such apparent 'similarity' as a confirmation of mainstream IR's claim to universality, or merely a consequence of the formative effect of the 'Western' education received by many scholars from the global South, we could begin our inquiries by reading IR scholarship originating from outside North America and Western Europe as responding to a world that is already worlded by IR.[5] In making this point, I follow Edward Said (2000: 205) who wrote that it is 'perfectly possible to judge misreadings (as they occur) as part of a historical transfer of ideas and theories from one setting to another'.

Yet, in doing so, I also differ from some of Said's interlocutors who warrant their call for national schools of IR by citing his essay on 'traveling theory'

Introduction 3

(Said, 2000), presuming that 'theory does not travel well' (Salter, 2010: 134). In contrast, I read Said as distinguishing between two different processes: that theories respond to a particular time and place, and that they assume new meanings and roles when they travel to other settings and are translated to fit the requirements of their new setting. I support my reading of Said by making two points. First, Said's essay entitled 'Travelling Theory' does not only point to trials and travails of theories as they move from one socio-political setting to another ('such movement into a new environment is never unimpeded', he wrote) but also underscores the need for 'borrowed, or traveling theory': 'For borrow we certainly must if we are to elude the constraints of our immediate intellectual environment' (Said, 1983: 226, 41). Second, given that Said himself borrowed liberally from other fields, approaches, geographies and cultures, and praised those few remaining 'genuine polymaths' (see Said's foreword in Schwab, 1950 [1984]), it would be difficult to reduce his discussion on 'travelling theory' to a question of geo-cultural origins. We would also not be doing justice to Said if we conflate his analysis of the worldliness of theories with assumptions of autonomous development of 'difference' (for a critique of the latter, see Narayan, 2000).

In present-day IR, 'worlding' is typically understood as reflecting on the situatedness of knowing (what John Agnew [2007] has called 'know-where'). However, there is another, equally important, dimension to 'worlding', which is about reflecting on the constitutive effects of knowing. This second understanding of 'worlding' (developed mostly in postcolonial studies) has been hardly visible in recent discussions.[6] In this book, I call for worlding IR in both senses of the term, which I characterise as 'worlding-as-situatedness' and 'worlding-as-constitutive'. I suggest that worlding IR in its twofold meaning would allow us to understand how others' insecurities, experienced in a world that is already worlded, have shaped (and have been shaped by) their conceptions of the international.

In calling for worlding IR in its twofold meaning, I follow R.B.J. Walker (1993: 6) who argued that 'theories of international relations are more interesting as aspects of world politics that need to be explained than as explanations of contemporary world politics'. This is not to downplay the significance of Ole Wæver's (1998b) call for inquiring into the sociology of knowledge in making sense of IR scholarship around the world. Rather I seek to underscore the politics of knowledge insofar as 'every study is positioned socially, which means that every study is political, whether the politics are admitted, or not' (Sylvester, 2012: 314). This is what I have previously referred to as the 'international political "sociology of IR"', invoking the title of Wæver's 1998 study which called for sociology of knowledge informed inquiries into IR (Bilgin, 2009). In the said piece, Wæver criticised prevalent accounts on the development of the field for focusing on 'the impact of developments in real-world international relations on developments within the discipline of IR'. Yet he also noted how this is done in a paradoxical manner insofar as those dynamics are not 'external' to the field, but are part of its 'quasi-positivist, progressivist self-understanding' (Wæver, 1998b: 691). Since then, inquiries utilising

4   Introduction

sociology of science explanations have increased in number. However, the paradox that Wæver pointed to remains unaddressed. For, while we now have better insight into the 'internal' dynamics of IR in various settings, relatively few studies inquire into the internal/external dynamics, that is, how IR outside North America and Western Europe has developed in a world that is already worlded by IR.

The building blocks of the answer I offer in this book are available to us in the scholarship on critical security studies and postcolonial studies. The former has focused on the constructedness of insecurities, and pointed to the ways in which one's 'basic ideas – political theories and philosophy – about what makes the world go round' shape his/her conceptions of security (Booth, 2007: 154). The latter has shown that thinking about international relations in a world characterised by a multiplicity of inequalities and differences entails becoming curious about others' conceptions of the international as shaped by those basic ideas (Inayatullah and Blaney, 2004, Seth, 2013).

Indeed, students of critical security studies thus far have not paid sustained attention to the relationship between our 'multiple complex inequalities' (Walby, 2009) and others' conceptions of the international. While important beginnings have been made in the study of 'strategic cultures' (Booth and Trood, 1999) or 'cultures of insecurity' (Weldes et al., 1999), these insights have not always been integrated into theorising about world security. This is not to imply the 'absence' of culture in mainstream approaches to IR and security. Rather, following Michael Williams (1998), I underscore the difference between approaches that engage with the dynamic relationship between culture and in/security, and others that fail to reflect on the cultural embeddedness of theorising about IR and security.

Students of postcolonial studies, in turn, have offered 'contrapuntal readings' (Said, 1993) of the coloniser and the colonised to point to re/production of colonial differences and postcolonial insecurities (Grovogui, 1996, 2006, Ling, 2002, Krishna, 1999). While it is generally accepted that the insights of post-colonial studies are relevant not only for the coloniser and the colonised but all those who have been shaped by 'the continuity and persistence of colonising practices' (Chowdhry and Nair, 2002: 11, also see Hall, 1996), students of postcolonial studies have not paid sustained attention to broader issues regarding world security (but see Biswas, 2001, Barkawi, 2005, Barkawi and Laffey, 2006, Jabri, 2007, 2013).

Over the years, these two bodies of scholarship (critical security studies and postcolonial studies) have not been in dialogue with each other.[7] Indeed, the students of critical security studies have not always paid sustained attention to the insights offered by the latter, while at the same time seeking to shield themselves against the latter's anti-Eurocentric critique (see, for example, Barkawi and Laffey, 2006, Peoples and Vaughan-Williams, 2010, Alker, 2005, Lee-Koo, 2007, Pettman, 2005). Students of postcolonial studies, in turn, have not been able to penetrate the consciousness of students of IR as regards the relevance of the insight they offer by giving voice to IR's 'constitutive outside'.

Introduction 5

If students of critical IR and security on the one hand and postcolonial studies on the other have had limited dialogue, this is partly because the former understand postcolonial studies as relevant only for the colonised and/or the colonial era. Even then, its relevance is considered as suspect for students of IR and security, given the 'cultural' focus of postcolonial studies (see below). Contra such narrow understandings of postcolonialism, I adopt Stuart Hall's (1996) understanding of postcolonialism as a 're-staged narrative' on world history. Following Hall, colonialism 'references something more than direct rule over certain areas of the world by the imperial powers'. Rather, it '[signifies] the whole process of expansion, exploration, conquest, colonisation and imperial hegemonisation which constituted the "outer face", the constitutive outside, of European and then Western capitalist modernity after 1492' (Hall, 1996: 249, cf. Shohat, 1992, McClintock, 1992). Insofar as colonialism 'refers to a specific historical moment' *as well as* 'a way of staging or narrating history', postcolonial studies re-stage this narrative by de-centring the coloniser and looking at the experiences and perspectives of the colonised as the 'constitutive outside' of modernity. Understood as such, postcolonial studies is already about the international, although the account it offers does not take forms that are instantly recognisable to students of IR and security. Indeed, one of the contradictions highlighted by the postcolonial critics is that students of IR do not recognise others' theoretical explorations of world politics as 'IR' even as they lament the 'absence' or 'invisibility' of contributions by scholars from the global South (see Chapter 3).

In what follows, I suggest that the task of addressing the question of thinking about security in a world characterised by a multiplicity of inequalities and differences calls on us to give heed to Hayward Alker's (2005: 190) advice and inquire into 'epistemologically and ontologically sensitive ways in which the reshapings of collective memories and imagined futures can be emancipatory' without 'neglecting to consider experiences of colonisation and imperialism' as underlined by Jan Jindy Pettman (2005: 159). More specifically, I suggest, students of critical security studies could turn to postcolonial studies to learn from and draw upon 'contrapuntal readings' of world history and politics offered by the latter.

Edward Said developed his method of 'contrapuntal reading' to be able to do research as if viewed through the eyes of 'the exile' (Said, 1984, 1994). Most people 'are principally aware of one culture, one setting, one home', Said observed in his 1984 essay 'Reflections on Exile'. 'The exile', however, is aware of at least two if not more. It is this plurality of vision, highlighted Said, that 'gives rise to an awareness of simultaneous dimensions, an awareness that – to borrow a phrase from music – is contrapuntal' (Said, 1984: 172).

Said defined 'contrapuntal awareness' as belonging to multiple worlds not only in terms of 'cultural' identity but also academic field, thereby defying disciplinary belonging and restraints. Such 'eccentricity' allows the exile not only 'the negative advantage of refuge', wrote Said, but also 'the positive benefit of challenging the system, describing it in language unavailable to those it has

6 *Introduction*

already subdued' (Said, 1993: 334). In his writings, Said drew upon various fields including but not limited to the humanities and social sciences. 'By looking at the different experiences contrapuntally, as making up a set of what I call intertwined and overlapping histories', wrote Said,

> a more interesting type of secular interpretation can emerge, altogether more rewarding than the denunciations of the past, the expressions of regret for its having ended, or – even more wasteful because violent and far too easy and attractive – the hostility between Western and non-Western cultures that leads to crises. The world is too small and interdependent to let these passively happen.
>
> (Said, 1993: 18–19)

Lamenting the passing of an era where intellectuals were expected to be fluent in several subject areas and languages, he maintained that '[t]he fantastic explosion of specialised and separatist knowledge is partly to blame' (Said, 1993: 320) for the present-day limits of our insight into 'intertwined and overlapping histories' of humankind.[8]

That said, my aim is not to seek a meta-theoretical warrant for answering our questions.[9] Nor do I wish to plea for 'bridging' postcolonial studies and IR (Darby and Paolini, 1994). Somewhat differently, I call for students of critical security studies to raise their 'contrapuntal awareness' and seek to learn from and draw on postcolonial studies, and, as they do so, to remain mindful of the latter's criticisms. Here, I take heed of Kimberly Hutchings's warning about '[t]he tendency of critical IR theory to remain trapped within unsolvable theoretical debates rather than turning attention toward redirecting empirical research and specific explanations' (Hutchings, 2001: 79).[10] My task in this study is to take stock of the literature on critical theorising about IR and security with a view to its limits and possibilities, re-think where we are in terms of responding to our questions, and pull together the building blocks of the answer I offer.

The plan

Chapter 1 considers the limits of theorising about IR and security in inquiring into others' conceptions of the international. This may come across as somewhat counter-intuitive in that mainstream approaches to security are often criticised for their external focus. However, focusing on external actors (be it state or non-state) is not the same as being curious about how 'they' approach the international, and/or be mindful of the limits of 'our' ways of accessing their conceptions of the international. More often than not, students of mainstream approaches to IR and security studies have studied others' material capacities based on 'our' assumptions regarding 'their' intentions. What these limits amount to is that mainstream approaches to IR and security have not been equipped to respond to the question of thinking about security in a world characterised by a multiplicity of inequalities and differences.

Introduction 7

Students of critical theorising about International Relations and security have sought to address these (and other) limits of mainstream approaches. Chapter 2 looks at the important strides made by critical theorising about IR and security and those issues that remain. Postcolonial studies scholars, among others, have highlighted those limits that have persisted (as with Eurocentrism). Yet, the insights of postcolonial studies have not always been appreciated and/or integrated into critical theorising about IR and security. In particular, reflections on others' conceptions of the international have been missing from IR and security studies scholarship. Indeed, the need for inquiring into 'others' as IR's 'constitutive outside' has barely registered in Critical IR debates on the limits of the field.

Chapter 3 turns to the difficulties involved in accessing others' conceptions of the international. In the attempt to find out about how 'others' approach the international, some IR scholars have looked at IR scholarship in other parts of the world to see how they do things differently. However, they were thwarted in their efforts in finding that IR scholarship in other parts of the world was not as 'different' as they expected. Another group of authors focused on the so-called 'non-Western' texts and contexts to see whether and/or how 'different' conceptions of the international were offered in texts from outside IR and/or the 'West', practices of 'everyday life' and 'non-Western thought'. Notwithstanding important insights provided by these two bodies of literature, we were left with the question: How is it that IR scholarship in other parts of the world does not reflect the kind of 'difference' found in texts and contexts outside IR and/or North America and Western Europe, but adopts the 'standard' concepts and theories of the field, notwithstanding their well-known limits?

I suggest that, rather than explaining away such apparent 'similarity' as confirmation of mainstream IR's assumptions of universality, or misplaced expectations of 'difference', we could begin our inquiries into others' conceptions of the international by reading their IR scholarship as an aspect of world politics, or, more specifically, as a response to their insecurities experienced in a world that is already worlded. Towards this end, I propose that we engage in 'worlding IR' in its twofold meaning, reflecting on the situatedness of IR scholarship *and* its constitutive effects. This is what I term as inquiring into 'security in the international, the international in security'. Chapters 4 and 5 flesh out the answer I offer.

Chapter 4 inquires into security in the international by worlding IR scholarship in China and security scholarship in Turkey. I suggest that if IR scholarship in these two contexts does not come across as 'different' as expected, this could be because they are responding to a world that is already worlded by IR. The example of China is noteworthy because of the relatively high volume of reflective studies (available in English) on the state of IR in China and on 'IR theory with Chinese characteristics'. The example of Turkey is chosen partly because of my ability to access primary resources in Turkish. That said, the case of Turkey is also noteworthy because it helps to highlight the insights that postcolonial studies has to offer in the study of a part of the world that was not formally colonised but was nevertheless caught up in hierarchies that

8   *Introduction*

were built and sustained during the age of colonialism and beyond. Taken together, these two cases are offered not as representative of IR scholarship in the global South, but to illustrate the broader point about reading others' IR scholarship as an aspect of world politics, as responding to a world that is already worlded.

Chapter 5 inquires into the international in security by studying others' 'discourses of danger' (Campbell, 1992). Drawing on the postcolonial studies literature on the origins and development of India's 'atomic weapon' (Abraham, 1998, 2009), I seek to tease out others' conceptions of the international from the 'discourses of danger' employed by the leadership, suggesting that India's nuclear (weapons) programme could be considered as responding to non-military and non-specific insecurities experienced by the new entrants to the international society. Doing so, I suggest, allows one to go beyond surface understandings of the postcolonial becoming 'almost the same but not quite' as mere imitation. Accordingly, I suggest that we understand 'emulation' as a security response by new entrants to the international society to remove the grounds for their less-than-equal treatment. Here, I contrast the English School's understanding of the international society as 'benevolent' vis-à-vis the 'others', with the latter's experiences of the former as 'Janus-faced' (Suzuki, 2005). I suggest 'hierarchy in anarchical society' as a concept that captures the hierarchical, anarchical and societal aspects of others' conception of the international. The chapter illustrates this argument by offering a reading of Turkey's secularisation as part of an attempt to address non-military and non-specific insecurities that the country's early twentieth-century leadership experienced in their encounters with the international society.

Chapter 6 seeks to illustrate how the book's answer to our questions works when considering contemporary insecurities. The example I chose is a project of world security, the Dialogue of Civilisations (DoC) initiative, offered as a way of averting a future shaped by a Huntingtonian 'clash of civilisations' scenario. Here, I present a critical security studies critique that draws on the insights of postcolonial studies. While the proponents of civilisational dialogue strive to replace clash with dialogue, I argue, they do not always reflect on how myriad insecurities are (re)produced through attempts at civilisational dialogue that are shaped by particular notions of dialogue (that is not always dialogical in ethics and/ or epistemology), civilisation (which is not conceptualised dialogically or studied contrapuntally) and security (undeniably statist and military-focused, devoid of reflections on others' conceptions of the international).

One final note before moving to Chapter 1. Calls for inquiring into inequalities and difference/s in the study of world politics are often rebuffed by the critics who state that these are 'no more than political moves by the relatively weak'. In contrast, they argue, the 'strong'

> employ reason, righteousness, interest and, when all else fails, necessity and power. It is the weaker party that argues that they do what they do because they are who they are, and claim that cultural arguments are trumps,

Introduction 9

because they have nothing else, not power, reason nor, perhaps, even justice on their side.

(Sharp, 2004: 362)

As highlighted by Paul Sharp, whose words I quoted above, such responses to 'cultural' arguments overlook the way in which the very notions of 'reason', 'righteousness', 'interest', 'necessity' and 'power' are defined by someone and for some purpose (to invoke Robert W. Cox (1981)). Students of postcolonial studies and feminist IR have invariably pointed to how prevalent understandings of 'reason' tend to be white and male (Haraway, 1988, Smith, 1999). Key notions such as those mentioned above, which are utilised by the 'strong' are embedded in the very cultures where they are produced; yet they deny their cultural embeddedness, portraying themselves as 'free' of culture, i.e. objective. That some are able to offer their culturally embedded concepts as 'objective', thereby rendering others' as 'subjective' or 'cultural' is an instance of the limits of our theorising about IR and security. This is where the book begins.

Notes

1 Throughout the text, 'International Relations' refers to the discipline of IR and 'international relations' to world politics (except in quotations, which were left untouched).
2 Critical security studies can be defined in one of two ways. Narrowly defined, it refers to the Aberystwyth School, whose students draw upon Frankfurt School Critical Theory in the study of security (Booth, 1991, 1995, 1997, 2005, 2007, Booth and Vale, 1997, Stamnes and Wyn Jones, 2000, Wyn Jones, 1999, 2005, Bilgin, 2000, 2004, 2008a, 2011, Williams, 2001). Broadly defined, it refers to all critical approaches to security, i.e. scholarship that builds upon critical thinking about IR in the study of security. See, for example, Aradau et al. (2006), Burke (2001, 2007), Burke and McDonald (2007), Weldes et al. (1999), Fierke (1998, 2007), Huysmans (1995, 1998a, 1998b, 2006), Buzan (1991), Guzzini and Jung (2004), Wæver and Buzan (2003), Wæver et al. (1993), Wæver (1989, 1995, 1998a, 2004, 2011), Krause and Williams (1996, 1997), Peoples and Vaughan-Williams (2010), Walker (1990, 1997), Jabri (2007, 2013), Sylvester (2010), Buzan and Hansen (2009), Hansen (2000, 2006), Bigo (2000, 2001), Burgess (2010, 2011), Aradau (2004).
3 Postcolonial studies originated in the humanities. Its insights were integrated into the social sciences, with some disciplines proving more open to reflecting on their limits than some others. Postcolonial studies is not a unified body of thought. Differences among postcolonial studies scholars encompass the definition of 'postcolonial', meanings of 'modernity' and the limits of postcolonial agency. In what follows, I will clarify my position vis-à-vis postcolonial studies by identifying differences within the literature as appropriate. Finally, there is also the question of differences between postcolonial and decolonial studies. Following Bhambra (2014), who emphasises the potential for dialogue between the two literatures, and in keeping with the dialogical spirit of the project, I will highlight points of convergence where possible. However, as will become clear, I draw mostly on Edward Said, and less on Spivak and Bhabha – all key authors of postcolonial studies.
4 Throughout the study, I use the terms 'Third World' and 'global South' interchangeably, remaining true to the choices made by scholars where possible. While

10   *Introduction*

remaining mindful of the declining utility of these concepts, I follow Albert Paolini (1999: 4) who noted that 'no matter how amorphous', such concepts are nevertheless useful insofar as they '[redirect] our attention to the edges of the Western gaze'. Indeed, as Matthew Sparke (2007: 117) noted, 'The Global South is everywhere, but it is also always somewhere, and that somewhere, located at the intersection of entangled political geographies of dispossession and repossession, has to be mapped with persistent geographical responsibility'. For example, the global South is where students in Southern Africa who are frustrated with the persistence of the legacy of apartheid would locate themselves (http://www.bbc.com/news/world-africa-34636419).

5   For an early formulation of this argument, see Bilgin (2008b).

6   As editors, Tickner and Wæver (2009b) introduced both understandings in setting up their framework. However, the second understanding is not integral to the analyses offered by the contributors to the 2009 volume.

7   Some have even cast doubt upon the potential for a 'postcolonial IR' (Krishna, 2001, cf. Darby and Paolini, 1994, Obendorf, 2015).

8   See, for example, Said's foreword to Raymond Schwab's *The Oriental Renaissance* (Schwab, 1950 [1984]).

9   On in/commensurability, see Campbell (1996), Wæver (1996), Guzzini (1998), Lukes (2000), Agnew (2007), Lichbach (2007), Kornprobst (2009), Burgess (2014). For a reading of Edward Said's 'contrapuntal reading' as 'a method, an ethos and a metaphor for IR', see Bilgin (2016).

10   Hutchings (2001) defines critical IR broadly.

Bibliography

Abraham, I. 1998. *The Making of the Indian Atomic Bomb: Science, Secrecy and the Postcolonial State*, New York, Zed Books.

Abraham, I. (ed.). 2009. *South Asian Cultures of the Bomb: Atomic Publics and the State in India and Pakistan*, Bloomington, Indianapolis, Indiana University Press.

Agnew, J. 2007. Know-where: Geographies of Knowledge of World Politics. *International Political Sociology*, 1, 138–148.

Alker, H. 2005. Emancipation in the Critical Security Studies Project. In: Booth, K. (ed.) *Critical Security Studies and World Politics*, Boulder, CO, Lynne Rienner.

Aradau, C. 2004. Security and the Democratic Scene: Desecuritization and Emancipation. *Journal of International Relations & Development*, 7, 388–413.

Aradau, C., Balzacq, T., Basaran, T., Bigo, D., Bonditti, P., Buger, C., Davidshofer, S., Guillaume, X., Guittet, E. P., Huysmans, J., Jeandesboz, J., Jutila, M., Lobo-Guerrero, L., Mccormack, T., Malksoo, M., Neal, A., Olsson, C., Petersen, K. L., Ragazzi, F., Akilli, Y. S., Stritzel, H., Van Munster, R., Villumsen, T., Wæver, O. and Williams, M. C. 2006. Critical Approaches to Security in Europe: A Networked Manifesto. *Security Dialogue*, 37, 443–487.

Barkawi, T. 2005. *Globalization and War*, Lanham, MD, Rowman & Littlefield Publishers.

Barkawi, T. & Laffey, M. 2006. The Postcolonial Moment in Security Studies. *Review of International Studies*, 32, 329–352.

Bhambra, G. K. 2014. Postcolonial and Decolonial Dialogues. *Postcolonial Studies*, 17, 115–121.

Bigo, D. 2000. When Two Become One: Internal and External Securitisations in Europe. In: Keltsrup, M. & Williams, M. C. (eds.) *International Relations Theory and* the Politics of European Integration: Power, Security, and Community, London, New York, Routledge.

Bigo, D. 2001. The Möbius Ribbon of Internal and External Securit(ies). In: Albert, M. E. A. (ed.) *Identities Borders Orders: Rethinking International Relations Theory*, Minnesota, University of Minnesota Press.

Bilgin, P. 2000. Regional Security in the Middle East: A Critical Security Studies Perspective. Ph.D., University of Wales, Aberystwyth.

Bilgin, P. 2004. *Regional Security in the Middle East: A Critical Perspective*, London, Routledge.

Bilgin, P. 2008a. Critical Theory. In: Williams, P. D. (ed.) *Security Studies: An Introduction*, London, Routledge.

Bilgin, P. 2008b. Thinking Past 'Western' IR? *Third World Quarterly*, 29, 5–23.

Bilgin, P. 2009. The International Political Sociology of a Not So International Discipline, *International Political Sociology*, 3, 338–342.

Bilgin, P. 2011. Continuing Appeal of Critical Security Studies. In: Brincat, S., Lima, L. and Nunes, J. (eds.) *Critical Theory in International Relations and Security Studies: Interviews and Reflections*, London, Routledge.

Bilgin, P. 2012. Security in the Arab World and Turkey, Differently Different. In: Tickner, A. and Blaney, D. (eds.) *Thinking International Relations Differently*, London, Routledge.

Bilgin, P. 2016. Edward Said's 'Contrapuntal Reading' as a Method, an Ethos and a Metaphor for Global IR. *International Studies Review*, 18, 1, 134–46.

Biswas, S. 2001. 'Nuclear Apartheid' as Political Position: Race as a Postcolonial Resource? *Alternatives: Global, Local, Political*, 26, 485–522.

Booth, K. 1991. Security and Emancipation. *Review of International Studies*, 17, 313–326.

Booth, K. 1997. Security and Self, Reflections of a Fallen Realist. In: Krause, K. and Williams, M. C. (eds.) *Critical Security Studies: Concepts and Cases*, Minneapolis, University of Minnesota Press.

Booth, K. (ed.) 2005. *Critical Security Studies and World Politics*, Boulder, CO, Lynne Rienner Publishers.

Booth, K. 2007. *Theory of World Security*, Cambridge, Cambridge University Press.

Booth, K. and Trood, R. B. (eds.) 1999. *Strategic Cultures in the Asia-Pacific Region*, New York, St. Martin's Press.

Booth, K. and Vale, P. 1997. Critical Security Studies and Regional Insecurity: The Case of Southern Africa. In: Krause, K. and Williams, M. (eds.) *Critical Security Studies: Concepts and Cases*, Minneapolis, University of Minnesota Press.

Burgess, J. P. (ed.) 2010. *The Routledge Handbook of New Security Studies*, London, New York, Routledge.

Burgess, J. P. 2011. *The Ethical Subject of Security: Geopolitical Reason and the Threat against Europe*, New York, Routledge.

Burgess, J. P. 2014. Commensurability and Methods in Critical Security Studies. *Critical Studies on Security*, 2, 356–358.

Burke, A. 2001. *Fear of Security: Australia's Invasion Anxiety*, Annandale, Pluto Press.

Burke, A. 2007. *Beyond Security, Ethics and Violence: War against the Other*, New York, Routledge.

Burke, A. & McDonald, M. (eds.) 2007. *Critical Security in the Asia-Pacific*, Manchester, Manchester University Press.

Buzan, B. 1991. *People, States, and Fear: An Agenda for International Security Studies in the Post-Cold War Era*, New York, Harvester Wheatsheaf.

12   Introduction

Buzan, B. and Hansen, L. 2009. *The Evolution of International Security Studies*, Cambridge, Cambridge University Press.

Campbell, D. 1992. *Writing Security: United States Foreign Policy and the Politics of Identity*, Manchester, Manchester University Press.

Campbell, D. T. 1996. Can We Overcome Worldview Incommensurability/Relativity in Trying to Understand the Other? In: Jessor, R., Colby, A. and Shweder, R. (eds.) *Ethnography and Human Development: Context and Meaning in Social Inquiry*, Chicago, The University of Chicago Press.

Chowdhry, G. and Nair, S. 2002. Introduction: Power in a Postcolonial World: Race, Gender, and Class in International Relations. In: Chowdhry, G. and Nair, S. (eds.) *Power, Postcolonialism, and International Relations: Reading Race, Gender, and Class*, London, Routledge.

Cox, R. W. 1981. Social Forces, States and World Orders: Beyond International Relations Theory. *Millennium – Journal of International Studies*, 10, 126–155.

Darby, P. & Paolini, A. J. 1994. Bridging International Relations and Postcolonialism. *Alternatives*, 19, 371–397.

Donnelly, J. 2006. Sovereign Inequalities and Hierarchy in Anarchy: American Power and International Society. *European Journal of International Relations*, 12, 139–170.

Enloe, C. 1997. Margins, Silences and Bottom Rungs: How to Overcome the Underestimation of Power in the Study of International Relations. In: Booth, K., Smith, S. and Zalewski, M. (eds.) *International Theory: Positivism and Beyond*, Cambridge, Cambridge University Press.

Fabian, J. 1983. *Time and the Other: How Anthropology Makes its Object*, New York, Columbia University Press.

Fierke, K. M. 1998. *Changing Games, Changing Strategies: Critical Investigations in Security*, Manchester, New York, Manchester University Press.

Fierke, K. M. 2007. *Critical Approaches to International Security*, Oxford, Polity.

Grovogui, S. N. 1996. *Sovereigns, Quasi-sovereigns and Africans: Race and Self-determination in International Law*, Minneapolis, University of Minnesota Press.

Grovogui, S. N. 2006. *Beyond Eurocentrism and Anarchy: Memories of International Order and Institutions*, New York, Palgrave Macmillan.

Guzzini, S. 1998. *Realism in International Relations and International Political Economy: The Continuing Story of a Death Foretold*, London, Routledge.

Guzzini, S. & Jung, D. (eds.) 2004. *Contemporary Security Analysis and Copenhagen Peace Research*, London, New York, Routledge.

Hall, S. 1996. When Was 'the Post-colonial'? Thinking at the Limit. In: Chambers, I. and Curti, L. (eds.) *The Post-colonial Question: Common Skies, Divided Horizons*, London, Routledge.

Hansen, L. 2000. The Little Mermaid's Silent Security Dilemma and the Absence of Gender in the Copenhagen School. *Millennium – Journal of International Studies*, 29, 285–306.

Hansen, L. 2006. *Security as Practice: Discourse Analysis and the Bosnian War*, New York, Routledge.

Haraway, D. 1988. Situated Knowledges, the Science Question in Feminism and the Privilege of Partial Perspective. *Feminist Studies*, 14, 3, 575–599.

Hindess, B. 2007. The Past is Another Culture. *International Political Sociology*, 1, 325–338.

Hobson, J. M. 2014. The Twin Self-Delusions of IR: Why 'Hierarchy' and Not 'Anarchy' Is the Core Concept of IR. *Millennium – Journal of International Studies*, 42, 3, 557–575.

Hutchings, K. 2001. The Nature of Critique in Critical International Relations Theory. In: Jones, R. W. (ed.) *Critical Theory and World Politics*, Boulder, CO, Lynne Rienner.

Huysmans, J. 1995. Migrants as a Security Problem: Dangers of 'Securitizing' Societal Issues. In: Thränhardt, D. & Miles, R. (eds.) *Migration and European Integration: The Dynamics of Inclusion and Exclusion*, London, Pinter.

Huysmans, J. 1998a. Revisiting Copenhagen: Or, On the Creative Development of a Security Studies Agenda in Europe. *European Journal of International Relations*, 4, 479–505.

Huysmans, J. 1998b. Security! What Do You Mean? From Concept to Thick Signifier. *European Journal of International Relations*, 4, 226–255.

Huysmans, J. 2006. *The Politics of Insecurity: Fear, Migration, and Asylum in the EU*, Milton Park, Abingdon, Oxon, New York, Routledge.

Inayatullah, N. & Blaney, D. L. 2004. *International Relations and the Problem of Difference*, London, Routledge.

Jabri, V. 2007. *War and the Transformation of Global Politics*, Basingstoke, England, New York, Palgrave Macmillan.

Jabri, V. 2013. *The Postcolonial Subject: Claiming Politics/Governing Others in Late Modernity*, London, Routledge.

Kornprobst, M. 2009. International Relations as Rhetorical Discipline: Toward (Re-) Newing Horizons. *International Studies Review*, 11, 87–108.

Krause, K. & Williams, M. C. 1996. Broadening the Agenda of Security Studies: Politics and Methods. *International Studies Quarterly*, 40, 229–254.

Krause, K. & Williams, M. C. (eds.) 1997. *Critical Security Studies: Concepts and Cases*, Minneapolis, MN, University of Minnesota Press.

Krishna, S. 1999. *Postcolonial Insecurities: India, Sri Lanka, and the Question of Nationhood*, Minneapolis, MN, University of Minnesota Press.

Krishna, S. 2001. Race, Amnesia, and the Education of International Relations. *Alternatives: Global, Local, Political*, 26, 401–424.

Lee-Koo, K. 2007. Security as Enslavement, Security as Emancipation: Gendered Legacies and Feminist Futures in the Asia-Pacific. In: Burke, A. & McDonald, M. (eds.) *Critical Security in the Asia-Pacific*, Manchester, Manchester University Press.

Lichbach, M. I. 2007. Theory and Evidence. In: Lebow, R. N. & Lichbach, M. I. (eds.) *Theory and Evidence in Comparative Politics and International Relations*, New York, Palgrave Macmillan.

Ling, L. H. M. 2002. *Postcolonial International Relations: Conquest and Desire between Asia and the West*, New York, Palgrave.

Lukes, S. 2000. Different Cultures, Different Rationalities? *History of the Human Sciences*, 13, 3–18.

McClintock, A. 1992. The Angel of Progress: Pitfalls of the Term 'Post-Colonialism'. *Social Text*, 31/32, 84–98.

Narayan, U. 2000. Essence of Culture and a Sense of History: A Feminist Critique of Cultural Essentialism. In: Narayan, U. & Harding, S. (eds.) *Decentering the Center: Philosophy for a Multicultural, Postcolonial, and Feminist World*, Bloomington, Indiana University Press.

Obendorf, S. 2015. Dangerous Relations? In: Bernard, A., Elmarsafy, Z. & Murray, S. (eds.) *What Postcolonial Theory Doesn't Say*, London, Routledge.

Paolini, A. J. 1999. *Navigating Modernity: Postcolonialism, Identity, and International Relations*, London, Lynne Rienner.

Pasha, M. K. & Murphy, C. N. 2002. Knowledge/Power/Inequality. *International Studies Review*, 4, 1–6.

14   Introduction

Peoples, C. & Vaughan-Williams, N. 2010. *Critical Security Studies: An Introduction*, New York, Routledge.

Pettman, J. J. 2005. Questions of Identity: Australia and Asia. In: Booth, K. (ed.) *Critical Security Studies and World Politics*, Boulder, CO, Lynne Rienner.

Said, E. W. 1983. *The World, the Text, and the Critic*, Cambridge, MA, Harvard University Press.

Said, E. W. 1984. Reflections on Exile. *Granta*, 13, 157–172.

Said, E. W. 1993. *Culture and Imperialism*, New York, Knopf.

Said, E. W. 1994. *Representations of the Intellectual: The 1993 Reith Lectures*, New York, Pantheon Books.

Said, E. W. 2000. Traveling Theory. In: Bayoumi, M. & Rubin, A. (eds.) *The Edward Said Reader*, New York, Vintage Books.

Salter, M. B. 2010. Edward Said and Post-colonial International Relations. In: Moore, C. & Farrands, C. (eds.) *International Relations Theory and Philosophy: Interpretive Dialogues*, London, Routledge.

Schwab, R. 1950 [1984]. *The Oriental Renaissance: Europe's Rediscovery of India and the East, 1680–1880*, New York, Columbia University Press.

Seth, S. (ed.) 2013. *Postcolonial Theory and International Relations: A Critical Introduction*, London, Routledge.

Sharp, P. 2004. The Idea of Diplomatic Culture and its Sources. In: Slavik, H. (ed.) *Intercultural Communication and Diplomacy*, Malta, DiploFoundation.

Shohat, E. 1992. Notes on the 'Post-Colonial'. *Social Text*, 31/32, 99–113.

Smith, L. T. 1999. *Decolonizing Methodologies: Research and Indigenous Peoples*, London, Zed Books.

Sparke, M. 2007. Everywhere but Always Somewhere: Critical Geographies of the Global South. *The Global South*, 1, 117–126.

Stamnes, E. & Wyn Jones, R. 2000. Burundi: A Critical Security Perspective. *Peace and Conflict Studies*, 7, 37–55.

Suzuki, S. 2005. Japan's Socialization into Janus-Faced European International Society. *European Journal of International Relations*, 11, 137–164.

Sylvester, C. 2010. Tensions in Feminist Security Studies. *Security Dialogue*, 41, 607–614.

Sylvester, C. 2012. The Elusive Arts of Reflexivity in the 'Sciences' of International Relations. *Millennium – Journal of International Studies*, 41, 309–325.

Tickner, A. & Herz, M. 2012. No Place for Theory? Security Studies in Latin America. In: Tickner, A. & Blaney, D. (eds.) *Thinking International Relations Differently*, London, Routledge.

Tickner, A. B. & Wæver, O. (eds.) 2009a. *International Relations Scholarship Around the World*, London, Routledge.

Tickner, A. B. & Wæver, O. 2009b. Introduction: Geocultural Epistemologies. In: Tickner, A. B. & Wæver, O. (eds.) *International Relations Scholarship Around the World*, London, Routledge.

Vitalis, R. 2005. Birth of a Discipline. In: Long, D. & Schmidt, B. C. (eds.) *Imperialism and Internationalism in the Discipline of International Relations*, Albany, State University of New York Press.

Wæver, O. 1989. Security, the Speech Act: Analysing the Politics of a Word. COPRI Working Paper. Copenhagen, Copenhagen Peace Research Institute.

Wæver, O. 1995. Securitization and Desecuritization. In: Lipschutz, R. D. (ed.) *On Security*, New York, Columbia University Press.

Wæver, O. 1996. The Rise and Fall of the Inter-paradigm Debate. In: Booth, K. & Smith, S. (eds.) *International Theory: Positivism and Beyond*, Oxford, Polity.

Wæver, O. 1998a. Insecurity, Security, and Asecurity in the West European Non-war Community. In: Adler, E. & Barnett, M. N. (eds.) *Security Communities*, Cambridge, Cambridge University Press.

Wæver, O. 1998b. The Sociology of a Not So International Discipline: American and European Developments in International Relations. *International Organization*, 52, 687–727.

Wæver, O. 2004. Aberystwyth, Paris, Copenhagen – New 'Schools' in Security Theory and their Origins between Core and Periphery. International Studies Association, Montreal, Canada.

Wæver, O. 2011. Politics, Security, Theory. *Security Dialogue*, 42, 465–480.

Wæver, O. & Buzan, B. 2003. *Regions and Powers: The Structure of International Security*, Cambridge, Cambridge University Press.

Wæver, O., Buzan, B., Kelstrup, M. & Lemaitre, P. 1993. *Identity, Migration and the New Security Agenda in Europe*, London, Pinter.

Walby, S. 2009. *Globalization and Inequalities: Complexities and Contested Modernities*, Los Angeles, Sage.

Walker, R. B. J. 1990. Security, Sovereignty and the Challenge of World Politics. *Alternatives*, 15, 3–28.

Walker, R. B. J. 1993. *Inside/outside: International Relations as Political Theory*, Cambridge, Cambridge University Press.

Walker, R. B. J. 1997. The Subject of Security. In: Krause, K. & Williams, M. C. (eds.) *Critical Security Studies: Concepts and Cases*, Minneapolis, MN, University of Minnesota Press.

Walker, R. B. J. 2002. International/Inequality. *International Studies Review*, 4, 7–24.

Weldes, J., Laffey, M., Gusterson, H. & Duvall, R. (eds.) 1999. *Cultures of Insecurity: States, Communities and the Production of Danger*, Minneapolis, University of Minnesota Press.

Wendt, A. & Friedheim, D. 2009. Hierarchy under Anarchy: Informal Empire and the East German State. *International Organization*, 49, 689–721.

Williams, M. C. 1998. Identity and the Politics of Security. *European Journal of International Relations*, 4, 204–225.

Williams, P. D. 2001. *Intellectuals and the End of Apartheid: Critical Security Studies and the South African Transition*, PhD. Aberystwyth, University of Wales.

Wyn Jones, R. 1999. *Security, Strategy and Critical Theory*, Boulder, CO, Lynne Rienner Publishers.

Wyn Jones, R. 2005. On Emancipation: Necessity, Capacity and Concrete Utopias. In: Booth, K. (ed.) *Critical Security Studies and World Politics*, Boulder, CO, Lynne Rienner.

Zhang, Y. 2007. Discourses of Security in China: Towards a Critical Turn? In: Burke, A. & McDonald, M. (eds.) *Critical Security in the Asia-Pacific*, Manchester, Manchester University Press.

1 Limits of theorising about IR and security

Chapter 1 considers the limits of our theorising about International Relations and security in inquiring into others' conceptions of the international, namely: ethnocentrism, parochialism and Eurocentrism. Each section of the chapter focuses on one such limit and highlights its implications for theorising about security. Before proceeding, let me address one question that is frequently raised by mainstream students of the field.

What limit?

Students of the social sciences are accustomed to addressing the limits of their existing explanations by identifying puzzles and seeking to answer them. We call those phenomena 'puzzles' that we fail to explain within our existing frameworks, using our existing concepts, categories or theories. Research projects in IR are expected to respond to puzzles. As he encouraged the students of IR to think theoretically, James N. Rosenau advised them to identify puzzles, defined as 'perplexity over specific and patterned outcome' (Rosenau and Durfee, 1995: 36). IR as a social science would advance through identifying and answering puzzles, he instructed the students of the field. Since then, thinking in terms of puzzles has become a recognised way of explaining how to think theoretically in IR (Guzzini, 2001).

What if we are not puzzled? That is because we presume that 'we already understand'. We think our existing concepts and theories suffice in making sense of what we encounter in world politics. I suggest that the question of 'what limits?' is based on the same presumption; if we do not see the limits of our theorising about IR and security in inquiring into others' conceptions of the international, this is because we presume that 'we already understand'. Let me elaborate on this with reference to an example: security dynamics in the Middle East.

Steven M. Walt's 1987 study on Middle East security entitled *The Origins of Alliances* focused on alliance politics in the Middle East. In this book, Walt (1987) pointed to a type of alliance behaviour that could not be accounted for by structural realist accounts. Whereas structural realist frameworks focused on power balancing, noted Walt, the dynamics of relations between Arab states suggested that they were responding to threats and not necessarily changes in military power. In response to this puzzling behaviour of Arab states, Walt offered a new concept: 'balance of threat'.

About a decade after the publication of Walt's study, Michael J. Barnett (1998) offered an alternative answer to the same puzzle. While Walt correctly diagnosed an aspect of Arab politics that was previously unaccounted for, argued Barnett, he could not fully explain what he observed, given the limits of the structural realist framework that he used. Instead, Barnett offered a social constructivist framework to analyse the same dynamics. If Arab states seemed to be balancing threats and not power, wrote Barnett, it is the relationship between identity and security policy that needed focusing on. As such, Barnett's study entitled *Dialogues in Arab Politics* (1998) offered an alternative way of responding to Walt's puzzle, that is, by studying the constructedness of identity and its relationship with security policy (also see Barnett, 1999, Telhami and Barnett, 2002).

There was, however, something that did not puzzle either Walt or Barnett: Arab leaders' conceptions of security. While Walt and Barnett sought to make sense of the balancing behaviour of Arab leaders, they presumed that they already understood what 'security' meant for the leaders of the Arab world. Accordingly, both authors bracketed 'security' as they inquired into the policy behaviour of the Arab leaders (Bilgin, 2004a).

Certainly Walt and Barnett are in good company. Such lack of interest in the Arab leaders' conceptions of security is sustained by our presumption, as students of IR and security studies, that 'we already understand' 'their' behaviour by analysing 'their' capabilities based on 'our' assumptions regarding 'their' intentions. As will be discussed in Chapters 1 and 2, these limits have shaped significant aspects of mainstream and critical IR. One way of responding to the 'what limit?' question, I suggest, is to raise our 'contrapuntal awareness' and draw on the insights of postcolonial studies (as well as critical IR and security studies) to learn how to identify the limits of our theorising about IR and security.

Ethnocentrism in IR theorising

The concept of ethnocentrism has its origins in anthropologists' concern with accessing other societies' cultures in a manner that is not 'contaminated' by the researcher's own concepts and categories (Cooper, 2012). In sociology, ethnocentrism is understood as a bias encountered when one approaches the others through one's own value system (sometimes but not necessarily) by privileging one's own (Sumner, 1906: 13). Students of anthropology and sociology recognise that ethnocentrism may impede one's understanding of others even when s/he does not consider him/herself to be superior (Merton, 1973: 108). Then, as a scholarly affliction, ethnocentrism occurs when scholars seek to make sense of other groups or societies through their own concepts and categories, and without necessarily reflecting on their limits (Merton, 1972).

In IR, ethnocentrism was initially problematised by students of international negotiation and conflict resolution as they sought to understand the dynamics

18 Limits of IR theorising

of inter-group relations in times of conflict and/or during negotiations (LeVine and Campbell, 1972, Druckman, 1968, Campbell and LeVine, 1961, Hammond and Axelrod, 2006). Academic strategists, who are tasked with understanding the strategic 'beliefs' or 'styles' of their counterparts in other countries, followed suit (Booth, 1979, Gray, 1981, 1986, 2013).

Identifying ethnocentrism as a perennial problem for IR, Ken Booth wrote:

> Societies look at the world with their own group as the centre, they perceive and interpret other societies within their own frames of reference, and they invariably judge them inferior. Ethnocentrism is a phenomenon which has ramifications in most if not all areas of international relations.
>
> (Booth, 1979: 13)

For example, consider Quỳnh Phạm and Himadeep Muppidi's (2013) discussion on a remark made by General Westmoreland when discussing US strategic failures in the Vietnam war. According to General Westmoreland, the difficulties encountered by the US side included the difference in emphasis placed on the 'value' of human life by their Vietnamese counterparts. His understanding was that the Vietnamese side was able to endure significant losses in human-power, because 'the Oriental doesn't put the same high price on life as does the Westerner'. This was because, he opined, '[l]ife is plentiful, life is cheap in the Orient'. He continued by making an Orientalist move to link the contemporary Vietnamese behaviour with a 'fixed' past driven from ancient texts (Said, 1978). He wrote: 'And as the Philosophy of the Orient expresses it: Life is not important' (quoted in Phạm and Muppidi, 2013: 180).

As such, General Westmoreland was not puzzled. He presumed that he already understood the Vietnamese. This was not because his parochialism (see section on 'Parochialism in IR theorising') prevented him from taking an interest in the Vietnamese others. He was reported to have kept a copy of his counterpart General Giap's writings in his collection (Phạm and Muppidi, 2013: 180). Rather, the General's remark could be viewed as an instance of ethnocentrism impeding his attempt to make sense of the value system of another group or society. The General presumed that he already understood the Vietnamese by looking through the prism of 'pricing life or measuring its value based on "plentiful-ness" or scarcity' (Phạm and Muppidi, 2013).

Over the years, IR scholars have taken important steps in raising students' awareness of their ethnocentric limits in understanding 'others'. This is considered to be the best that IR scholars can do (Cooper, 2012). As Thierry Hentsch wrote, it is widely accepted that

> [e]thnocentrism is not a flaw to be simply set aside, nor is it a sin to be expunged through repentance. *It is the precondition of our vision of the Other.* Far from offering us absolution, this precondition compels us constantly to return to our point of departure, if only to grasp the internal and external imperatives which shape our curiosity about the Other.
>
> (Hentsch, 1992: xiv) [original emphasis]

Be that as it may, when IR's postcolonial critics point to ethnocentrism as a limit, they do not only point to individual researchers' biases and the need for vigilant self-reflection. They also point to the ways in which IR trains its students not to inquire into others' perspectives because we presume that 'we already understand' 'their' behaviour. Let me elaborate on this point by focusing on security theorising.

Ethnocentrism in theorising about security

The classical study on the ethnocentric limits of security theorising is Ken Booth's *Strategy and Ethnocentrism* from 1979. In this (then pioneering and now classical) study, Booth identified ethnocentrism as 'one of the important and pervasive sources of misjudgement which have so often affected the theory and practice of strategy' (Booth, 1979: 180).[1] Almost two decades after the first publication of his study, Booth reflected on how he first became aware of ethnocentrism's effects on the study of strategy. 'Trying to understand the Soviet Union, and the variety of Western thinking about it' he noted, 'revealed the ethnocentric character of Anglo-American strategic studies in particular and International Relations in general' (Booth, 1997: 96).

Efforts to understand Soviet behaviour led another student of strategic studies to inquire into Soviet strategic 'culture'. Jack Snyder's (1977) RAND Report entitled *The Soviet Strategic Culture: Implications for Limited Nuclear Operation* highlighted the ethnocentric limits of deterrence theorising in the United States. That said, Snyder's focus was on understanding Soviet behaviour and less so on identifying and addressing the limits of deterrence theorising. Colin Gray (Gray, 1981, 1986) built on the insights offered by Snyder and Booth to reflect on the limits of US strategic thinking when he wrote:

> There is a discernible American strategic 'culture': that culture referring to modes of thought and action with respect to force, derives from perception of the national historical experience, aspiration for self-characterisation (e.g., as an American, what am I?, how should I feel, think, and behave?), and from all of the many distinctively American experiences (of geography, political philosophy, of civic culture, and 'way of life') that characterise an American citizen.
>
> (Gray, 1981: 22)

However, these efforts by three forthcoming scholars of strategic studies were not integrated into deterrence theorising in the following years. Indeed, throughout the Cold War students of security studies presumed that they already understood Soviet behaviour through their existing frameworks: by analysing Soviet capabilities based on US assumptions regarding Soviet intensions. When others' strategic beliefs were studied, these were treated as deviation from the rule. The 'rule' was presumed to be deterrence theorising based on rational choice assumptions. During these years, there was little evidence of

20   *Limits of IR theorising*

questioning as to whether it was American 'beliefs' that shaped deterrence theorising, and whether this constituted a challenge for the claim to universal relevance.

This recounting of Cold War writings of students of strategic studies points to two aspects to the ethnocentric limits of theorising about security. In Neta Crawford's formulation:

> on the one hand ethnocentrism affects the ability of scholars to understand other societies' strategic beliefs. On the other hand, ethnocentrism prevents scholars from critically evaluating their own strategic beliefs and looking beyond their own culture for insights into problems.
>
> (Crawford, 1991: 302)

While Booth and Gray seemed to highlight both aspects, students of strategic studies at best focused on the first – as with Snyder and others' studies on strategic and security culture which flourished after the end of the Cold War (see Chapter 2). However, as Crawford noted, the challenge was not only the ethnocentrism of individual researchers and/or understanding particular countries, but also the ethnocentric limits of deterrence theorising as a body of knowledge.

Among students of security studies, it was a practitioner-turned-scholar, Michael MccGwire whose analysis hinted at the intricate relationship between these two aspects, which he discussed in terms of (1) the absence of 'serious Sovietologists' from the policy discussions on the Soviet Union and (2) the 'axiomatic nature' of deterrence theorising.

MccGwire was a British Naval officer before he turned to academic studies (Booth et al., 1998). The gist of MccGwire's argument in his 1985 study entitled 'Deterrence: The Problem – not the Solution' was that deterrence theorising proved less helpful in US encounters with the Soviet Union than its celebratory portrayals suggested. In this ground-breaking article, MccGwire pointed to how the Soviet policymakers devised their own precepts in nuclear strategy even as US strategists presumed the Soviets to be playing in the same 'deterrence game' as they did. Perhaps most devastatingly, MccGwire suggested that deterrence policies might, at times, have exacerbated the problems between the two superpowers.[2]

(1) To start with the absence of 'serious Sovietologists' from policy discussions, US strategists failed to understand the Soviet perspective on nuclear strategy partly because the area experts were not invited to join the debates on deterrence, wrote MccGwire (1985: 57). This was particularly problematic, he argued, because 'theories of limited war and escalation depended on assumptions about the Soviet reaction under given circumstances'. It was because US strategists' calculations were based on the capabilities of their opponents and their own assumptions regarding the opponents' intentions that deterrence thinking became a problem rather than the solution it was assumed to be, wrote MccGwire.

Limits of IR theorising 21

Instead of building US nuclear strategy on intelligence reports on Soviet capabilities[3] and US assumptions regarding Soviet intentions, wrote MccGwire, 'Soviet intentions must be examined directly'. He wrote:

> At the national level, intentions are remarkably consistent; radical change results from political shifts of a kind which have not occurred in the Soviet Union since the 1919 revolution. The evidence of more than sixty-five years of Soviet action and pronouncements, when combined with an analysis of Soviet interests and set in the historical context of geography and social inertia, produces a fairly clear picture of Soviet intentions, particularly on such fundamental matters as peace and war.
>
> (MccGwire, 1985: 59)

That said, MccGwire did not call for privileging area expertise (in this case Soviet studies) over theorising about IR and security. Rather, his was a plea for the insights of area studies to be brought into the discussions on nuclear strategy so that the 'axiomatic nature' of deterrence theorising would be problematised (MccGwire, 1985: 59).

(2) Regarding the 'axiomatic nature' of US strategic thinking, MccGwire argued, deterrence theorising rested on

> a definition of rational behaviour which, in political terms, was at best arational and more often irrational, and favoured models like the 'prisoners' dilemma' in preference to studying the political psychology of opponents and allies.
>
> (MccGwire, 1985: 57)

Soviet ways of reasoning regarding reasoning about nuclear strategy were not inquired into, wrote MccGwire, because US strategists presumed that they already understood their counterparts' intentions via recourse to the rationality assumption of deterrence theorising.

Of the two aspects of ethnocentrism identified by Crawford, MccGwire prioritised the first one, i.e. the ways in which the ethnocentric limits of deterrence theorising conditioned US security analysts' understanding of Soviet strategy. Hence his call for bringing in the insights of Sovietologists into security thinking. That said, his emphasis on the particularity of the notion of 'rationality' that shaped deterrence theorising also hinted at the intricate relationship between the two aspects of ethnocentrism. Highlighting the second aspect, in turn, would have required focusing on the implications, for deterrence theorising, of US security analysts' lack of interest in the Soviet (or any other counterparts') perspectives. Arguably, it was US strategists' lack of interest in studying Soviet reasoning on nuclear strategy that allowed for ethnocentric readings of American experiences to shape their thinking on what counted as 'rational' strategic behaviour. To reiterate, the challenge for the students of security studies is not only their own ethnocentric bias as

22 Limits of IR theorising

individual analysts, but also the ethnocentric limits of deterrence theorising as a body of knowledge.

Parochialism in IR theorising

The Oxford Dictionary defines parochialism as 'a limited or narrow outlook, especially focused on a local area; narrow-mindedness'.[4] Understood as such, parochialism may come across as 'an almost inevitable and universal characteristic of IR globally' insofar as 'there are "national" IR disciplines and that these quite naturally tend to be concerned with their own national interests', as Gunther Hellmann (2011: 1300) noted. For instance, scholars in those parts of the world that are adversely affected by environmental degradation may prioritise green politics, while scholars who are citizens of great powers may focus on their countries' hegemonic ambitions and those of the other aspiring hegemons. Be that as it may, what renders parochialism a challenge for IR is not that scholars in different parts of the world may have their narrow (geographical or topical) areas of concentration, but that they sometimes mistake their own narrow window on the world for the 'universal'.[5]

Aforementioned aspects of parochialism are identified by Thomas J. Biersteker (2009) as 'geographic', 'topical' and 'epistemological'. When IR's parochial limits are problematised, it is done mostly on epistemological terms (see, for example, Alker and Biersteker, 1984, Jarvis, 2001, Smith, 2004, Hellmann, 2011). Biersteker (2009: 311) defined epistemological parochialism as 'giving primacy to a single approach to scholarly analysis, or a synthesis of different traditions, as in the case of the English School's integration of history, philosophy and law'. In the case of IR in the United States, primacy has been given to rational choice theorising. Steve Smith, among others, has argued that the reason why mainstream IR has not been able to come to terms with its parochial limits could be sought in American IR's predilection for making IR a Social Science (narrowly defined), and the prevalence of rational choice theory among IR's 'scientists'. As Smith (2004: 503) wrote:

> rational choice theory treats identities and interests as given, and never enquires into how these come about. As such it buys into a political economy of the possessive individual, itself a creation of seventeenth century social contract theorists such as Hobbes and Locke. It takes the relationship between economics and politics as given, whereas in fact they were always taught as political economy until the nineteenth century. Crucially it treats these features of the social world, especially as they have unfolded in the U.S., as if they apply throughout the world and apply for all time, even projecting them backwards into history.

Over the years, mainstream IR orientated its students to think that the 'universal' relevance of 'rational choice' theorising rendered it unnecessary to inquire into others' perspectives.

Limits of IR theorising 23

It is significant to note here that IR is not the only social science discipline that has been conditioned by epistemological parochialism. All social sciences, in one way or another, are shaped by what the political geographer John Agnew called 'know-where', that is, the way in which

> much knowledge about world politics…involves the universalising of what can be called 'doubtful particularisms'. These are interpretive projections from the knowledge experiences of specific places/times onto all places/times.
>
> (Agnew, 2007: 138)

Somewhat different from some other social sciences, however, IR is expected to be cognisant of such limits, given its interest in 'the international'. Indeed, some consider IR as 'particularly well placed to escape' such limits (Jahn, 2000: 168).

But then, why has it proven so difficult to de-parochialise a field that is otherwise expected to caution everyone else against looking through their narrow windows on the world? Arguably, parochialism in IR has persisted for a long time because there is only partial awareness of its implications. On the one hand, there is widespread awareness of the need for students to be trained in other languages and cultures (Robles Jr., 1993, Hovey, 2004, cf. Blaney, 2002). On the other hand, our awareness about the parochial limits of IR theorising has been partial insofar as others' perspectives have seldom been brought to bear on IR theorising. Indeed, training students of IR in other cultures and languages may help with addressing geographical and topical parochialism, but is likely to leave epistemic parochialism untouched so long as others' explorations of world politics do not get recognised as 'IR'.

That others' perspectives gets categorised as 'area expertise' is an instance of the parochial limits of IR theorising in defining what counts as 'IR'. Amitav Acharya (2000: 8) observed this hierarchical categorisation in the following manner:

> While the introductory historical chapters of many textbooks on IR, dealing with the evolution of the international system, may these days include a section on China or India, and a few quotes from Kautilya or Confucius or Sun Tzu, this recognition of non-Western contributions stops as one moves to the discussion of more contemporary issues such as power, interdependence, and hegemony. Here, the overwhelming majority of theorists are Western, mostly American. It is as if, when it comes to International Relations, nothing of substance or significance has ever been said by anyone who grew up in Calcutta or Ulan Bator, Jakarta or Nairobi.

So long as others' perspectives are defined out of 'IR', the parochial limits of IR theories go undetected.

In those rare instances when others' perspectives are brought to bear on IR theorising (mainstream and critical) its parochial limits become apparent, as Naeem Inayatullah and David Blaney showed. For example, they wrote:

24 *Limits of IR theorising*

in both Waltz and Wendt an appeal to a state-of-nature condition is required to fill the gap in determinacy left by an undertheorization of international society; that is, an ahistorical and acultural state of nature displaces a more specific analysis of international society as a world of cultures and cultural interactions.

(Inayatullah and Blaney, 1996: 67)

L.H.M. Ling (2002: 16) concurred, reminding that such assumptions about the 'state of nature' do not come from nowhere but derive from a certain strand of 'Western political philosophy rooted in the experiences and perspectives of one group of people who happen to be white, propertied, and male'. As will be discussed in Chapter 2, these ideas about the 'state of nature' did not evolve in a vacuum but through 'European' encounters with 'non-European' others following the 'discovery' of America (Jahn, 2000). It is another instance of the parochial limits of IR theorising that this historical context and the roles played by IR's 'constitutive outside' (Inayatullah and Blaney, 2008, Ahluwalia, 2005) have been left out of discussions on the 'state of nature', upon which so much of mainstream IR has drawn.

Parochialism in theorising about security

Some consider the parochialism of security studies to be a 'natural' outcome of scholars' prioritisation of security concerns in their own regions as with scholars in India focusing on Pakistan, Turkey on Greece, etc. (Azar and Moon, 1988b, Baylis, 1998). Be that as it may, the parochial limits of security studies are not confined to giving a 'particular' regional focus to security scholarship. As with IR, what renders parochialism a limit for security thinking is the way in which 'particular' assumptions driven from one's own narrow outlook have become embedded into security thinking as 'theory'.

A case at hand is 'democratic peace' theorising that has sought to explain the relative absence of wars between democracies (Doyle, 1986, Russett, 1994, cf. Barkawi and Laffey, 1999, 2001). Ido Oren's historical investigation into the notion of 'democracy' as utilised by students of 'democratic peace' pointed to the particularity of this definition and democratic peace scholars' lack of reflection on this particularity. Oren wrote:

> Political scientists' current understanding of 'democracy' is the product of a historical process partly shaped by America's international rivalries. Those aspects of democracy that made America appear similar to its enemies have been marginalized over time, whereas those that magnify the apparent distance between America and its enemies have become privileged.
>
> (Oren, 2003: x)

The issue at hand is not merely 'methodological' but has shaped the findings of democratic peace research insofar as scholars looked back to history in search for what they expected to find. This is because

Limits of IR theorising   25

when we project our present definitions of democracy upon the past, it should not be surprising that our analyses validate scientific claims about the mutual peacefulness of democracies, for the concept of democratic peace is a product of the very same historical patterns against which the claims are being 'tested'.

(Oren, 2003: x)

Tarak Barkawi and Mark Laffey interrogated the definition of 'war' adopted by the same body of theory, pointing to the ways in which a particularly narrow definition of war is used to generate the data set and much of democratic peace theorising (Barkawi and Laffey, 1999, 2001). Notwithstanding such efforts, however, the parochial limits of democratic peace theorising in particular and security theorising in general have gone unacknowledged.[6]

It was not a student of security studies, but an anthropologist, Hugh Gusterson (1999) who unmistakably identified the parochialism of security theorising. Surveying articles published during 1986–1989 in *International Security*, one of the leading journals of security studies, Gusterson noted that those

readers who relied on the journal *International Security* alone for their understanding of world politics would have been taken more or less completely by surprise by the end of the Cold War in the fall of 1989.

(Gusterson, 1999: 319)

The point Gusterson made was not about (failures in) prediction in the study of security. Rather he argued that

authors in the journal constructed a discursive world within which the indefinite continuation of the Cold War was plausibly presumed and what we would in retrospect narrate as signs of the impending end of the Cold War were rendered dubious or invisible.

(Gusterson, 1999: 323)

Put differently, Gusterson's analysis highlighted how Anglo-American security concerns and a particular approach to these concerns had become embedded into the epistemology of security studies. Gusterson suggested that those scholars who relied on the journal for insight into the dynamics of world security likely became unable to even consider the possibility of the Cold War coming to an end. 'The problem with the dominant discourse in security studies in the 1980s was not that its construction of the international system was wrong', wrote Gusterson (1999: 324) 'but that it so marginalised discussion of competing constructions.' What led to parochialism in the study of security, argued Gusterson, was not only the search for prediction though utilising a particular way of thinking about world politics, but the sub-field's failures in thinking outside that particular way of thinking, often without recognising its particularity.

26 *Limits of IR theorising*

One body of scholarship that could have helped to identify the parochial limits of security thinking is the 'Third World' critics of security studies. Scholars contributing to this literature pointed to the limits caused by the imposition of the superpower conflict as the political framework and 'standard' approaches to IR as the theoretical framework when studying dynamics in other parts of the world. However, what the 'Third World' critics of security studies focused on was the 'different' characteristics of 'Third World' states but not necessarily the limits of the notion of 'security' that prevailed in security studies. As such, students of security in the 'Third World' offered new concepts to capture insecurities of developing statehood, as with the 'insecurity dilemma' (Job, 1992), 'wars of the third kind' (Holsti, 1996), 'software side of security' (Azar and Moon, 1988a), and 'subaltern realism' (Ayoob, 1997) (also see Al-Mashat, 1985, Bobrow and Chan, 1988, cf. Vale, 2003). The title of a chapter by Caroline Thomas (1989) crystallised this group of scholars' thinking: 'Southern instability, security and western concepts: On an unhappy marriage and the need for a divorce'. The implication of this group of studies was that what security studies needed was new concepts suited for the 'Third World', and not necessarily de-parochialising existing ones.

My point being that the 'Third World' critics of security studies pointed to the particularity of 'Third World' states and highlighted how security theorising failed to capture that particularity. As such, they left untouched the parochial limits of security studies. At the same time, this eventuality allowed for new parochialisms to emerge in the study of security in the 'Third World' (see below).

To reiterate, the challenge of parochialism as a limit for IR and security studies is not only geographical or topical but also epistemological. This is also why IR's parochial limits have gone unaddressed for so long, notwithstanding a myriad attempts to train students in other languages and cultures. IR's epistemic parochialism has remained untouched insofar as others' perspectives have not been recognised as IR and their insights were not utilised to de-parochialise 'our' thinking about IR and security.

Eurocentrism in IR theorising

Two different conceptions of Eurocentrism can be found in IR literature. Depending on which conception is adopted, Eurocentrism could be viewed as less or more of a challenge for IR. The first one views Eurocentrism as a fallacious approach to international history. Eurocentrism as a limit for IR is understood as building upon fallacious international historical accounts that put 'Europe' at the centre of world history even when it was not (yet) central to world politics. Adding de-centred histories to existing narratives is seen as a remedy to Eurocentrism understood as 'world history centred upon Europe'. The second conception draws upon economist Samir Amin (1989), and understands Eurocentrism as a 'consciousness' that has allowed the aforementioned accounts to prevail notwithstanding the availability of de-centred histories. As evidence of this second form of Eurocentrism in IR, scholars point to the prevalence of Eurocentric accounts of world history notwithstanding the availability of non-Eurocentric 'micro-histories' of various parts of the world (Shilliam, 2008).

Of the two conceptions of Eurocentrism I have identified above, Barry Buzan and Richard Little (2001, 2002) have built upon the first kind (world history centred upon Europe) and provided appraisals of IR scholarship that build upon fallacious accounts on world history (cf. Buzan and Lawson, 2013, 2015). Particularly problematic, Buzan and Little argued, were those studies that put Europe at the centre when looking at periods of world history when Europe was not (yet) at the centre. Indeed, as Hobson (2004, 2012) also reminded, it is only after the Industrial Revolution that Europe becomes 'central' to world history in the way presupposed by some IR scholarship.

While offering an important corrective to Eurocentric accounts of international history, what rendered Buzan and Little's critique of Eurocentrism in IR partial is the implication of their argument – that putting Europe at the centre of one's research may not necessarily be a problem when looking at those periods of world history when Europe was indeed at the centre. In contrast, Siba Grovogui (2006) maintained that Eurocentrism should not be viewed as a problem that only emerges when looking at periods prior to Europe's ascent. John Hobson (2004, 2009) concurred, noting that Eurocentrism imposes limits on research when studying periods of European ascent as well as the years prior to such ascent. This is because, argued Hobson, Eurocentrism results in portraying European achievements as products of autonomous development, whereas non-Eurocentric research agendas reveal relations of give-and-take and learning between world peoples across centuries.

But then, why is it that such fallacious approaches to world history pervade IR notwithstanding the availability of de-centred accounts?[7] An answer to this question is offered in Samir Amin's (1989) conception of Eurocentrism as 'consciousness'. According to Amin, this particular belief came about during the Renaissance and especially the age of Enlightenment, as 'Europe' sought to make a break with the past of seeking foundations for knowledge in religion and sought to anchor knowledge in 'science'. As Martin Bernal (1987) and Walter Mignolo (2003) have argued, albeit in reference to different contexts, Europe's self-understanding was re-drafted during this period by drawing an almost straight line from Ancient Greece to 'Europe', thereby entrenching a Eurocentric account of world history. This Eurocentric account narrated a history of 'Europe' as autonomously developed, almost as if no substantive debts were incurred by 'Europeans' to 'others' on the way.

In line with this Eurocentric account of world history, learning between the 'Europeans' and 'non-Europeans' is portrayed as having been unidirectional, with the former shaping the latter.[8] 'The asymmetry is striking', observed Edward Said:

> On the one hand we assume that the whole of history in colonial territories was a function of the imperial intervention; on the other, there is an

28 *Limits of IR theorising*

equally obstinate assumption that colonial undertakings were a phenomenon marginal and perhaps even eccentric to the central activities of the great metropolitan cultures.

(Said, 1986: 58–59)[9]

In contrast to such portrayals are historical accounts that document mutual learning between 'Europeans' and 'non-Europeans'. For instance, writing about Japan's relations with the Dutch prior to the expansion of the European international society, Shogo Suzuki noted that

> while many conventional historical studies…tended to concentrate heavily on examining Japan's relations with the Netherlands, Japan was at this time in a position to impose its own norms of diplomatic conduct to 'foreign' polities, and this would mean that the Netherlands would be incorporated into the social structures of a particular international order based on the terms of the Japanese.
>
> (Suzuki, 2014: 81)

Suzuki was writing with reference to the English School, but his observation is relevant for other Eurocentric accounts of world history. The point being, if Eurocentric approaches to world history have prevailed (in IR and elsewhere), this is no mere fallacy but a consequence of the persistence of Eurocentrism as a consciousness. Notwithstanding the availability of de-centred accounts that point to myriad relations of give-and-take, learning and mutual constitution between 'Europeans' and 'non-Europeans' they have yet to be brought to bear on macro accounts, as Eric Wolf also argued in his ground-breaking *Europe and the People Without History* (1982).

It is in this sense that Eurocentrism is not a mere historical fallacy, wrote Amin (1989), but a belief in the specificity of 'Europe' – a belief that is created through the writing of this particular historical narrative and sustained through successive narrations. Nor is Eurocentrism a form of ethnocentrism (see section on 'Eurocentrism in IR theorising') but an instance of 'culturalism', 'an apparently coherent and holistic theory based on the hypothesis that there are cultural variants able to persist through and beyond possible transformations in economic, social, and political systems' (Amin, 1989: 7). During the Crusades, wrote Amin, both the Crusaders and the Muslims looked at each other from their ethnocentric perspectives. However, the Crusaders were not (yet) Eurocentric in their self-understanding – no more than the Muslims were 'Islamocentric', noted Amin. The emergence of Eurocentrism, then, cannot be explained away as a phase in world history (as implied by the first understanding of Eurocentrism as 'world history centred on Europe') but as the production of a particular self-understanding that constituted 'Europe' and its relations with others.

Sandra Halperin (1997, 2006) laid out the challenge for students of IR when she wrote that the issue is not de-centring 'Europe' in world history through examining other parts of the world. For, Eurocentrism as consciousness has shaped the history of both 'Europe' and the rest of the world (Seth, 2011). Furthermore, it is through the concepts and categories developed in/by 'Europe' that students of IR make sense of their own and others' past and present. Accordingly, Halperin argued that the challenge for students of IR is learning how to look at 'Europe' anew, as reflected 'in the mirror of the Third World' (the title of Halperin's book). As yet, the Eurocentric limits of IR, argued Halperin (1997: viii, ix), did not allow researchers to see how 'the pattern displayed in contemporary Third World dependent development is analogous to the pattern of development in pre-1945 Europe'. However, she noted, in many cases, 'knowledges and practices universalised by Europeans…neither originated in Europe nor were even part of the European experience' (Halperin, 2006: 43).

For example, by way of shaping concepts and categories with which statehood and state development has been understood, Eurocentrism circumscribed our understanding of what is popularly referred to as 'state failure' (Bilgin and Morton, 2002, 2004). In Jennifer Milliken and Keith Krause's neat formulation, 'what has collapsed is more the vision (or dream) of the progressive, developmental state that sustained generations of academics, activists and policy-makers, than any real existing state' (Milliken and Krause, 2002: 762). That said, and following Halperin, it is not only state development in faraway lands that eludes IR, but also in Europe. Eurocentrism as a form of 'consciousness' is limiting for our understanding of state development here, there and everywhere (Halperin, 1997: viii, ix).

To summarise, depending on which conception of Eurocentrism is adopted, it could be viewed as less or more limiting for IR theorising. Those IR scholars who have adopted the first conception of Eurocentrism as 'world history centred upon Europe' consider it to be a challenge for IR insofar as scholarship draws upon fallacious accounts of world history. They seek to fix this problem by adding de-centred histories of other parts of the world. Those scholars who have adopted the second conception of Eurocentrism as 'consciousness' see Eurocentrism as a more fundamental problem for IR. This is because they understand Eurocentrism as a particular narrative about 'Europe' and its place in world history that has been constitutive of Europe's self-understanding, its understanding of others, others' understanding of 'Europe' and their own self-understanding. This latter group of scholars maintain that rendering IR less Eurocentric is not about adding on de-centred narratives to the existing accounts of world history, but inquiring into the constitutive relationships between 'Europe' and 'non-Europeans' and locating in these relationships the beginnings of the ideas and institutions of humankind (as with Said's emphasis on 'contrapuntal readings'). This eventuality is in tune with developments in other fields such as political theorist Susan Buck-Morss's (2000, 2003, 2009) emphasis on 'universal history', historian Sanjay Subrahymanyam's (1997, 2005) research on 'connected histories', and sociologist Gurminder Bhambra's (2007, 2010) call for 'connected sociologies'.

30 Limits of IR theorising

Eurocentrism in theorising about security

Eurocentrism in security studies is understood mostly in terms of the geo-cultural 'situatedness' of the contributors. Published in 1994, Ken Booth and Eric Herring's *Keyguide to Information Sources in Strategic Studies* pointed to how much of scholarship on security originated from the United States, and that this began to change only later with the increase in contributions by scholars from Western Europe.[10] Barry Buzan and Lene Hansen's *The Evolution of International Security Studies*, which came out 15 years later in 2009, highlighted the issue of what they called the 'Western-centrism' of security studies in terms of the geographical situatedness (also see Buzan and Wæver, 2010). Pointing to the limited number of sources written by authors located outside North America and Western Europe, Buzan and Hansen maintained that the sub-field had been 'Western-centric' and that this has generated a 'blind-spot' in the study of security whereby perspectives from outside North America and Western Europe did not get reflected in security studies (Buzan and Hansen, 2009: 19).[11]

Be that as it may, seeking to capture the Eurocentric limits of security studies through worlding the contributions only in terms of their geo-cultural situatedness ('worlding-as-situatedness') misplaces the problem insofar as the analyses offered by students of security writing from outside North America and Western Europe have also exhibited Eurocentric characteristics. The latter, in turn, could only be captured through worlding these contributions with an eye on the constitutive effects of security scholarship (worlding-as-constitutive) (see Chapter 3).

Over the years, the 'constitutive' dimension of Eurocentrism in security studies has gone largely unacknowledged (but see Vale, 2003, Barkawi and Laffey, 2006, Bilgin, 2010, Jabri, 2013). Indeed, the emergence of analyses, from the 1980s onwards, focusing on insecurities in the 'Third World' did little to remedy the Eurocentrism of security studies (see, for example, Azar and Moon, 1988b, Korany, 1986, Ayoob, 1997). This was not only because students of security in the 'Third World' were relatively few in numbers (as highlighted by Buzan and Hansen, see above). It was mostly because they exhibited what Immanuel Wallerstein (1997) termed, 'anti-Eurocentric Eurocentrism' by offering Euro-centric accounts of security in the 'Third World', even as they were critical of Eurocentrism of security studies. Over the years, the students of security studies have come to understand 'security' here, there and everywhere as viewed through the Eurocentric categories and concepts of the field. Students of security writing from the 'Third World' were no exception to this (see above).[12]

The constitutive dimension of Eurocentrism in security studies was highlighted by Tarak Barkawi and Mark Laffey (2006). Defining Eurocentrism in terms of both a fallacious historical account of 'world history centred on Europe' and a 'consciousness', Barkawi and Laffey pointed to the way in which Eurocentrism has shaped the sub-field. They wrote:

> questions of war and peace raised by great power competition are foun-
> dational for security thought and practice. As a result, security studies

Limits of IR theorising   31

provides few categories for making sense of the historical experiences of the weak and the powerless who comprise most of the world's population.
(Barkawi and Laffey, 2006: 332, also see Barkawi, 2005)

In advancing their critique, Barkawi and Laffey echoed students of security in the 'Third World' who underscored the limits of the military-focused Cold War framework in accounting for insecurities outside North America and Western Europe. However, where Barkawi and Laffey sought to identify and address the Eurocentric limits of security studies, students of security in the 'Third World' invariably offered Eurocentric critiques.

Consider, for instance, the writings of Abdulmonem Al-Mashat. In *National Security in the Third World* (1985) Al-Mashat highlighted the inadequacy of the concept of 'national security', which, he argued,

is a complex phenomenon that in developing countries is a more serious problem than in other countries…Such complexity can be approached by concentrating on two basic elements of national security in these countries; namely, tranquillity and well-being.
(Al-Mashat, 1985: 51)

However, what Al-Mashat was critical of was not conceptions of statehood, nationhood and security that were based on a particular story about European experiences (see above), but their utilisation in analysing security in the 'Third World'. Accordingly, Al-Mashat's critique left the concept of 'national security' untouched so long as it was used when analysing 'Europe'. Nor did he discuss the relationships between the 'First' and the 'Third World' in the production of insecurities. However, as Barkawi and Laffey (1999) argued, the emergence of a 'non-war community' in Western Europe cannot be explained in isolation from the persistence of wars in other parts of the world. Likewise, the emergence and persistence of 'failed states' is another instance of the Eurocentric limits of security studies. The very notion of 'failed states' makes sense in a discursive economy of 'failure' that overlooks the dynamic relationship between the 'First' and 'Third World' (Bilgin and Morton, 2002, 2004).

Also consider Caroline Thomas who played a central role during the 1990s in pushing security in Africa onto the agenda of security studies (Thomas, 1987, 1989, 1991, 1999, 2001, Thomas and Wilkin, 1999). At a time when security studies focused on the United States, its allies and their regional interests as referents of security in the 'Third World', Thomas's analyses looked at African states and peoples as security referents.[13] She wrote:

The traditional approach to security in the Third World, based on the Realist conception of international relations, fails to identify and address the most pressing current security concerns of the poorer states. This state-centric, geopolitical approach identifies physical threats outside the territorial boundary of the state, and sees the build-up of military power as the

32　*Limits of IR theorising*

appropriate response to the perceived external challenge...the primary physical threats to the security of the overwhelming number of Third World states are internal, not external; they result from granting of international legitimacy to states which lack domestic legitimacy.

(Thomas, 1991: 266)

However, as with Al-Mashat, Thomas highlighted the limits of standard concepts in accounting for insecurities in Africa. In doing so, she problematised assumptions regarding the relevance of these concepts for understanding insecurities in Africa, but not the concepts themselves. Again, as with Al-Mashat, Thomas did not consider the eventuality that what is needed may not be different concepts fit for different dynamics in the Third World, but re-thinking security studies concepts themselves with an eye on the global connections between the 'First' and 'Third World' in the context of colonial pasts and postcolonial presents (Thomas, 1989).

The point being that while students of security in the 'Third World' successfully highlighted the Eurocentric limits of security studies in accounting for insecurities outside North America and Western Europe, they did not discuss Eurocentrism as a limit of the concepts themselves but in terms of their utilisation in accounting for insecurities in the 'Third World'. In doing so, they fell short of challenging Eurocentrism in security studies, or identifying its limits fully for security theorising. Insofar as students of security in the 'Third World' continued to produce Eurocentric accounts, the Eurocentric limits of security theorising persisted. This eventuality, in turn, has had implications for the study of security not only in the 'Third World' but security studies in general (Barkawi and Laffey, 2006, Bilgin, 2010).

To summarise, the Eurocentric limits of security studies cannot be reduced to the prevalence of studies authored by scholars writing from North America and Western Europe (worlding-as-situatedness). Eurocentrism has been constitutive of security studies, the sub-field's core concepts and categories, as well as our knowledge about insecurities in different parts of the world. Indeed, even some of the critics of security studies specialising in the 'Third World' have exhibited Eurocentrism in their writings by way of finding fault with the utilisation of security studies concepts and categories outside North America and Western Europe, but not extending their critique to Eurocentric limits of the sub-field when making sense of security dynamics worldwide. I will revisit this point in the concluding section of this chapter.

Conclusion

Chapter 1 considered the limits of theorising about International Relations and security in inquiring into others' conceptions of the international. I focused on three main issues as raised by the critics: ethnocentrism, parochialism and Eurocentrism. In identifying the limits of mainstream theorising about IR and security, I raised my contrapuntal awareness and drew upon the criticisms raised by students of postcolonial studies.

Limits of IR theorising 33

Chapter 2 will consider the extent to which critical theorising about IR and security has addressed these limits. Before moving on, let me revisit the question I asked in the beginning of this chapter: 'what limit?' Now that I have discussed three main issues as identified by IR's (postcolonial) critics, let me try to address a second question that usually follows this one. It goes: 'Enough of pointing to limits. What do you propose as an alternative?'

By way of responding to this question, let me seek help from critical IR/International Political Economy scholar Craig Murphy (1996), who highlighted a similar kind of challenge that was issued to feminist IR in 1995 by the then president of the International Studies Association (ISA), Susan Strange (1995). Murphy wrote:

> In her presidential address Susan Strange expressed her guarded support for the new scholarship on women and gender in international relations but pleaded for its authors to stop the whining and just get on with it, by which Strange meant they should just get on with research demonstrating that attention to women and gender will tell us something important about the traditional subjects that have been at the core of research in the field.
>
> (Murphy, 1996: 532)

I quoted Murphy at length, because Susan Strange's challenge to feminist IR scholars comes across as prescient of contemporary sceptics' reservations vis-à-vis postcolonial studies. Is Strange's advice to feminist IR scholars ('just get on with it') also relevant to students of IR who seek to draw from the insights of postcolonial studies to point to IR's limitations?

Murphy argued that the formulation of the question that Strange directed to IR's feminist critics misplaces the problem, for pointing to the limits of IR theorising is one way of 'getting on with it'. Murphy identified the limits of Strange's challenge in the following way:

> much of the writing that Strange dismissed as whining can be seen as the work of scholars dedicated to getting on with the hard work of detailed empirical research. The problem is that many scholars would not identify the object of that research – specifying and explaining the limits on the rights of women – as a central task of international relations. They would see it as a small subset of the issue of compliance with international human rights norms, which itself would be a very small subset of the topics that should be addressed by the field as a whole.
>
> (Murphy, 1996: 532)

In a similar fashion, those students who draw from postcolonial studies to identify the limits of theorising about IR and security could be viewed as 'getting on with the hard work' of doing IR.

While students of mainstream (and some critical) IR expect the critics to offer an entirely new approach to international relations (in the form of, say, a Chinese or Iranian theory of IR), I suggest that the limits of IR cannot be

34   *Limits of IR theorising*

addressed by calling on 'others' to produce their own 'different' theories. Indeed, as will be discussed in Chapter 3, the very question 'why is there no Chinese or Iranian IR theory?' misplaces the problem. After all, to quote cultural studies scholar Arif Dirlik, 'it is possible to reverse the question, and ask not why Chinese do not have theory, or do not seem to be willing to do theory like "we" do, as if that were a failure, and ask instead why "we" have theory and do theory the way "we" do?' (Dirlik, 2011: 150–151).

Put differently, the way in which we ask the questions, 'what limit?' and/or 'what do you propose as an alternative?' gives away IR's limits in reflecting on its limits, and the ways in which those limits have been constitutive of IR. Chapter 2 will consider how critical IR fared in identifying and addressing these limits.

Notes

1 See Gray (2013) on the 'timeless significance' of Booth's study.
2 For detailed analyses of the track record of deterrence policymaking during the Cold War, see Lebow and Stein (1994, 1998).
3 It is also worth noting that intelligence gathering is not an exact science that is devoid of ideological or bureaucratic politics. A case at hand is the so-called 'missile gap' and 'bomber gap' fears in the United States during the late 1950s and early 1960s. See, for example, Johnson (1996).
4 'Parochialism', Oxford Dictionary, OUP online, http://www.oxforddictionaries. com/definition/english/parochialism. Accessed 13 May 2014.
5 The literature often singles out parochialism of IR in the United States. Perhaps the most well-known critique of parochialism of IR teaching in the United States is Hayward Alker and Thomas Biersteker's (1984) article entitled 'The Dialectics of World Order: Notes for a Future Archaeologist of International Savoir Faire'. 'If a future archaeologist were to take it upon him/herself to study IR in the United States', Alker and Biersteker argued, s/he will reach two findings. A library-based research would reveal a rich and diverse literature representing 'recognizable variants of each of the major research traditions'. An analysis of course syllabi, especially in 'leading' US universities, on the other hand, would reveal 'parochialism of IR teaching' (Alker and Biersteker, 1984: 128). Quarter of a century later, Thomas Biersteker found that parochialism persisted in IR teaching in the United States. He wrote: 'The nature of American IR parochialism is that it is rationalist, positivist, U.S.-centric, monolingual, recently published, and written by men' (Biersteker, 2009). How are we to make sense of the relatively larger number of studies on parochialism of IR scholarship in the United States when compared to other countries? Is IR in the United States more parochial than elsewhere? Even if IR in the United States is no more parochial than others, argued Thomas Biersteker (2009: 311) 'the prevalence of parochialism in the interpretation of international relations across the globe does not exonerate us from efforts to reduce it'. Does IR in other parts of the world fare any better? Studies on parochialism of IR outside the United States remain scant. A significant exception is Jonas Hagmann and Thomas Biersteker's (2014) comparative analysis of IR teaching in Europe and the United States. The authors' finding is that while IR teaching in the United States is more parochial than Europe, both have failed to integrate non-North American and non-European perspectives. Correspondingly, even if IR in the United States were indeed more parochial than others, this would not exonerate others from addressing their own parochialisms. Furthermore, focusing almost exclusively on parochialisms of IR in the United States may result

Limits of IR theorising 35

in leaving other parochialisms untouched (or invite new parochialisms in the form of national IR schools).

6 For instance, consider Tarak Barkawi's (2015) rejoinder to a recent piece on democratic peace theorising, which highlights the persistence of parochialism in this body of theory.

7 See, for example, Abu-Lughod (1989), Trouillot (1995), Gilroy (1993) and Mignolo (2003).

8 Iver Neumann quotes Charles Halperin to remind that '[i]t was endemic on the medieval religious frontier not to admit consciously that one had borrowed institutions from conquered or conquering peoples of a different religion. This was true of Crusader Valencian 13th century Spain about Islamic Moorish institutions, of the Arab Umayyad dynasty from the 7th century or the Ottoman Empire from the 14th century about Byzantine institutions, and of the French Crusader Kingdom of Jerusalem from the 12th century about Islamic Institutions' (Halperin quoted in Neumann, 2014: 12).

9 For an IR example, see Brown (1988). For a discussion that contests such unidirectional accounts, see Pieterse and Parekh (1995).

10 See, for example, Aradau et al. (2006), Wæver et al. (1993), and Wæver (2012).

11 Buzan and Hansen use 'Eurocentric' and 'Western-centric' interchangeably.

12 This argument was initially developed in Bilgin (2010). The following discussion draws upon this article.

13 A case at hand is regional security in the 'Middle East'. See Bilgin (2000, 2004a, 2004b).

Bibliography

Abu-Lughod, J. L. 1989. *Before European Hegemony: The World System A.D. 1250–1350*, New York, Oxford University Press.

Acharya, A. 2000. Ethnocentrism and Emancipatory IR Theory. In: Arnold, S. & Bier, J. M. (eds.) *Displacing Security*, Toronto, Centre for International and Security Studies, York University.

Agnew, J. 2007. Know-Where: Geographies of Knowledge of World Politics. *International Political Sociology*, 1, 138–148.

Ahluwalia, P. 2005. Out of Africa: Post-Structuralism's Colonial Roots. *Postcolonial Studies*, 8, 137–154.

Al-Mashat, A. M. M. 1985. *National Security in the Third World*, Boulder, CO, Westview Press.

Alker, H. & Biersteker, T. J. 1984. The Dialectics of World Order: Notes for a Future Archaeologist of International Savoir Faire. *International Studies Quarterly*, 28, 121–142.

Amin, S. 1989. *Eurocentrism*, New York, Monthly Review Press.

Aradau, C., Balzacq, T., Basaran, T., Bigo, D., Bonditti, P., Buger, C., Davidshofer, S., Guillaume, X., Guittet, E. P., Huysmans, J., Jeandesboz, J., Jutila, M., Lobo-Guerrero, L., Mccormack, T., Malksoo, M., Neal, A., Olsson, C., Petersen, K. L., Ragazzi, F., Akilli, Y. S., Stritzel, H., Van Munster, R., Villumsen, T., Wæver, O. & Williams, M. C. 2006. Critical Approaches to Security in Europe: A Networked Manifesto. *Security Dialogue*, 37, 443–487.

Ayoob, M. 1997. Defining Security: A Subaltern Realist Perspective. *Critical Security Studies*. In: Krause, K. & Williams, M. C. (eds.) Critical Security Studies: Concepts and Cases. Minneapolis: University of Minnesota Press.

Azar, E. E. & Moon, C.-I. 1988a. Legitimacy, Integration and Policy Capacity: The 'Software' Side of Third World National Security. In: Azar, E. E. & Moon, C.-I.

36 Limits of IR theorising

(eds.) *National Security in the Third World: The Management of Internal and External Threats*, Aldershot, Edward Elgar.

Azar, E. E. & Moon, C.-I. 1988b. Rethinking Third World National Security. In: Azar, E. E. & Moon, C.-I. (eds.) *National Security in the Third World: The Management of Internal and External Threats*, Aldershot, Edward Elgar.

Barkawi, T. 2005. *Globalization and War*, Rowman & Littlefield Publishers.

Barkawi, T. 2015. Scientific Decay. *International Studies Quarterly*, 59, 4, 27–29.

Barkawi, T. & Laffey, M. 1999. The Imperial Peace: Democracy, Force and Globalization. *European Journal of International Relations*, 5, 403–434.

Barkawi, T. & Laffey, M. (eds.) 2001. *Democracy, Liberalism, and War: Rethinking the Democratic Peace Debate*, Boulder, Co, Lynne Rienner Publishers.

Barkawi, T. & Laffey, M. 2006. The Postcolonial Moment in Security Studies. *Review of International Studies*, 32, 329–352.

Barnett, M. N. 1998. *Dialogues in Arab Politics: Negotiations in Regional Order*, New York, Columbia University Press.

Barnett, M. N. 1999. Culture, Strategy and Foreign Policy Change: Israel's Road to Oslo. *European Journal of International Relations*, 5, 5–36.

Baylis, J. 1998. International and Global Security in the Post-Cold War Era. In: Smith, S. & Baylis, J. (eds.) *The Globalization of World Politics*, Oxford, Oxford University Press.

Bernal, M. 1987. *Black Athena: The Afroasiatic Roots of Classical Civilization*, New Brunswick, NJ, Rutgers University Press.

Bhambra, G. K. 2007. *Rethinking Modernity: Postcolonialism and the Sociological Imagination*, New York, Palgrave.

Bhambra, G. K. 2010. Historical Sociology, International Relations and Connected Histories. *Cambridge Review of International Affairs*, 23, 127–143.

Biersteker, T. J. 2009. The Parochialism of Hegemony: Challenges for 'American' International Relations. In: Tickner, A. B. & Wæver, O. (eds.) *Global Scholarship in International Relations: Worlding Beyond the West*, London, Routledge.

Bilgin, P. 2000. Inventing Middle Easts? The Making of Regions through Security Discourses. In: Vikor, K. (ed.) *The Middle East in a Globalized World*, Oslo, Nordic Society for Middle Eastern Studies.

Bilgin, P. 2004a. *Regional Security in the Middle East: A Critical Perspective*, London, Routledge.

Bilgin, P. 2004b. Whose Middle East? Geopolitical Inventions and Practices of Security. *International Relations*, 18, 17–33.

Bilgin, P. 2010. The 'Western-Centrism' of Security Studies: 'Blind Spot' or Constitutive Practice? *Security Dialogue*, 41, 615.

Bilgin, P. & Morton, A. D. 2002. Historicising Representations of 'Failed States': Beyond the Cold-War Annexation of the Social Sciences? *Third World Quarterly*, 23, 55–80.

Bilgin, P. & Morton, A. D. 2004. From 'Rogue' to 'Failed' States? The Fallacy of Short-termism. *Politics*, 24, 169–180.

Blaney, D. L. 2002. Global Education, Disempowerment, and Curricula for a World Politics. *Journal of Studies in International Education*, 6, 268–282.

Bobrow, D. B. & Chan, S. 1988. Simple Labels and Complex Realities: National Security for the Third World. In: Azar, E. E. & Moon, C.-I. (eds.) *National Security in the Third World: The Management of Internal and External Threats*, Cheltenham, Edward Elgar.

Limits of IR theorising   37

Booth, K. 1979. *Strategy and Ethnocentrism*, New York, Holmes & Meier.

Booth, K. 1997. Security and Self: Reflections of a Fallen Realist. In: Krause, K. & Williams, M. C. (eds.) *Critical Security Studies: Concepts and Cases*, Minneapolis: University of Minnesota Press.

Booth, K. & Herring, E. (eds.) 1994. *Keyguide to Information Sources in Strategic Studies*, London, New York, Mansell.

Booth, K., Daniel, D., Herman, M., Mcdonnell, J., Clarke, M. & Dauber, C. E. 1998. A Cold War Life, and Beyond. In: Booth, K. (ed.) *Statecraft and Security: The Cold War and Beyond*, Cambridge, UK & New York, Cambridge University Press.

Brown, C. 1988. The Modern Requirement? Reflections on Normative International Theory in a Post-Western World. *Millennium – Journal of International Studies*, 17, 339–348.

Buck-Morss, S. 2000. Hegel and Haiti. *Critical Inquiry*, 26, 821–865.

Buck-Morss, S. 2003. *Thinking Past Terror: Islamism and Critical Theory on the Left*, New York, Verso.

Buck-Morss, S. 2009. *Hegel, Haiti, and Universal History*, Pittsburgh, PA, University of Pittsburgh Press.

Buzan, B. & Hansen, L. 2009. *The Evolution of International Security Studies*, Cambridge, Cambridge University Press.

Buzan, B. & Lawson, G. 2013. The Global Transformation: The Nineteenth Century and the Making of Modern International Relations. *International Studies Quarterly*, 57, 620–634.

Buzan, B. & Lawson, G. 2015. *The Global Transformation: History, Modernity and the Making of International Relations*, Cambridge, Cambridge University Press.

Buzan, B. & Little, R. 2001. Why International Relations has Failed as an Intellectual Project and What to Do about It. *Millennium – Journal of International Studies*, 30, 19–39.

Buzan, B. & Little, R. 2002. International Systems in World History: Remaking the Study of International Relations. In: Hobden, S. & Hobson, J. M. (eds.) *Historical Sociology of International Relations*, Cambridge, Cambridge University Press.

Buzan, B. & Wæver, O. 2010. After the Return to Theory: The Past, Present and Future of Security Studies. In: Collins, A. (ed.) *Contemporary Security Studies*, Oxford, Oxford University Press.

Campbell, D. T. & Levine, R. A. 1961. A proposal for cooperative cross-cultural research on ethnocentrism. *Journal of Conflict Resolution*, 5, 1, 82–108.

Cooper, E. E. 2012. Ethnocentrism. *Oxford Bibliographies*, Oxford University Press http://www.oxfordbibliographies.com/view/document/obo-9780199766567/obo-9780199766567-0045.xml. Accessed 20 May 2014.

Crawford, N. C. 1991. Once and Future Security Studies. *Security Studies*, 1, 283–316.

Dirlik, A. 2011. Culture in Contemporary IR Theory: The Chinese Provocation. In: Shilliam, R. (ed.) *International Relations and Non-Western Thought: Imperialism, Colonialism and Investigations of Global Modernity*, London, Routledge.

Doyle, M. 1986. Liberalism and World Politics. *American Political Science Review*, 80, 1151–1169.

Druckman, D. 1968. Ethnocentrism in the Inter-nation Simulation. *Journal of Conflict Resolution*, 12, 45–68.

Gilroy, P. 1993. *The Black Atlantic: Modernity and Double Consciousness*, Cambridge, MA, Harvard University Press.

Gray, C. S. 1981. National Style in Strategy: The American Example. *International Security*, 62, 2, 21–47.

38 Limits of IR theorising

Gray, C. S. 1986. *Nuclear Strategy and National Style*, Lanham, MD, Hamilton Press.

Gray, C. S. 2013. The Strategic Anthropologist. *International Affairs*, 89, 1285–1295.

Grovogui, S. N. 2006. *Beyond Eurocentrism and Anarchy: Memories of International Order and Institutions*, New York, Palgrave Macmillan.

Gusterson, H. 1999. Missing the End of the Cold War in International Security. In: Weldes, J., Laffey, M., Gusterson, H. & Duvall, R. (eds.) *Cultures of Insecurity: States, Communities and the Production of Danger*, Minneapolis, University of Minnesota Press.

Guzzini, S. 2001. The Significance and Roles of Teaching Theory in International Relations. *Journal of International Relations and Development*, 4, 98–117.

Hagmann, J. & Biersteker, T. J. 2014. Beyond the Published Discipline: Toward a Critical Pedagogy of International Studies. *European Journal of International Relations*, 20, 2, 291–315.

Halperin, S. 1997. *In the Mirror of the Third World: Capitalist Development in Modern Europe*, Ithaca, NY, Cornell University Press.

Halperin, S. 2006. International Relations Theory and the Hegemony of Western Conceptions of Modernity. In: Jones, B. G. (ed.) *Decolonizing International Relations*, Lanham, MD, Rowman & Littlefield.

Hammond, R. A. & Axelrod, R. 2006. The Evolution of Ethnocentrism. *Journal of Conflict Resolution*, 50, 926–936.

Hellmann, G. 2011. International Relations as a Field of Study. In: Badie, B., Berg-Schlosser, D. & Morlino, L. (eds.) *International Encyclopedia of Political Science*, London, Sage.

Hentsch, T. 1992. *Imagining the Middle East*, Montréal & New York, Black Rose Books.

Hobson, J. M. 2004. *The Eastern Origins of Western Civilization*, Cambridge, Cambridge University Press.

Hobson, J. M. 2009. The Myth of the Clash of Civilizations in Dialogical-Historical Context. In: Bilgin, P. & Williams, P. D. (eds.) *Global Security, in Encyclopedia of Life Support Systems (EOLSS)*, Oxford, UNESCO, EoLSS Publishers.

Hobson, J. M. 2012. *The Eurocentric Conception of World Politics: Western International Theory, 1760–2010*, Cambridge, Cambridge University Press.

Holsti, K. J. 1996. *The State, War, and the State of War*, Cambridge: Cambridge University Press.

Hovey, R. 2004. Critical Pedagogy and International Studies: Reconstructing Knowledge through Dialogue with the Subaltern. *International Relations*, 18, 241–254.

Inayatullah, N. & Blaney, D. L. 1996. Knowing Encounters: Beyond Parochialism in International Relations Theory. In: Lapid, Y. & Kratochwil, F. V. (eds.) *The Return of Culture and Identity in IR Theory*, Boulder, CO, Lynne Rienner Publishers.

Inayatullah, N. & Blaney, D. L. 2008. International Relations from Below. In: Reus-Smit, C. & Snidal, D. (eds.) *Oxford Handbook of International Relations*, Oxford, Oxford University Press.

Jabri, V. 2013. *The Postcolonial Subject: Claiming Politics/Governing Others in Late Modernity*, London, Routledge.

Jahn, B. 2000. *The Cultural Construction of International Relations: The Invention of the State of Nature*, London, Palgrave Macmillan.

Jarvis, D. S. L. 2001. International Relations: An International Discipline? In: Crawford, R. A. & Jarvis, D. S. (eds.) *International Relations – Still an American Social Science? Toward Diversity in International Thought*, Albany, NY, State University of New York Press.

Job, B. L. 1992. The Insecurity Dilemma: National, Regime and State Securities in the Third World. In: Job, B. L. (ed.) *The Insecurity Dilemma*, Boulder, CO, & London, Lynne Rienner.

Johnson, L. K. 1996. Analysis for a New Age. *Intelligence and National Security*, 11, 657–671.

Korany, B. 1986. Strategic Studies and the Third World: A Critical Evaluation. *International Social Science Journal*, 38, 547–562.

Lebow, R. N. & Stein, J. G. 1994. *We All Lost the Cold War*, Princeton, NJ, Princeton University Press.

Lebow, R. N. & Stein, J. G. 1998. Nuclear Lessons of the Cold War. In: Booth, K. (ed.) *Statecraft and Security: The Cold War and Beyond*, Cambridge: Cambridge University Press.

Levine, R. A. & Campbell, D. T. 1972. *Ethnocentrism: Theories of Conflict, Ethnic Attitudes, and Group Behavior*, New York, Wiley.

Ling, L. H. M. 2002. *Postcolonial International Relations: Conquest and Desire between Asia and the West*, New York, Palgrave.

MccGwire, M. 1985. Deterrence: The Problem – Not the Solution. *International Affairs*, 62, 55–70.

Merton, R. K. 1972. Insiders and Outsiders: A Chapter in the Sociology of Knowledge. *American Journal of Sociology*, 78, 1, 9–47.

Merton, R. K. 1973. *The Sociology of Science: Theoretical and Empirical Investigations*, Chicago, The University of Chicago Press.

Mignolo, W. 2003. *The Darker Side of the Renaissance: Literacy, Territoriality, and Colonization*, Ann Arbor, University of Michigan Press.

Milliken, J. & Krause, K. 2002. State Failure, State Collapse, and State Reconstruction: Concepts, Lessons and Strategies. *Development & Change*, 33, 753.

Murphy, C. N. 1996. Seeing Women, Recognizing Gender, Recasting International Relations. *International Organization*, 50, 513–538.

Neumann, I. B. 2014. Europeans and the Steppe: Russian Lands under the Ongol rule. In: Suzuki, S., Zhang, Y. & Quirk, J. (eds.) *International Orders in the Early Modern World: Before the Rise of the West*, London, Routledge.

Oren, I. 2003. *Our Enemies and US: America's Rivalries and the Making of Political Science*, Ithaca, Cornell University Press.

Phạm, Q. & Muppidi, H. 2013. Wresting the Frame. In: Tickner, A. B. & Blaney, D. (eds.) *Claiming the International*, London, Routledge.

Pieterse, J. N. & Parekh, B. 1995. Shifting Imaginaries: Decolonization, Internal Deco-lonization, Postcoloniality. In: Pieterse, J. N. & Parekh, B. (eds.) *The Decolonization of Imagination: Culture, Knowledge and Power*, London, Zed Books.

Robles Jr., A. C. 1993. How 'International' Are International Relations Syllabi? *PS: Political Science and Politics*, 26, 526–528.

Rosenau, J. N. & Durfee, M. 1995. *Thinking Theory Thoroughly: Coherent Approaches to an Incoherent World*, Boulder, CO, Westview Press.

Russett, B. 1994. *Grasping the Democratic Peace: Principles for a Post-Cold War World*, Princeton, NJ, Princeton University Press.

Said, E. W. 1978. *Orientalism*, London, Penguin.

Said, E. W. 1986. Intellectuals in the Post-Colonial World. *Salmagundi*, 70/71, 44–64.

Seth, S. 2011. Postcolonial Theory and the Critique of International Relations. *Millennium – Journal of International Studies*, 40, 167–183.

Shilliam, R. 2008. What the Haitian Revolution Might Tell us about Development, Security, and the Politics of Race. *Comparative Studies in Society and History*, 50, 778–808.

Smith, S. 2004. Singing Our World into Existence: International Relations Theory and September 11. *International Studies Quarterly*, 48, 499–515.

40 Limits of IR theorising

Snyder, J.L. 1977. *The Soviet Strategic Culture. Implications for Limited Nuclear Operations.* Santa Monica, CA: RAND Corporation.

Strange, S. 1995. Presidential Address: ISA as a Microcosm. *International Studies Quarterly*, 39, 289–295.

Subrahmanyam, S. 1997. Connected Histories: Notes Toward a Reconfiguration of Early Modern Eurasia. *Modern Asian Studies*, 31, 735–762.

Subrahmanyam, S. 2005. On World Historians in the Sixteenth Century. *Representations*, 91, 26–57.

Sumner, W. G. 1906. *Folkways: A Study of the Sociological Importance of Usages, Manners, Customs, Mores, and Morals*, New York, Ginn.

Suzuki, S. 2014. Europe at the Periphery of the Japanese World Order. In: Suzuki, S., Zhang, Y. & Quirk, J. (eds.) *International Orders in the Early Modern World: Before the Rise of the West*, London, Routledge.

Telhami, S. & Barnett, M. N. (eds.) 2002. *Identity and Foreign Policy in the Middle East*, Ithaca, Cornell University Press.

Thomas, C. 1987. *In Search of Security: The Third World in International Relations*, Boulder, CO, Lynne Rienner.

Thomas, C. 1989. Southern Instability, Security and Western Concepts: On an Unhappy Marriage and the Need for a Divorce. In: Thomas, C. & Saravanamuttu, P. (eds.) *The State and Instability in the South*, Basingstoke, Macmillan.

Thomas, C. 1991. New Directions in Thinking about Security in the Third World. In: Booth, K. (ed.) *New Thinking about Strategy and International Security*, London, Harper Collins.

Thomas, C. 1999. Where is the Third World now? *Review of International Studies*, 25, 225–244.

Thomas, C. 2001. Global Governance, Development and Human Security: Exploring the Links. *Third World Quarterly*, 22, 159–175.

Thomas, C. & Wilkin, P. (eds.) 1999. *Globalization, Human Security, and the African Experience*, Boulder, CO, Lynne Rienner Publishers.

Trouillot, M.-R. 1995. *Silencing the Past: Power and the Production of History*, Boston, Beacon Press.

Vale, P. 2003. *Security and Politics in South Africa: The Regional Dimension*, Boulder, CO, Lynne Rienner Publishers.

Wæver, O. 2012. Aberystwyth, Paris, Copenhague: The Europeness of New 'Schools' of Security Theory in an American Field'. In: Tickner, A. B. & Blaney, D. (eds.) *Thinking International Relations Differently*, London, Routledge.

Wæver, O., Buzan, B., Kelstrup, M. & Lemaitre, P. 1993. *Identity, Migration and the New Security Agenda in Europe*, London, Pinter.

Wallerstein, I. 1997. Eurocentrism and its Avatars: The Dilemmas of Social Science. *New Left Review*, I, 226, 93–108.

Walt, S. M. 1987. *The Origins of Alliances*, Ithaca, Cornell University Press.

Wolf, E. R. 1982. *Europe and the People Without History*, Berkeley, Universitty of California Press.

2 Critical theorising about IR and security

'Who does the theorising?'

Chapter 2 considers how critical approaches fared in identifying and addressing IR's limits as discussed in Chapter 1. I do this by focusing on the question, 'who does the theorising?' – a question initially raised by K.J. Holsti (1985) and elaborated upon by the postcolonial critics of IR. Writing from today's vantage point, where critical IR is found wanting in addressing this question and its various implications, one may fail to appreciate the roles played by critical IR scholars in opening up the field to allow a variety of voices to be heard.[1] Indeed, beginning from the early 1980s, the field of International Relations witnessed concerted efforts designed to re-think IR.[2] By the early 1990s, the project of 're-thinking IR' was considered to have gained significant ground. Jim George (1994: 216) applauded the critical approaches for having 'broken down' what Holsti (1985) referred to as the 'three-centuries long intellectual consensus' in IR. In the following years, others joined George in commending the critical approaches for 'introducing doubt' (Wyn Jones, 2001b: 2) into the study of world politics, even if the positivist edifice of the mainstream remained standing (also see Smith, 2002a, Krishna, 1993, Neufeld, 1995, Walker, 2002).

Arguably, it was these very accomplishments of critical IR scholarship in opening up the discipline that have also rendered visible the ways in which some of the pillars of the 'three-centuries long intellectual consensus' were still standing. Among IR scholars, George was not alone in overlooking the question 'who does the theorising?' as he applauded the accomplishments of critical IR. Michael Banks (1986), when highlighting what was at stake in the 'third debate' between realists, structuralists and pluralists, mentioned 'the South' only with reference to economic inequalities and conflicts, but not in epistemological terms (cf. Maghroori and Ramberg, 1982). Yosef Lapid (1989: 237, also see Lapid, 2002), who clarified the terms of the 'third debate', did not problematise the question of 'who does the theorising?' even as he endorsed re-thinking IR in a manner that paralleled 'the intellectual ferment' that other social sciences were experiencing at the time (cf. Biersteker, 1989). Finally, Steve Smith (2002b, 2004), who has done much to challenge mainstream IR's parochialism and ethnocentrism, was also criticised for failing to reflect upon the Eurocentric

42 Critical IR theorising

limits of his own critique (Chan, 1997). That having been said, some strands of critical IR thinking have been more attentive to the question 'who does the theorising?' and the implications of the answer (see below).

Chapter 2 begins with a discussion on how critical scholars sought to identify and address IR's limits. The sections that follow consider the contributions of critical theorising about IR and security. The concluding section suggests that if some of critical IR's Eurocentric limits have remained, this is because the students of critical IR understood the limits of IR in terms of the geo-cultural origins and/or location of scholars whose voices were apparently absent from the debates. To invoke the conceptual vocabulary introduced in the Introduction, where asking the question 'who does the theorising?' calls for worlding IR in the first sense ('worlding-as-situatedness'), inquiring into its implications invites worlding IR in the second sense ('worlding-as-constitutive'). Indeed, as will be seen below, the need for inquiring into 'others' as IR's 'constitutive outside' has barely registered in critical IR debates on the limits of the field.

I borrow the notion 'constitutive outside' from Stuart Hall (1996) whose definition of postcolonialism I presented in the Introduction. Pal Ahluwalia (2005) elaborated on IR's 'constitutive outside' in a discussion on 'post-structuralism's colonial roots' (also see Go, 2013). Ahluwalia sought to capture the 'ambivalence of deconstruction', which he formulated as

> the contradiction between the marginality, and indeed provisionality, of the Algerian experience that seeks to challenge the master discourse of the West, and the simultaneous disavowal of that marginality which puts deconstruction at the very centre of the European thought.
>
> (Ahluwalia, 2005: 145)

Put differently, postcolonial experiences are already there even when they are left out of the post-structuralist writings; and the task of critical scholars is to point to their apparent absence from, and the constitutive effects such absence has had on, post-structuralist thinking.

David Blaney and Naeem Inayatullah invoked the notion of IR's 'constitutive outside' when they argued against 'bridging' IR and postcolonial studies, and called for an 'excavation'. This is because, where 'bridging' implies two things that are about to be brought together, in the case of postcolonialism and IR, the relationship is constitutive. Hence they called for

> a mining of the culture of international relations in order to reveal the representational practices that hide what is central to its constitution and through which we may find the resources for international relations' reimagination.
>
> (Blaney and Inayatullah, 2008: 670)

Drawing on these insights, the following suggests that if some of IR's limits remained, notwithstanding the best efforts of critical thinking about IR and security, this could be understood as a consequence of understanding those limits in terms of the geo-cultural situatedness of IR scholars ('who does the theorising?'), but not always reflecting on the ways in which the ideas and experiences of 'others' have been constitutive of IR even as they were apparently absent from debates.

Critical IR and the limits of theorising about IR and security

During the 1980s and 1990s, critical IR scholars were invariably concerned with producing 'better theory' (Banks, 1986: 17) to counter the 'poverty of neorealism' (Ashley, 1984) and moving 'beyond positivism' (Smith, 1996). While critical IR scholars did not agree as to their definition of 'better theory', they were in agreement regarding the basics: 'concrete, self-reflexive, nuanced, and theoretically-informed research' (Biersteker, 1989: 267, Price and Reus-Smit, 1998, Hutchings, 2001). The 'world-making nature of theory' (George, 1994: 3) was underscored by Robert W. Cox (1981), who pointed to neo-realism as a 'problem-solving theory' that helped to constitute the neo-liberal world order as it sought to fix its glitches. Theory as 'everyday political practice' (George, 1994: 3) was underscored by R.B.J. Walker (1993: 6) when he maintained that '[t]heories of international relations are more interesting as aspects of contemporary world politics that need to be explained than as explanations of contemporary world politics'. Cynthia Enloe (1990, 1996) pointed to gendered practices of world politics that were overlooked not only by those who consider theories as explanations of world politics, but also by those who understand theories as aspects of world politics. In sum, the efforts of critical IR scholars were directed toward producing 'a different kind of knowledge and knowledge of a different reality' (Tooze and Murphy, 1996: 698, Murphy, 2001). For, from a critical IR perspective, the theory/practice relationship is understood not merely as shaping policy by whispering into the ears of those in power. There is a larger role that theories play in shaping world politics through interrogating what is accepted as the 'common sense', informing (and being informed by) social movements, and teaching (Booth, 1997a, Smith, 1997, Murphy, 2007).

Contra those who 'measure' the efficacy of critical approaches by the standards of the mainstream (see, for example, Keohane, 1988, Walt, 1991), critical IR scholars insisted that their contributions be assessed differently, i.e. 'through an awareness of the distinctiveness of various perspectives and their respective relation to existing structures of power' (Duvall and Varadarajan, 2003: 77). Accordingly, critical IR scholars disavowed empiricism while calling for increased emphasis to be put on empirical research. Steve Smith (2002a: 202) emphasised the need for conducting empirically grounded studies when he wrote that 'the acid test for the success of alternative and critical approaches is the extent to which they have led to empirically grounded work that explores the range and variety of world politics'. Critical IR scholars who focused on empirical cases produced important studies analysing how 'national interests', 'crises' (Weldes, 1996, 1999), 'sovereignty' (Peterson, 1992, Weber, 1995) and 'national identity' (Campbell,

44 *Critical IR theorising*

1992, 1993) are socially constructed; how constructions of security shape the dynamics of societies and world politics (Wæver et al., 1993, Huysmans, 1995, 2006b, Booth, 1991c, Deudney, 1983, Campbell, 1992, Tickner, 1992); NATO as a 'cultural' community of identity (Milliken, 2001, Klein, 1990, Williams and Neumann, 2000); and the political economy of world order (Murphy, 2006, Cox, 1987, Murphy, 1994).

One question that was not very high on the agenda of the aforementioned critical IR scholars was 'who does the theorising?'. Writing in 1985, Holsti had invited IR scholars to consider the question '*who* does the theorising' (original emphasis), for he expected the answer to have significant implications for the study of world politics. This question was important for Holsti not because he was committed to opening up the field for its own sake. Rather, he argued that since IR 'reflected the historical experience of the European state system in the past, and the Cold War more recently', one should expect 'serious challenges' to come from those who did not share these experiences or experienced them differently (Holsti, 1985: viii). 'The problem of *what* kind of theories we use to understand and explain the world of international politics is not divorced from *who* does the theorising', Holsti (1985: viii) wrote (original emphasis). Consequently, Holsti challenged critical IR scholars to go beyond introducing or subtracting '"essential" actors' and/or changing 'the core subjects of the field' (which he viewed to be the focus of the critical IR agenda) and ask '*who* does the theorising' so that they would be in a position to offer a 'serious challenge' to the field of IR. What Holsti (1985: viii) had in mind was inquiring into the perspectives of those who seemed to be underrepresented in IR journals as revealed by the analysis of bibliometric data, i.e. scholars from outside Western Europe and North Africa.[3]

In the years that followed, Holsti's question was taken up by some other critical scholars who problematised the limits of IR on similar terms, i.e. the geo-cultural situatedness of scholars. In the late 1990s, Ole Wæver offered an updated analysis of bibliometric data on IR scholarship and reached conclusions similar to those of Holsti. IR was a discipline that was 'not so international' wrote Wæver (1998b). While the focus of Wæver's 1998 study was American and European IR, during the 2000s he inquired into various aspects of IR's lack of 'openness' through the 'geocultural epistemologies and IR' project (with Arlene B. Tickner, see Chapter 3). More recently, Peter Markus Kristensen (2015) extended and updated Wæver's bibliometric data analysis. His findings suggested that while there has been some progress in the past decade or so, it was relatively small.

It is significant to note here that IR is by no means exceptional in terms of the low number of contributions by scholars from outside Western Europe and North America (measured in terms of contributions to 'top' journals). Indeed, Kristensen's findings suggested that

> IR is not the most Anglo-Saxon social science either. Political science, psychology, economics, and sociology are all more dominated by

Anglo-Saxon-based scholars. Anglo-Saxons only account for a smaller share of publications in anthropology and in the full sample of law articles. Comparatively speaking, IR is not the most American or Anglo-Saxon social science. Nor is IR the social science with the highest proportion of Anglo-Saxon and Continental European contributions taken together.

(Kristensen, 2015: 257)

That said, it is worth underscoring the point that some of the critics focus on the question 'who does the theorising?' not necessarily because IR's record is any worse than some other social science disciplines. Rather, they ask this question because while IR is *the* scholarly discipline where one expects to find research into the constitution and functioning of the international (Seth, 2013), there is little interest within IR on the perspectives of those 'others' who also helped to constitute 'the international' (Jabri, 2013). Indeed, such discrepancy between what IR promises (an explanation or understanding of the international) and what mainstream perspectives delivered (a 'particular' perspective on the international that is offered as the 'universal' story) is what the critics have problematised. What is at stake in debates about 'who does the theorising?', then, is not merely IR opening up to the writings of differently situated authors, but opening up to those perspectives that may question IR's self-understandings regarding the constitution of the international and the contours of what counts as 'IR'.

On the one hand, IR's problems with reflecting on 'others' as its 'constitutive outside' should not come across as surprising given that mainstream IR reflects prevalent narratives about its founding in the United Kingdom and the United States in the aftermath of the two world wars. However, asking 'who does the theorising?' requires us to go beyond reflecting on the situatedness of IR's founders in North America and Western Europe, to consider the constitutive effects of such situatedness. As Vivienne Jabri highlighted,

> The scripting of global politics in terms that subsume the postcolonial world confers agency, and hence authorship and legitimacy to the West, thereby generating a conceptual schema that is not only inadequate to the task of understanding the international, but one that is framed in universalist and normative terms.

(Jabri, 2014: 378–379)

The point being that addressing the limits of IR is not merely a matter of reflecting on the geo-cultural situatedness of its founders or current contributors, but conditioned by the way we narrate the story of how the international is constituted and how we draw the contours of what counts as 'IR', i.e. by leaving out the perspectives of those who also help to constitute the international. The issue is not merely *who* does the theorising, but also what they *say*, and whether others' writings on the international are received as 'IR' (Acharya, 2000, 2014, Shilliam, 2009, 2011).

46 *Critical IR theorising*

The following sections look at three strands of critical IR thinking: Frankfurt School IR, post-structuralist IR, and feminist IR.[4] These three approaches are chosen for the pivotal role they have played in re-thinking IR. Treating all three approaches as 'constellations' (Wyn Jones, 2001b), I will not attempt to reflect their richness but discuss how they contributed to addressing the limits of theorising about IR. Each section includes a spotlight sub-section on security scholarship inspired by that body of critique.

Frankfurt School IR and the limits of IR theorising

What has distinguished Frankfurt School IR scholars from other critical approaches is their explicit commitment to augmenting emancipatory thinking and practices in world politics (Neufeld, 1995, Wyn Jones, 2001a, Brincat et al., 2012). Andrew Linklater (1982, 1990, 1992, 1998, 2005) sought to go 'beyond Realism and Marxism' as he pointed to the possibility of extending moral community beyond citizens in search for emancipation. Ken Booth (1991b, 1997b, 2005c, 2007) argued that security and emancipation should be viewed as 'two sides of the same coin'.[5]

The critics of Frankfurt School IR have long cautioned that such 'commitment to "changing the world" implies a commitment to a particular vision of what the changed world ought to look like' (Duvall and Varadarajan, 2003: 83). More specifically, the critics pointed to the particularity of universals such as emancipation, and critiqued Frankfurt School IR for being unwilling to let go of the ideas and ideals of the Enlightenment, understood as an 'authoritative and exclusionary' approach to emancipation (Hutchings, 2001: 83). Adopting such a notion of emancipation, they argued, would amount to imposing particular universals on others who do not (want to) share these ideas and ideals (Brown, 1988, Shani, 2007, 2008, cf. Wyn Jones, 2001b).

A critical question that does not get asked by Frankfurt School IR theorists, noted Kimberly Hutchings, is the following: 'whose imagination is shaping the contours of utopia?' This is not only a question about '*who* does the theorising?', which is important in itself, as highlighted above. However, Hutchings's question is also about the internal consistency of Frankfurt School critical IR theorists. For,

> from the critical theorists' point of view, how the world is understood matters for how the values of equity, peace, emancipation, and solidarity have meaning and traction in any given context, whether as a premise of argument or a requirement for action. The claims of critical theory are authoritative only insofar as the audience of those claims recognizes and endorses them. In this respect, the critical theorist is always in a political relation to his or her audience that is implicitly democratic.
>
> (Hutchings, 2012: 211)

Put differently, Hutchings argued that, from a Frankfurt School IR perspective, inquiring into others' approaches to the international should have been central to the project of theorising critically about the world.[6] Writing about social theory in general, Jan Naderveen Pieterse (1992: 32) concurred, noting that the 'moral horizon' involved in emancipatory thinking 'cannot be one's own' but 'needs to be located in our already existing communications about moral horizons'. I will revisit this issue below, when discussing Frankfurt School inspired approaches to security theorising. Suffice it to say here that Habermasian communicative ethics is yet to tap into and learn from humankind's already existing communications and contributions to discussions about moral horizons (Buck-Morss, 2003, Grovogui, 2005, also see Dussel, 1993).

It is significant to note that the criticisms directed at the particularity of universals favoured by Frankfurt School IR are not only about the geo-cultural situatedness of scholars and institutions (which we uncover by worlding IR in the first sense). Criticisms are also directed at the particularity of the Enlightenment origins of their ideas, *and* Frankfurt School IR's limited reflection on the constitutive effects of such particularity (which invites worlding IR in the second sense). Indeed, IR's postcolonial critics have argued that the limits of Frankfurt School IR should be understood in broader terms; not merely about the geographical and/or institutional 'origins' of some ideas, but the ways in which the 'origins' and 'particularity' of those ideas have been understood, and how they have been put into practice.[7] What follows looks at three major issues identified by the postcolonial critics by focusing on the 'human rights' debates.

To begin with, the Frankfurt School IR approach is often criticised for seeking to impose 'universally' what are 'particular' definitions of 'human rights'. Such criticisms of the particularity of universals, however, need not be taken as a rejection of universals as it is sometimes suggested. Consider Chris Brown (1988: 342), who maintained that the fact that human rights notions were learned either 'by direct intervention or by creating a situation which ensured that the only way to resist direct intervention was to adopt Western ways' should serve as a reminder that they are, in fact, not universal. On the one hand, Brown's reminder about colonial encounters through which such universals have been produced is pertinent and constitutes an instance of reflection on the particularity of liberal universalism. On the other hand, Brown's assumption that colonial encounters only shaped the colonised but not the coloniser does not allow developing a fuller critique of the nature of the particularity of those ideas.

When the critics point to the 'particular' framework within which prevalent conceptions of human rights have come about, they are highlighting the ways in which that framework has been 'constituted by the particular and by the exclusion of other particulars' (Bhambra and Shilliam, 2009a: 7). Such criticism should not be conflated with those proponents of 'Asian values' who seek to '[revive] pre-Western social forms' that Brown (1988: 342) was critical of. This is not only because of the impossibility of such a recovery, as Brown also highlighted, but mostly because what the postcolonial critics are concerned about is not the notion of universals, but the practice of applying particular universals without reflecting on their particularity, and without thinking about ways of making them less exclusionary (Grovogui, 2005, 2011).

48   *Critical IR theorising*

A second related problem that the critics have identified with Frankfurt School IR is its students' limited reflection on the ways in which universals have been applied arbitrarily, thereby resulting in an erosion of trust among peoples regarding concrete instantiation of such universals (Rao, 2010). Responding to Andrew Linklater's (1982, 1998) call for extending the moral boundaries of political community to include those who were previously excluded, Siba Grovogui wrote:

> Linklater's generosity assumes full knowledge of postcolonial criticism of the problems of international politics. But he is mistaken about related criticisms of modernity, rationalism, and philosophical and political universalism. Such criticisms do not conceive prior misapplication or suspension of international morality (likened metonymically to a liberal constitutional regime) as a mere problem of exclusion. They involve considerations of the very terms of the constitutional order – the implicated political imaginaries, juridical and moral systems, and their base-notions of communities and obligations – as mechanisms of exclusion.
>
> (Grovogui, 2006b: 48–49)

Beate Jahn (1998: 631) noted that thinkers such as Samuel von Pufendorf and Emmerich de Vattel, whose writings Linklater has built upon, 'did not develop universal ideas but rather universal *yardsticks* which were supposed to provide them with a justification *not* to extend equal rights to others' (original emphasis). Accordingly, argued Jahn, Linklater's model excludes others at the moment of inclusion:

> For it is on the basis of the 'inclusion' into humanity defined as European rationality, European political organization, European capitalism or forms of communication and morality that alternative forms of rationality, political organization, modes of production or forms of communication and morality are excluded, not only from the higher echelons of humanity, but also from certain concrete legal and moral rights.
>
> (Jahn, 1998: 636–637)

Put differently, what the postcolonial critics consider problematic about Frankfurt School IR is not only that particular universals are imposed in seeking to 'better' the human condition in different parts of the world, but also that such universals have been imposed arbitrarily, and that the proponents of these ideas and ideals in IR have had precious little to say about such arbitrariness (Grovogui, 2005, 2006b, 2011).

A third problem that the postcolonial critics identify with Frankfurt School IR is that universals are portrayed as having a single (Western) origin, thereby overlooking others' contributions and contestations. One way of rendering prevalent notions of human rights less exclusionary would be, the critics noted, to problematise assumptions regarding the 'Western' origins of human rights (Bhambra and Shilliam, 2009b) *and* the assumption that ideas have a single origin as opposed to 'beginnings' (recalling the discussion on Said in the Introduction).

Distinguishing between 'establishing the "origins of Western notions"' and inquiring into the '"Western origins" of human rights', Grovogui (2011: 43) argued that where the former allows us to question the particularity of prevalent human rights notions, the latter rests on Eurocentric assumptions that 'self-consciously or not…appropriate the human genius for "Europe" or the "West"' thereby overlooking others' contributions to and contestations of what are portrayed as 'Western' ideas (Grovogui, 2006a: 4). Grovogui wrote:

> To be sure, social and critical theorists are cognizant of temporal and spatial intellectual pluralism and the hybridity and the fluidity of ideas and institutions. But they assume Western origination of crucial ones. By implication, the methods and canons of analysis necessarily remain 'Western' while the antiseptic gazes, the ones seeking cures for global pathologies, necessarily turn toward the non-West.
>
> (Grovogui, 2006a: 4–5)

Indeed, even notions that were developed in and through colonial encounters are portrayed as having developed autonomously without input by others – be it in the form of contribution or contestation (as discussed by Jahn, see above).

Consider critical theorist Enrique Dussel (1993: 65) who took issue with those who portray modernity as exclusively 'European', noting that it is 'one constituted in a dialectical relation with a non-European alterity that is its ultimate content'. Furthermore, it is not only self/other dialectics that Dussel viewed as constitutive of 'Europe' but also material give-and-take. In a lecture delivered in Frankfurt, Dussel said:

> It was a Jew from my country [Argentina] involved in the export trade in agricultural commodities between Argentina and Great Britain, who provided the initial subsidy for the institute that Horkheimer and others founded in this city. That is, it was the value produced by the labour of the gauchos and peons of the pampa, objectivized in wheat or beef and appropriated by the great landowning and merchant families of Argentina, that, transferred to Germany, gave birth to the Frankfurt school.
>
> (Dussel, 1993: 66)

In identifying the links between 'Europe' and its 'constitutive outside', Dussel added another dimension from his own biography, disclosing to his listeners that

> In 1870, a poor carpenter, a socialist and Lutheran from the town of Schweinfurt am Main only a few kilometers from here, arrived in Buenos Aires looking for work, freedom from persecution, and peace. His name was Johannes Kaspar Dussel. He was welcomed in Argentina, given

50 *Critical IR theorising*

opportunities to make good, and he raised a family and died in those lands. He was my great grandfather.

(Dussel, 1993: 66–67)

Here, in one lecture by Dussel, we locate 'beginnings' of the ideas of the Frankfurt School scholars as well as their postcolonial critics.

To recap, postcolonial scholars have been critical of Frankfurt School IR not only for (1) seeking to impose particular universals, but also (2) imposing them arbitrarily, and (3) defining them without due consideration for and acknowledgement of others' contributions and contestations. As such, the postcolonial critique is not directed against the notion of universals, but the marshalling of particular universalisms in the service of 'liberal cosmopolitanism' (Jabri, 2012) or 'liberal peace' (Sabaratnam, 2013).

Such 'slippage from establishing the "origins of Western notions" to one of the "Western origins" of those notions' (Grovogui, 2011: 43) was not without implications for the students of Frankfurt School IR (or human rights activists around the world). In those parts of the world which were written out of the history of ideas about universals, it has become more difficult to make a case for the relevance of universals (such as human rights). The narrowing of the discussion on the universals has meant that debates regarding the 'particularity' of universals in IR theorising (as with 'liberal cosmopolitanism') and their selective employment in practice (as with 'liberal peace'), got tied up with debates regarding the need for having universals in theory and practice. In such instances, critiquing the particularity of some forms of universalism was conflated with critiquing the need for or the possibility of having universals. Such conflation in theory has had further consequences for practice insofar as it was used by some as a stepping stone to make a case for 'lighter' human rights regimes in some parts of the world – as with the 1990s debates on 'Asian values' (see Burke, 2007: chapter 4) or with the 2000s debates on 'Dialogue of Civilisations'. Indeed, as will be discussed in Chapter 6, civilisational dialogue initiatives do not reflect on non-state referents' insecurities but focus on world security understood as stability in inter-state relations. Such stability, in turn, is sought by giving up on universals in theory and practice, and accepting 'lighter' definitions of 'human rights' as offered by self-styled representations of civilisations. The point made by IR's postcolonial critics, that the universals could be re-thought through incorporating others' contributions and contestations, does not have influenced the discussions on civilisational dialogue (see Chapter 6).

Indeed, conflating the critiques of the particularity of universals with critiques of the idea of having universals has meant that the challenge of the postcolonial critics to expand the debates on cosmopolitanism was overlooked. For, some postcolonial IR scholars have defended the need for universals through focusing on 'strategic essentialism' (Krishna, 1993, Agathangelou and Ling, 2009b) and re-thinking cosmopolitanism through engaging with those 'intellectual agendas, beliefs, attitudes, values, institutions and idioms which, although not organically linked to theirs, seek to enhance ethical existence' (Grovogui, 2005: 103, also

Critical IR theorising 51

see Rao, 2010). The point being that, reading contrapuntally the writings by the students of postcolonial studies and critical security studies is likely to produce fruitful communications on the universals.

Frankfurt School inspired approaches to critical security theorising

The origins of the Frankfurt School inspired approaches to security theorising can be traced back to Ken Booth's (1991b) epochal article entitled 'Security and Emancipation'. Booth and his students at the Aberystwyth University played key roles in the development of this approach. Hence the label, the Aberystwyth School.[8] Richard Wyn Jones's (1999) book entitled *Security, Strategy and Critical Theory* located Booth's critical approach to security vis-à-vis the Frankfurt School Critical Theory tradition.[9] Booth's other students and colleagues at and beyond Aberystwyth developed different conceptual aspects of the approach by offering empirical case studies.[10] Booth's 2007 book developed a theory of world security drawing upon a number of critical traditions including but not limited to Frankfurt School Critical Theory (also see Booth, 2005a).[11]

Central to Booth's approach to security has been problematising three main characteristics of the mainstream approaches, namely, statism, military-focus, and the problem-solving approach to security. Statism is a normative approach that privileges the security of states in research design and policy advice.[12] Problem-solving approaches to security are problematised for privileging those issues that are put on the security agenda by the powerful, and their study through a commitment to scientific-objectivist understanding of theory and theory/practice dynamics (which, in turn, renders invisible aforementioned privileging of the security agenda of the powerful). The military-focus of security studies is problematised not only in terms of priority attached to military insecurities but also in terms of the preference given to militarised solutions in addressing myriad (military and non-military) problems (Booth, 1991b, 1997b, 2005b, 2007, Booth and Vale, 1995, Wyn Jones, 1999, Bilgin et al., 1998, Bilgin, 2000b).

As an alternative, Booth offered a social constructivist conception of security and reflexive understanding of theory and theory/practice dynamics, coupled with a commitment to emancipatory practices. Social constructivist conception of security refers to understanding security as a 'derivative concept', derived from one's view of the world, insofar as human beings make sense of the material world through inter-subjective categories and frameworks ('security is what we make it' [Booth, 2005a: 272]). Reflexivity is understood as 'the application of a theory back on its own ideas and practices' (Booth, 2005a: 259) and acknowlededges the role played by the theorist in shaping and being shaped by practice, expecting critical approaches to constantly question and renew themselves. Emancipatory politics is the most controversial of all three and distinguishes Booth's approach to security from other critical approaches in terms of an explicit commitment to pursue 'concrete utopias', i.e. seeking to better the

52   Critical IR theorising

human condition by removing barriers that prevent human beings from realising themselves (Booth, 1991b, 2005c, 2007, Wyn Jones, 1999, 2005).

As such, addressing the problem of 'who does the theorising?' did not top the agenda of the students of Frankfurt School inspired approaches to critical security theorising. Rather, as with many other students of critical IR, Booth expected the limits of IR to be addressed through re-thinking security (as with his contributions to the debates on ethnocentrism and parochialism, see Chapter 1) and offering an alternative framework. Over the years, Booth encouraged the students of security to think beyond their own immediate insecurities and pay attention to others' insecurities, with an eye on the well-being of human beings around the world (Booth, 2005a: 276).

Yet, Frankfurt School inspired approaches to critical security theorising have not persuaded their critics with regard to their attentiveness to the question 'who does the theorising?' Highlighting the paucity of voices from outside North America and Western Europe in this body of writings, Amitav Acharya (2000: 16) cautioned that what is needed is encouraging emancipatory practices without 'marginalising the emancipatory strategies of the multitude of non-Western voices'. Hayward Alker (2005: 201) also noted that in their discussions on emancipatory security practices, Frankfurt School inspired authors' references were all to 'secular rationalist thinkers, identified positively with key aspects of modernity that some 'non-Western or postcolonial writers (and some post-modernists) reject'. By way of a solution, Alker (2005: 200) called for locating the roots of emancipation in 'non-Western' thinking (his choice of term), while allowing that 'there may be meta-physical, religious, or more general cultural differences in how these notions are defined, applied and responded to'. The gist of Acharya and Alker's critique was, then, directed at the Frankfurt School inspired critical security scholars' reliance on a self-referential history of ideas about emancipation (but see Booth, 2007).

Jan Jindy Pettman concurred, arguing that failing to reflect on the roles played by the colonial experiences in constituting the international and others' perspectives on the international would likely result in overlooking the inse-curities generated by those experiences and their present-day shadows. Pettman wrote:

> Neglecting to consider experiences of colonisation and imperialism can obscure both the legacy and force of anti colonial nationalism in Asian states and the deep desire to escape from the 'abject status' of colonisation. It also facilitates the reproduction of older readings of difference and encourages complicity with new Orientalisms that replicate the boundary between Asia and the West, Them and Us.
>
> (Pettman, 2005: 167)

Being attentive to the question 'who does the theorising?', Pettman suggested, would not only help understand a range of insecurities tied up with colonialism and neo-colonialism, but also help generate awareness about the Eurocentric limits of Frankfurt School inspired approaches to critical theorising about security. That said, it is significant to highlight here that the aforementioned critiques by Alker and Pettman were published in Booth's 2005 edited volume entitled *Critical Security Studies and World Politics*. The point being that Frankfurt School inspired approaches to critical theorising about security carry within the potential to reflect on their limits through 'reflexive self-monitoring' (also see Lee-Koo, 2007, Bilgin, 2012).

On the one hand, understanding security as a 'derivative concept', as Booth does, opens up room for inquiring into different worldviews and conceptions of the international and in/security. On the other hand (and following the discussion above), the problem of Eurocentrism is not only about the geographic and institutional situatedness of scholars, but also about the constitutive effects of such situatedness. The assumption that ideas have a single origin, which is warranted by self-referential histories of ideas, is one aspect of Eurocentrism that has been a persistent feature of Frankfurt School IR and critical security thinking that it has inspired.

Arguably, this is where raising their contrapuntal awareness and drawing on contrapuntal readings of history would become essential for students of Frankfurt School inspired critical security theorising. As noted above, emancipatory approaches to security are almost always criticised for their reliance on self-referential narratives on ideas about emancipation. Drawing on postcolonial studies would allow students of this body of critical security theorising to adopt a twofold strategy. On the one hand, they could point to multiple historical instances where emancipation has served as an 'ideal and a rallying cry', including struggles of 'Jews in Europe, slaves in the United States, blacks in the West Indies, the Irish in the British state, and serfs in Russia' (Booth, 2007: 111). On the other hand, they could inquire into the beginnings of their core ideas in different parts of the world, without giving up on the idea of a 'moral horizon' guiding security practices (Pieterse, 1992, also see Grovogui, 2005).

Post-structuralist IR and the limits of theorising about IR and security

Post-structuralist IR scholars have refrained from prescribing a particular vision (and therefore universals) but rather focused on 'unmasking the relations of dominance, and making possible (creating a space for) a politics of resistance' (Duvall and Varadarajan, 2003: 83).[13] Committed to increasing our 'understanding of how power and knowledge are intertwined in all representations of politics', students of post-structuralist IR have conducted genealogical analyses to 'illuminate how particular historical evolutions created the type of world we live in today', and deconstruction to 'expose values and power relations that are entailed – either explicitly or implicitly – in particular texts, ranging anywhere from political speeches to legal documents and popular magazines' (Bleiker, 2007: 91).

Notwithstanding their best scholarly efforts that have revealed self/other dialectics in the making of the 'West', and opening up space for 'different'

54 *Critical IR theorising*

articulations of world politics, students of post-structuralist IR, too, have come under criticism. Arguably, this was because in responding to the question: 'who does the theorising?' post-structuralist IR scholars concentrated their efforts in opening up space for those who are differently situated, i.e. voices from outside North America and Western Europe (worlding-as-situatedness). In doing so, they have not always focused on the constitutive effects colonialism has had on post-structuralist thought (worlding-as-constitutive). In particular, post-structuralist IR has been criticised for resting on a self-referential narrative of modernity as 'Western', which, the critics argued, has resulted in (1) overlooking the role of the 'constitutive outside' in the making of the 'West' and modernity (Bhambra, 2007a, Ahluwalia, 2005, Jabri, 2007a, 2014, Krishna, 1993), and (2) a failure to allow room for postcolonial subjectivity and agency (Bhambra, 2007b, Jabri, 2007a, 2013, Agathangelou and Ling, 2009b, Ling, 2002, Krishna, 1993). Let us consider each point in turn.

(1) Post-structuralist IR's focus on critiques of modernity has come under criticism by virtue of resting on 'a remarkably self-contained and self-referential view of the West' that is inherited from social theory (Krishna, 1993: 403).[14] Focusing on Michel Foucault's writings, which many students of IR have drawn upon, Sankaran Krishna wrote:

> whereas Foucault's meticulous genealogies of the micropolitics of power in discursive practices have had such a tremendous impact, his work itself geopolitically isolates the West and is completely oblivious to a whole history of imperialism that surely has much to do with the very practices that he investigates.
>
> (Krishna, 1993: 403)

It is not only the colonial heritage that is overlooked, noted Vivienne Jabri, but also inter-societal dynamics between 'Europe' and its 'constitutive outside'. Jabri wrote:

> While Foucault…provides the tropes through which we think critically, and indeed, provide a conception of what it means to be 'critical', at the same time his is a spatialised ethos that most definitely does not consider non-European moments of critique and self-reflection.
>
> (Jabri, 2013: 13)

It is important to highlight here that this limit is not isolated to Foucault or to post-structuralist authors. As Gurminder Bhambra highlighted,

> [w]hat modernist and anti-modernist understandings fail to consider is the idea that the very definition of the conditions of modernity only emerged with the establishment of sociology as a discipline. While histories of sociology unquestioningly delineate its formation 'in the nineteenth century struggle to understand the combined upheavals of the great political

revolutions and the industrial revolution', they rarely consider the impact of the East–West construct in this endeavour.

(Bhambra, 2007b: 53)

Jabri agreed, pointing to how Foucault's writings on Iran illustrated the trappings of post-structuralist thought in accounting for others and their difference/s. Foucault's failure was not due to a lack of interest in others, noted Jabri; on the contrary he took great interest in the Iranian revolution, writing multiple essays as it evolved, and visiting the country immediately after the revolution. Nor was it due to a failure to accord agency to the Iranian revolutionaries; Foucault took interest in their resistance against the rationalist streak in modernist thought and the promise of spiritual injections into the political realm, which he considered the Iranian revolution to be offering (Jabri, 2007a). Rather, argued Jabri, Foucault failed to account for the Iranians and their difference/s by virtue of seeking to understand 'Iranian' and 'Western' approaches to modernity (and its trappings) as having evolved autonomously, without paying due attention to inter-societal interactions, thereby betraying a less-than-sociological conception of the international.

It was because Foucault did not consider the international as constituted by and constitutive of both 'Western' and 'non-Western' modernity, Jabri suggested, that he failed to detect those particular sensibilities that conditioned his own understanding of Iranian dynamics. Put differently, the Iranians' role in the constitution of the international and the ways in which the international has shaped Iran was not a part of Foucault's analysis. Jabri wrote:

Where [Foucault] saw modernisation as an imposed structure on the 'Islamic societies' of the Middle East, those very societies possess their own experiences and interpretations of the modernising imperatives of national identity, imperatives that were central to their liberation from colonial rule as well as being core to the transformation of the lived experience of many, essentially, transformations expressive of liberation from religious doctrine.

(Jabri, 2007a: 78)

The limits of Foucault's analysis of the 'West', and modernity and its trappings have shaped post-structuralist IR and its Eurocentric conception of the international, Jabri concluded.

As discussed in Chapter 1, Eurocentrism of IR has taken many forms, one of which is uncritical adoption of Eurocentric accounts of world history in the analysis of world politics. While some post-structuralist scholars have carefully avoided Eurocentrism (see, for example, Costas Constantinou's [2000] genealogy of diplomacy) others did not. This is because, Sandra Halperin argued,

While critical perspectives have done much to elucidate European representations of non-European 'others', they have left wholly unexamined

56 *Critical IR theorising*

Europe's representation of itself. Consequently, they tend to reproduce Europe's profoundly erroneous, highly ideological representation of its own history. They frequently assume, wrongly, that knowledges and practices universalized by Europeans were grounded in European history when, in many cases, these neither originated in Europe nor were even part of the European experience.

(Halperin, 2006: 43)

Accordingly, the issue is not merely one of recognising 'other modernities, whether or not concurrent with the Western one' (Grovogui, 2006a: 51, cf. Blumi, 2011), but also one of reflecting on instances of – what Krishna (1993: 388) termed as – an 'intimate dialogue between "Western" and "non-Western" economies, societies, and philosophies that underwrite the disenchantment with modernity that characterizes the present epoch'.[15]

One example of (the need for) such a dialogical account to inform our understanding of history and accounts on the international is Pal Ahluwalia's discussion on the links between post-structuralist thought (that post-structuralist IR draws upon) and postcolonial thought (that postcolonial IR builds upon). Postcolonial thought is often criticized for its indebtedness to post-structuralism, and sometimes found wanting because of its presumed derivativeness (Neufeld, 2012). Whereas, as Ahluwalia has argued,

in order to understand the project of French post-structuralism, it is imperative both to contextualise the African colonial experience and to highlight the Algerian locatedness, identity and heritage of its leading proponents. It is precisely the failure to confront or explicitly acknowledge the colonial experience that problematises the conflation of postcolonialism and post-structuralism.

(Ahluwalia, 2005: 140)

As such, Ahluwalia turned the criticisms regarding the apparent derivativeness of postcolonial thought on its head when he asked:

Isn't it plausible that the questions which have become so much a part of the post-structuralist canon – otherness, difference, irony, mimicry, parody, the lamenting of modernity and the deconstruction of the grand narratives of European culture arising out of the Enlightenment tradition – are possible because of their postcolonial connection?

(Ahluwalia, 2005: 138)

To give a more specific example, consider post-structuralist thinker Pierre Bourdieu. Bourdieu's experiences in Algeria (military service and later teaching at the University of Algiers) are well known (Gurtaudon, 2012). Yet, as Julian Go (2013) highlighted, little is made of such experiences by his admirers who produce self-referential histories of Bourdieu's ideas, or by his critics who question the relevance of his ideas beyond Europe due to their presumed Eurocentrism. Arguably, it is through those self-referential narratives, which render invisible the formative influence Bourdieu's situatedness in French colonial Algeria had on his thinking, that his thought comes under criticism for overlooking its 'constitutive outside' and being Eurocentric.

This is not to suggest that Bourdieu's ideas are immune to anti-Eurocentric criticism. Rather the point here is that anti-Eurocentric critique of Bourdieu's thought or its relevance should be grounded differently – other than pointing to the apparently 'European' geo-cultural origins of his ideas. This is not enough partly because Bourdieu's ideas had their beginnings in the colonising France and colonised Algeria. It is also not enough because the significance of excavating the colonial context of Bourdieu's thinking is not only about responding to his anti-Eurocentric critics. More importantly, it points to the need for raising our contrapuntal awareness and studying what Said called the 'connectedness' of things.[16] Responding to the anti-Eurocentric critics of Bourdieu, then, becomes a matter of recovering his early works *and* showing how he developed the key concepts of 'habitus' and 'field' during his studies in Algeria (Go, 2013). That such connections are often not made, and that modernity's limits are discussed in a self-referential manner, gives away enduring Eurocentrism in post-structuralist IR.

(2) If overlooking the role of inter-societal dynamics in the making of the 'West' and modernity is one of the limits of post-structuralist IR, a second one is a failure to allow for so-called 'non-Western' subjectivity and agency. This is somewhat surprising. After all, post-structuralist IR is commended for successfully de-centring 'Western' subjectivity. However, it has also come under criticism for 'simultaneously closing off the avenue into retrieving a global politics in which Eastern subjectivity/agency is accorded significance' (Hobson, 2007b: 101, also see Ling, 2002). Jabri agreed, highlighting that 'this scripting out of the postcolonial is not confined to realist or liberal perspectives in international theory, but also has been apparent in much critical and poststructuralist work' (Jabri, 2013: 9).

In response to what they viewed as post-structuralist IR's reluctance to accept a 'reference point in relation to which its own account of international politics is better' (Hutchings, 2001: 85) and 'preserve some notion of a politically enabling subjectivity' (Krishna, 1993: 402), some have called for 'strategic essentialism' following Spivak (1995). 'What is perhaps necessary', noted Krishna (1993: 405) 'is a greater degree of attention to the question of how… does one construct provisional and strategically essentialised subjectivities to enable a progressive politics?' Indeed, utilising 'strategic essentialisms' to constitute 'mobile' subjectivities and agency is no inconsequential task given the ways in which

> the late modern reinscription of imperial power and the 'racial ordering of the world' are currently being articulated in twenty-first century colonisations and their displays through military power, carceral power, confinement,

58 *Critical IR theorising*

administration, acquisition through dispossession, and the 'training' of local populations into societies amenable to self-discipline, self-regulation, and self-government (referred to variously as 'state-building' or 'nation-building').

(Jabri, 2007a: 74)

Insofar as post-structuralist IR has not allowed some notion of subjectivity and agency for the 'greatest victims of the West's essentialist conceits (the excolonials and neocolonials, Blacks, women, and so forth)', Krishna (1993: 406) argued, it has failed to 'garner the emancipatory potential of such essentialisms' in resisting violence – however 'provisional' and 'mobile' they may be.

Jabri (2013: 1) suggested another way of recovering the postcolonial subject: at the moment of reclaiming of the political by peoples around the world as they stood up against 'local as well as global structures of domination and control and their complex and contingent intersections'. Consequently, Jabri sought to circumvent the limits of existing approaches that either do not accord agency to the postcolonial subject, or circumscribe their agency. She wrote:

> The achievement of the postcolonial critique in international social and political thought is at once both deconstructive and generative of a research programme that seeks to script the postcolonial into the analytics of international and global politics. This scripting is not based on modernization theory and its 'developmental' discourse, one that provides the edifice upon which concepts such as 'failed states' are built. Rather, the lens shifts toward questions relating to postcolonial agency, not in a generalizing, simplifying, idealising mode, but in revealing its complex intersection with matrices of power and domination and their contingencies.
>
> (Jabri, 2013: 9)

The point being that, it is by way of opening up the post-structuralist research agenda to 'others' as constitutive of the international that Jabri's analysis was able to recover postcolonial agency while avoiding the problem of 'fixity' – be it in 'identities' or notions of emancipation.

To recapitulate, post-structuralist IR has come under criticism regarding the limits of its attentiveness to the question 'who does the theorising?' by virtue of its reliance on self-referential narratives on modernity as 'Western', and somewhat meagre interest in the constitutive roles played by others in the making of the 'West' and modernity. While de-centring 'Western' subjectivity, argued the critics, post-structuralist IR has failed to acknowledge 'West'/'non-West' intersocietal dynamics across history 'that underwrite the disenchantement with modernity that characterises the present epoch', or allow for 'strategic essentialisms' to constitute 'mobile' subjectivities and agency (Krishna, 1993: 388). Put differently, while students of post-structuralist IR have made significant contributions in considering the situatedness of IR scholars and bringing in the perspectives of those that are differently situated (worlding-as-situatedness), they have yet to address fully the implications of overlooking the roles played by Europe's 'constitutive outside' in the making of social theory and IR (worlding-as-constitutive). As exemplified in the writings of Vivienne Jabri (2007a, 2007b, 2013, 2014) and Costas Constantinou (2000), being more open to reflecting on others' contributions to and contestations of theorising about the international would likely allow post-structuralist IR to begin to address its Eurocentric limits.

Post-structuralist approaches to security theorising

Post-structuralist approaches to the study of security have developed since the 1980s, building on the critique of security studies developed by students of post-structuralist IR. R.B.J. Walker's (1997) chapter entitled 'The Subject of Security' is a key text of post-structuralist thinking on IR and security (also see Campbell and Dillon, 1993, Campbell, 1998, Huysmans, 1998, 2006a, 2006b, Huysmans et al., 2006, Burke, 2001, 2007). Anthony Burke (2013: 77) remarked that 'the most far-reaching contribution of post-structural approaches to security is to have brought the very idea of security under fundamental scrutiny'. During the late 1980s and early 1990s, post-structural contributions helped to cast doubt on Cold War security thinking and policies justified with reference to such thinking (Klein, 1990, 1994, Walker, 1990, Shapiro, 1990, Campbell, 1992). Following the September 11 attacks, which allowed a return to statist and military-focused security practices reminiscent of the Cold War years, post-structuralist approaches to security focused on the study of 'exception', 'risk' and 'the camp', thereby challenging those who predicted a return to the complacency of Cold War thinking (Burke, 2001, 2007, Rasmussen, 2004, Walker, 2006, Huysmans, 2006a).

Over the years, students of post-structuralist approaches to security have followed a twofold research track. While some studies have focused on the study of political theories which critical approaches to security have drawn upon, other studies adopted sociological methods to look at specific instances of 'securitisation' as developed in Ole Wæver's (1987, 1990, 1993, 1998a) approach to securitisation theory and 'insecuritisation' as articulated by Didier Bigo, among others (Aradau, 2004, Huysmans, 1995, 1998, 2006a, 2006b, Huysmans et al., 2006, Bigo, 2000, 2001, 2002, Bigo and Guild, 2005). More recently, considerations about the postcolonial as a subject and agent have been integrated into post-structuralist approaches to security by Vivienne Jabri (2007a, 2013), who pointed to IR's limits, with implications for post-structuralist theory inspired approaches to security.

In terms of empirical focus, most post-structuralist approaches to security have focused on case studies on Western Europe and North America (but see Jabri, 2013, Burke, 2001). Furthermore, in a manner similar to Frankfurt School approaches to security, post-structuralist scholars also have drawn on the self-referential history of ideas, institutions and practices. For all the stress put on the sociological dimension of international politics, post-structuralist approaches to security are only beginning to inquire into inter-societal

60 Critical IR theorising

interactions between Europe and its 'constitutive outside' in the making of the international (Jabri, 2007a, 2013, 2014).

In what follows, I will focus on how the students of securitisation theory sought to identify and address its limits. More so than other approaches to critical security studies, securitisation theory has been adopted and utilised outside North America and Western Europe. As such, it is worth inquiring into its 'success' in appealing to students of security in other parts of the world.

The securitisation theory approach originated in Ole Wæver's (1987, 1990, 1993, 1998a) writings that have drawn from post-structuralist thinking with an admixture of realism (Wæver 1989). His collaboration, during the 1990s, with Barry Buzan (1991) and Jaap de Wilde at the Copenhagen Peace Research Institute was labelled by Bill McSweeney (1996) as 'the Copenhagen School'. The key statement of the Copenhagen School is the 1998 book entitled *Security: A New Framework for Analysis* (Buzan et al., 1998). Securitisation theory has since grown beyond Copenhagen, being adopted by scholars throughout Western Europe (*Security Dialogue*, 2011), North America (Nyers, 2009, Bourbeau, 2011) and beyond (Caballero-Anthony et al., 2006, Emmers et al., 2006, Bilgin, 2011).

The securitisation theory approach has offered four sets of arguments: historical, theoretical, normative and strategic.[17] The historical argument of the securitisation theory approach rests upon Wæver's (1995: 60) fresh reading of post-World War II experience in Western Europe as a process of 'turning threats into challenges and security into politics' (also see Guzzini, 2015). Western Europe was able to distance itself from the violent experiences that characterised the first half of the twentieth century, argued Wæver, by re-setting intra-European relations outside security terms. In so doing, statist and militarist thinking and practices were marginalised. The 'successes' of desecuritisation in Western Europe were later extended to relations with Eastern Europe, Wæver wrote

> A great deal of the East-West dialogue of the 1970s and 1980s, especially that on 'non-military aspects of security', human rights and the whole Third Basket of the Helsinki Accords could be regarded as a discussion of where to place boundaries on a concept of security.
>
> (Wæver, 1995: 60)

By challenging the 'securityness' of previously securitised issues (that is, by asking '[t]o what degree were Eastern regimes "permitted" to use extraordinary instruments to limit societal East-West exchange and interaction?'), the parties were able to 'turn threats into challenges', thereby taking the necessary (but not always sufficient) steps towards overcoming them, argued Wæver (1995: 60).

The theoretical argument builds upon Austin's 'speech act' theory. Contesting mainstream security approaches' assumption that threats exist 'out there' independent of 'us' knowing about and/or representing them, Wæver offered a social constructivist understanding, arguing that what makes an issue a 'threat' to security is not a function of its 'objective' qualities but inter-subjective

Critical IR theorising 61

dynamics of interpretation and representation (Wæver, 1989, 1995, 1998a, Buzan et al., 1998).[18] An issue does not become a 'security' issue unless it is labelled as such by the relevant actors who have the authority to do so, noted Wæver. Since the state establishment has traditionally been the 'powers-that-be' in the realm of security, it has identified issues as 'threats' and decided what the security agenda should look like. Although the audience also plays a crucial role in accepting or rejecting such securitisation attempts, the power and authority enjoyed by the state elite over the production of security as a 'good' and 'knowledge' cannot be denied. Thus, building from the historical argument above, security is theorised as a tool that has traditionally been used by the state elite for 'framing' and 'handling' an issue, which 'organizes social relations into security relations' (Huysmans, 1998: 232).

The normative argument of the securitisation theory is, arguably, the most controversial one. It rests on Wæver and Buzan's caution that the widest possible concept of security need not be viewed as the most progressive, and that security, when broadly defined, could potentially result in the militarisation of wider societal fields (Wæver 1989, 1993, Buzan et al., 1998, Buzan, 1991). By way of this argument, Buzan and Wæver parted ways with some other critics of Cold War approaches to security (see, for example, Mathews, 1989, Knudsen, 2001). Labelling the latter's approach as 'conservative', Wæver (1995: 46) maintained that they shared a basic premise of mainstream approaches to security insofar as both treated security as 'a reality prior to language', which is 'out there (irrespective of whether the conception is "objective" or "subjective", is measured in terms of threat or fear)'. As such, Wæver was critical of broadening the security agenda without considering the 'securityness' of issues.

In contrast to Frankfurt School inspired approaches to security theorising that allow for broader conceptions of security to make room for governmental security agendas to be challenged from the perspective of multiple referents (see above), Wæver (1999: 334) insisted that each attempt to securitise an issue should be met with the following questions: 'why do you call this a security issue? What are the implications of doing this – or of not doing it?' As a consequence of such scrutiny, concluded Wæver (1995), fewer 'security' issues would likely be left over which powers-that-be can claim extraordinary powers. Accordingly, the Copenhagen School has underscored the political choices involved in deciding which issues are labelled as 'security' problems, for such labelling has implications insofar as those issues then get taken outside 'ordinary' political processes and handled through the adoption of 'extraordinary' measures.

Finally, the strategic argument of securitisation theory rests on what Wæver (2011) has called the 'politics of theory design'. I have refrained from labelling it as the political argument, for there are multiple facets to the politics of securitisation theory. As Wæver (2011: 466) argued, a theory is political in multiple ways, and not only through its explicit discussion on politics; theory is political 'through the way it conditions analyses, because a theory is a construct that enables particular observations about cases'. Accordingly, Wæver (2011: 469) presented the politics of the securitisation theory as the 'structural features of a theory that condition

62 Critical IR theorising

what can and cannot be done with it'. As will be suggested below, it is this strategic argument of securitisation theory that has rendered it attractive to scholars beyond Western Europe and North America. Furthermore, it could be argued that Eurocentrism of securitisation theory has proven to be its source of strength insofar as it has conditioned '*the political effects of using this theory*' [original emphasis] (Wæver, 2011: 466). In what follows I will first identify criticisms regarding the Eurocentric limits of securitisation theory and then discuss how those very limits may be viewed as its strategic source of strength.

The critics of securitisation theory have argued that securitisation theory is Eurocentric and therefore should not be expected to be able to account for contexts that are characterised by radically different configurations of state–society dynamics (Wilkinson, 2007, Caballero-Anthony and Emmers, 2006a, 2006b, Bilgin, 2007). This should not come across as surprising. Wæver et al. developed the securitisation theory approach by studying historical cases from Western Europe and in an attempt to make sense of security dynamics in contemporary Europe (Wæver, 1995, 1998a, Guzzini, 2015). Furthermore, over the years, securitisation theory has been developed mostly through the study of empirical cases drawn from Western European experiences (with some focus on North America). As such, the centrality to securitisation theory of concepts and categories driven from European experiences is only to be expected.

That said, the critics have taken issue with Wæver's (1995) caution that while securitisation may be a tactical move in certain times and places depending on the historical context and power configuration of various actors, the ultimate aim would remain one of desecuritisation (Wæver, 2011, Buzan et al., 1998). In particular, IR's postcolonial critics have noted that this stance may be particularly problematic in those parts of the world where civil societal actors are not able and/or willing to challenge established ways of thinking about and doing security. Indeed, it could be argued that securitisation theory's reliance on the agency of societal actors does not take into account the imprint that processes of state-building and/or violent conflict leave on a given society, which, in turn, render the society a site of the reproduction of the very security understandings and practices that societal actors are expected to challenge (Pasha, 1996, also see Bilgin, 2007, Wilkinson, 2007).

Acknowledging such dynamics observed in different parts of the world, Wæver further clarified his stance by noting that securitisation theory's

> 'preference' for desecuritisation is not of the 'political stance' type, but an effect produced by the kinds of analysis that securitisation theory spurs: it fosters critical attention to the costs of securitisation but allows for the possibility that securitisation might help society to deal with important challenges through focusing and mobilizing attention and resources.
>
> (Wæver, 2011: 465)

Indeed, where many students of securitisation theory have focused on studying the 'costs of securitisation', the ways in which securitisation may 'help society

Critical IR theorising 63

deal with important challenges' was illustrated by Elbe (2006) and Bilgin (2007), among others.

More recently, Copenhagen School securitisation theory has begun to be adopted increasingly to study cases where all or some of the aforementioned difficulties can be observed. These sites include Hong Kong (Caballero-Anthony and Emmers, 2006a, Curley and Wong, 2008, Lo Yuk-ping and Thomas, 2010), India (Upadhyaya, 2006), Indonesia (Panggabean, 2006), Bangladesh (Siddiqui, 2006), Singapore (Caballero-Anthony et al., 2006, Hyun et al., 2006, Liow, 2006, Mak, 2006), South Korea (Hyun et al., 2006), and Turkey (Aras and Polat, 2008, Karakaya Polat, 2008, Kaliber, 2005, Kaliber and Tocci, 2010). At first glance, this list may come across as too short to deserve critical scrutiny. Then again, when viewed against the background of what Tickner and Wæver (2009: 335) termed as the 'invisibility of theory in much of the world', the presence of securitisation theory outside of Western Europe and North America does deserve critical scrutiny. For, while the number of studies that utilise securitisation theory may be relatively small, they nevertheless constitute a not-too-insignificant fraction of critical security scholarship outside North America and Western Europe (Bilgin, 2011).

On the one hand, such interest in Copenhagen School securitisation theory outside North America and Western Europe seems to affirm Wæver's (2004) expectations regarding its potential to travel to other contexts. This is because, Wæver argued, very much like European civil societal activists of the 1980s, scholars in contexts outside Western Europe and North Africa may be distrustful of the ways in which 'security arguments are often (mis)used by rulers and elites for domestic purposes'. He wrote:

> Especially in Latin America, there is a wide-spread consciousness about the ways security rhetoric has been used repressively in the past, and therefore a wariness about opening a door for this by helping to widen the concept of security.
>
> (Wæver, 2004: 25)

On the other hand, what seems to enhance the securitisation theory's potential for adoption by scholars outside Western Europe and North America may be a matter of how it is utilised in that particular context. Raising a point about the 'uses of theory' in discussing its potential for travel, then, goes to the heart of what Wæver (2011: 465) termed the 'politics of securitisation theory', understood as 'tracking what kinds of analysis the theory can produce and whether such analysis systematically impacts real life political struggles'. Wæver expected securitisation theory to be embraced outside North America and Western Europe, not only because of his confidence that it can better account for security dynamics in such contexts, but also because he expected scholars situated in those contexts to reflect upon their 'actorness' even as they acted as 'analysts' (Bilgin, 2011, Wæver, 2011).

The broader point being that the reason why scholars make a choice in favour of adopting one body of concepts and theories over another may have

64 Critical IR theorising

to do with scholars' conception of the international and how those conceptions are shaped by IR. Making sense of how theories in general and securitisation theory in particular travel, then, calls for worlding IR in its twofold meaning: considering the situatedness of scholars who utilise securitisation theory and how IR (including securitisation theory) has worlded the world. I will revisit this point when discussing worlding IR in Chapter 3.

Feminist approaches and the limits of theorising about IR and security

Of the three critical IR approaches considered here, feminist IR may be the one that has been most attentive to criticisms regarding the question 'who does the theorising?'[19] Feminist IR as a constellation has shared an interest in studying 'the rarely discussed work of women in world politics' (Murphy, 1996), and the gendered character of our practices including the study of world politics (Enloe, 1990, 1996, 2000, Cohn, 1987a, Peterson, 1992, Pettman, 1996, Sharoni, 1993, Tickner, 1992, 1997, Sylvester, 1994). Over the years, multiple facets of 'difference' and 'openness' in IR have been central to debates within feminist approaches to IR. Somewhat more recently, the issue of 'cultural' difference has also been addressed.[20]

Feminist IR's increasing visibility in the field dates back to the early 1990s when the *Millennium – Journal of International Studies* special issue on 'Women and International Relations' (1988) was followed by a series of key feminist statements on IR by Cynthia Enloe (1990), J. Ann Tickner (1992), Christine Sylvester (1994), and Jindy Jan Pettman (1996). IR scholarship by women (some of whom focused on issues related to women and gender while some others did not), however, predate such visibility. The apparent invisibility of early contributions by women IR scholars has, in itself, been a subject of research in feminist IR. Indeed, Craig Murphy has suggested that

> there may be a regular pattern of innovation in international relations by scholars who are attentive to issues of women and gender, who are central to important social movements, and who later leave the discipline and are then forgotten by those who maintain the record of the discipline's past.
>
> (Murphy, 1996: 233)

Murphy considered the Wellesley economist Emily Greene Balch an example of such a pattern of innovation. Balch was a key figure in early twentieth-century debates on world order and received a Nobel Peace Prize in 1946 in recognition of her work. While she is not remembered in the field, wrote Murphy (1996), her male contemporaries (such as Angell, Hobson and Mitrany) are remembered.

As such, feminist IR, from the very beginning, has pursued a twofold agenda: making women visible (Enloe's question: 'where are the women?'), and making visible those dynamics that have rendered women less-than-visible. As such, the critics' concern with 'who does the theorising?' (understood in terms of both the situatedness of authors and the gendered effects of such situatedness) has been central to feminist IR – although in a different way than discussed by IR's postcolonial critics, as will be seen below.[21]

In the early years of feminist IR, feminist scholars' sensitivity to the question of 'who does the theorising', by virtue of their concerns with IR's gendered bias, did not always translate into curiosity regarding the sociology of the field (or the international). Sarah White (1999) viewed this eventuality as ironical when she discussed the criticisms brought against feminists for failing to register differences among women. The irony, she argued 'is that the arguments for attending to cultural difference are in fact made on very similar terms to those advanced by feminists within the western context' regarding IR's failure to attend to gendered differences (White, 1999: 128). Identifying three forms of difference (namely, 'women's difference from men', 'contrasts in the constitution of gender relations across cultures', and 'differences between and within women'), White (1999: 119) underscored the need to pay attention to all three.

However, gradually feminist IR responded to Chandra Talpade Mohanty (1984) and Deniz Kandiyoti's (1988) anti-Eurocentric critique of feminist scholarship. The gist of Mohanty's critique was that while 'non-Western' women's issues had been a central concern for feminist scholars, the perspectives of those women from outside North America and Western Europe were not always reflected upon. Kandiyoti, in turn, pointed to the agency of women outside North America and Western Europe, which went unrecognised if and when it took forms that could not be grasped through the existing categories of IR. Feminist IR scholars drew their lesson; while seeking to highlight how the international is gendered, they had been rather slow to integrate others' perspectives on gender and the international.

Indicative of the gradual change in Feminist IR are two special issues published by the LSE-based journal *Millennium*. While the special issue that came out in 1988 included articles by authors from North America and Western Europe, the 1998 special issue opened with the postcolonial scholar Gayatri Chakravorty Spivak's (1998) keynote address to the conference. From the late 1980s to the 1990s, then, the shift in emphasis from 'women' to 'gender' in feminist IR was coupled with an increased sensitivity to 'multiple subjectivities of women and the plurality of their experiential locations' (O'Gorman and Jabri, 1999: 2).

Cynthia Enloe's works where she integrated her area studies expertise into IR research have played particularly key roles in bringing in others' perspectives into the study of how the international is gendered (Enloe, 1990, 1993, 1996, 2000, also see Enloe, 2012). Another key author in bringing about the shift in feminist IR was Jindy Jan Pettman. In *Worlding Women*, Pettman (1996) focused on the problem of Eurocentrism in the study of women in world politics, calling for sensitivity to experiences and perspectives beyond North America and Western Europe, experiences that are shaped by culture and class as well as gender.[22]

Enloe and Pettman's efforts were reinforced by Vivienne Jabri and Eleanor O'Gorman (1999) who took on board the anti-Eurocentric critique of feminism,

66 Critical IR theorising

and called for looking into differences beyond North America and Western Europe. Jabri and O'Gorman's edited volume entitled *Women, Culture, and International Relations* (1999) focused on the limits of critical IR in accounting for multiple differences and argued that

> Interpreting and representing experiences of 'others' and defining means of change, resistance, or escape are intricately bound up in the context of knowledge creation and the self who writes…the building of critical knowledge through understandings of difference is not simply a concern of mapping out the self/other axis. To settle here is to leave the power-inscribed epistemic context in place.
>
> (O'Gorman and Jabri, 1999: 11)

That having been said, Enloe, Pettman, Jabri and O'Gorman's writings indicate that feminist IR has gone further than the two other strands of critical IR discussed above in responding to the question of 'who does the theorising?' (cf. Hobson, 2007b).

In this respect, L.H.M. Ling and Anna Agathangelou's postcolonial feminist analyses of world politics and global economy are worth highlighting (Agathangelou and Ling, 2003, 2004, 2009a, Agathangelou, 2004, Ling, 2002, 2014). In particular, their studies on inter-societal interactions in producing gendered conceptions of the international have pointed to the kind of insight that considering others' perspectives on the international would bring to IR scholarship.

Feminist approaches to security theorising

Over the years, feminist scholars have been at the forefront of advancing critical approaches to security. Feminist approaches have not only shifted the focus of security analysis from states to (gendered) people, but also revealed the gendered character of the international. What is said, how it is said, and what is left unsaid – all should become the subject of our analyses, feminist scholars of security underscored. Cynthia Enloe's (2000: xxi) statement, that '*in*attention is a political act' (original emphasis) highlighted the (unacknowledged) politics of theorising about IR and security. In doing so, feminist scholars have drawn upon the insights of anthropology, sociology, sociology of science, and (perhaps more importantly for the purposes of this study) the perspectives of feminists from outside North America and Western Europe.

In many ways, feminist scholars have been forerunners of key moves in the development of critical approaches to security. Ken Booth, in particular, has identified feminist approaches as one of the most significant influences on his journey 'from Cold War Strategic Studies to Critical Security Studies'. In the said piece, Booth wrote that '[t]o talk about security without thinking about gender is simply to account for surface reflections without examining deep down below the surface' (Booth, 1997b: 101).

The twofold moves of feminist IR (making women's agency and insecurities visible, and making visible those dynamics that render women's agency and insecurities less-than-visible) have also crystallised in the study of security. Enloe's question 'where are the women?' challenged the state-based ontology of security studies, showing how the security practices of states benefit from women's agency while at the same time overlooking their insecurities (if not exacerbating them). Both women's agency and insecurities were rendered less-than-visible by approaches that focused on states and their insecurity, feminist scholars noted. 'Diplomatic wives' (Enloe, 1990) constitute an instance of the former, as revealed by Simona Sharoni's (1996) discussion on how women's agency was overlooked in portrayals of the Oslo peace negotiations between Israelis and Palestinians in the early 1990s. Insecurities experienced by sex workers who live next to military bases in Southeast Asia (Enloe, 1990), and wives or girlfriends of men who returned home the 'morning after' the signing of the peace agreement in Northern Ireland (Sharoni, 1998) constitute an instance of the latter.

Making visible those dynamics that render women's agency and insecurities less-than-visible has been a multifaceted effort. Among the crucial steps taken in this direction we may count Carol Cohn's (1987a, 1987b, 1993) studies on the gendered language of security experts, which revealed 'playful' language tricks used by experts to (make it possible to) discuss annihilation of thousands of people; Cynthia Enloe's (1996: 186) essay entitled 'Margins, Silences and Bottom Rungs: How to Overcome the Underestimation of Power in the Study of International Relations', which highlighted the 'amounts and varieties of power it takes to form and sustain any given set of relationships between states'; and J. Ann Tickner's (1992, 1995, 1997) writings on the gendered study of IR and security, which showed how women and their apparent 'absence' have been rendered invisible by the prevalence of positivist epistemology. Cohn, Enloe and Tickner's efforts underscored that even as states insecured their citizens (including women) in the name of 'national security', mainstream approaches to security, with their state-focused research design and purportedly value-free stance toward their subject matter, did not allow seeing/showing the gendered character of our insecurities or our knowledge.

I noted above that feminist IR scholars responded earlier than some other critical approaches to the question 'who does the theorising?' How did the feminist approaches to security fare in this regard? Consider, for instance, Lene Hansen's 'The Little Mermaid's Silent Security Dilemma and the Absence of Gender in the Copenhagen School'. Here, Hansen showed how the securitisation theory's focus on the 'speech act' as a method of studying securitisation did not allow studying insecurities of those who cannot speak (Hansen, 2000). To illustrate her argument, Hansen focused on the case of rape of women in Pakistan that, when brought to court led to *zina* (adultery) convictions, and resulted in 'honour killings' when left outside the judiciary process. These examples, argued Hansen, highlighted the insecurities of women who fear the implications of verbalising their insecurities and, accordingly, the limits of

68   Critical IR theorising

the securitisation theory's reliance on speech act as a method of security analysis. She wrote:

> the use of the concept of securitisation as the analytical criteria for the identification of security problems cannot elucidate the case of the Pakistani honour killings.
>
> (Hansen, 2000: 297)

This is because, the Pakistani women's 'attempt to securitise [their] situation would in these cases, paradoxically, activate another threat posed to these women by their "own" society' (Hansen, 2000: 294). Accordingly, noted Hansen, they have often resorted to 'silence, denial, or if the incident has become known, flight', as opposed to verbalising their insecurities (Hansen, 2000: 295).

Hansen's feminist critique of securitisation theory highlights the Eurocentric limits of securitisation theory insofar as everyone (including women) is assumed to be capable of constituting themselves as agents and voicing their insecurities (see above). Yet it is within the same Eurocentric framework that Hansen highlighted the gendered limits of securitisation theory: 'if women themselves do not articulate their concerns, how to study their insecurities?', she asked. While Hansen's emphasis was not on 'cultural' but gendered 'differences' (i.e. the differences between 'men' and 'women' as gendered subjects of security) the issue of how 'men' and 'women' are differently gendered in different 'cultural' settings, with implications for their capacity to constitute their agency, also came up in her discussion. That having been said, Hansen's critique of securitisation theory was shaped by another aspect of Eurocentrism insofar as the author did not consider the Pakistani women's 'patriarchal bargains' (Kandiyoti, 1988), i.e. that women's relationship to patriarchy may work differently in different settings.

The term 'patriarchal bargain' was offered by Deniz Kandiyoti when pointing to the different ways in which women strategise in response to their 'concrete constraints', which may vary according to 'class, caste and ethnicity' and take forms of 'active' or 'passive resistance' (Kandiyoti, 1988: 275). In the Pakistani context, which fits Kandiyoti's category of 'classic patriarchy', young women are subordinated not only to the men they marry but also to the older women of his household ('especially the mother-in-law'). Pakistani women's 'patriarchal bargain' has taken shape in such a context that has rendered women's contributions to production 'invisible', thereby allowing women to exercise power only rather late in their lives, and insofar as they can 'ensure the loyalty' of their married son/s. As such, women's 'patriarchal bargain' in Pakistan has involved living by the 'rules' until it is their turn to assume the position of the senior women in the family to exercise control 'through their married sons'. What this has meant for women's security is that senior women have a vested interest in holding on to the only kind of power they can exercise under conditions of 'classic hierarchy'. More specifically, senior women have a 'vested interest in the suppression of romantic love between youngsters to keep the conjugal bond secondary and to claim sons' primary allegiance' (Kandiyoti, 1988: 278–280).

Pointing to the 'patriarchal bargain' dimension of women's insecurities need not be viewed as diminishing Hansen's (2000: 291) argument that so-called honour killings in Pakistan 'should be understood as part of a rigid, patriarchal definition of female transgressive behaviour articulated and sustained by the legal-religious political establishment'. Rather, the point here, following Kandiyoti, is that there are multiple aspects to women's insecurities, and that there are multiple dimensions to the strategies they adopt in addressing those insecurities. Women's silence in the face of honour killings, in other words, may be conditioned by not only 'the legal-religious political establishment' (as Hansen highlighted), but also by their 'patriarchal bargain', as shaped by the context of diminished life chances for women in a society that has been shaped by 'classic patriarchy'.

The broader point being that reflecting on the Eurocentric limits of feminist approaches to security adds another layer of gendered difference to feminist security analysis, thereby revealing yet another dimension to women's agency and insecurities. Hence the significance of raising our contrapuntal awareness and drawing on those contrapuntal readings that offer glimpses into others' conceptions of security – as opposed to, that is, theorising through applying 'our' theories to 'their' experiences.

Conclusion

Critical IR theorising has come a long way in addressing IR's limits. Nevertheless, critical IR theorising has also inherited some of IR's problems, Eurocentrism in particular. IR's Eurocentrism has had two inter-related aspects: sociological analyses of IR as a field revealed it to be 'not so international' (to invoke Ole Wæver's phrase); IR's understanding of 'the international' was not sociological, as highlighted by Stephen Chan (1997) and Justin Rosenberg (2006). Critical approaches to IR and security have tried to respond to the question 'who does the theorising?' by seeking to increase the number of differently situated contributions (i.e. scholars from outside North America and Western Europe). However, the persistence of Eurocentric limits of IR theorising revealed the need for reflecting on the constitutive effects of such situatedness by (1) adopting a more sociological understanding of the international that incorporates inter-societal interactions; and (2) focusing on the perspectives of those who also have played a constitutive role in its making (whose contributions have heretofore been overlooked).

Indeed, the constitutive effects of IR's Eurocentric limits are so influential that even as we seek to address them, we reveal our conditioning, The debates that surrounded the question 'why is there no non-Western IR theory?' (Acharya and Buzan, 2007) is a good example of how our Eurocentric conditioning has shaped debates on the state of IR around the world. As Arif Dirlik (2011) highlighted, the formulation of the question gives our conditioning in

70   Critical IR theorising

that we ask others why they do not have IR theory (in the way we know how to recognise it), as opposed to asking ourselves why it is that we look at the world through our own particular 'IR'. To quote Dirlik:

> Is it possible to reverse the question, and ask not why Chinese do not have theory, or do not seem to be willing to do theory like 'we' do, as if that were a failure, and ask instead why 'we' have theory and do theory the way 'we' do? Instead of subjecting Chinese ways of doing things to the scrutiny of 'our' ways, and judging them by the standards of 'our' practices, is it possible to inquire if the way they do things may have something to tell us about the nature and shortcomings of the ways 'we' do things?
>
> (Dirlik, 2011: 150)

This is not to question the relevance of 'theory' (Guzzini, 2001), but to highlight how we are conditioned by the Eurocentric limits of IR theorising, even as we seek to reflect on the perspectives of the differently situated.

That having been said, inquiring into whether 'the way they do things may have something to tell us about the nature and shortcomings of the ways "we" do things', as Dirlik advised, has also turned out to be a difficult task. This is what I turn to, in Chapter 3.

Notes

1 A key role was played by the journal *Alternatives: Local, Global, and Political* that has been published in association with the Center for the Study of Developing Societies in India. Under R.B.J. Walker's editorship, *Alternatives* has 'sought to promote a wide range of approaches to political, social, cultural and ecological developments, and to encourage more creative and imaginative ways of thinking and acting globally'. http://www.sage pub.com/press/2011/april/SAGE_publishingAlternatives.sp. Accessed 14 May 2014.

2 *Rethinking International Relations* is the title of a book by Fred Halliday published in 1994. A number of significant works produced during this period were presented by their authors as 're-thinking' or 're-visioning' different aspects of the study of IR. See, for example, Hutchings (1999), Tooze and Murphy (1996), Tickner (1995), Booth (1991a), Halliday (1994), Azar and Moon (1988), Buzan (1997), Williams (1992). Other critical works that are surveyed throughout Chapter 2 also sought to re-think different aspects of IR in different ways, although without portraying their efforts in these terms.

3 Also see E.H. Carr cited in Barkawi and Laffey (2006).

4 This is not to underestimate the contributions of constructivist scholars of both the more conventional (Wendt, 1992, 1999) and the more critical (Weldes, 1996, Weldes et al., 1999) persuasions who have played crucial roles in shaping critical approaches to IR from the 1990s onwards. Constructivism is not treated separately partly because most constructivist scholars consider it as a way of studying world politics, and not as a separate approach to IR. The English School (Dunne, 1998, Buzan, 2001, 2004, Epp, 1998) is also not treated separately because its contributions, since the late 1990s, have been directed mostly on reviving the international society approach as an alternative explanation of world politics. Both these approaches have been criticised for failing to move beyond mainstream IR's 'Eurocentrism' (Suzuki et al., 2014). On the English School, see Chapter 5.

Critical IR theorising 71

5 More extensive treatment of Frankfurt School IR and its critics is beyond the mandate of this chapter. For Frankfurt School IR, also see Haacke (1996), Brincat et al. (2012), Rengger (2001), Haacke (2005), Neufeld (1995, 2004), Levine (2012).

6 But see Linklater's more recent writings that incorporate Elias (Linklater, 2007); also see Neufeld (2012).

7 The significance of stories about 'origins' is highlighted by Dussell (1993) in his Frankfurt lectures.

8 In earlier texts, the same approach is referred to as the 'Welsh School' of critical security studies. See Bilgin et al. (1998), Booth (2005b), Smith (2005).

9 For Booth's writings, see Booth (1991a, 1991b, 1991c, 1995, 1997b, 1998, 2005b, 2007).

10 On 'regional security' and the case of the Middle East, see Bilgin (2000a, 2004a, 2004b). On 'the role of security intellectuals' and the case of South Africa, see Williams (2000, 2007). Also see Stamnes and Wyn Jones, (2000), Stamnes (2004), Vale (2003), Ruane and Todd (1996), *International Relations* (2004).

11 While both Booth and Wyn Jones identified Frankfurt School Critical Theory as the philosophical basis of their critical approach to the study of security, Booth's approach in particular draws upon a number of other critical traditions, as discussed in his chapter entitled 'Security and Self: Reflections of a Fallen Realist' (Booth, 1997b). These other influences include feminist approaches, academic peace research, World Order Models Project, peace movement, arms control and disarmament movements, and critical approaches to Third World security (Bilgin et al., 1998).

12 And some critical approaches that fail to move away from statism by virtue of state-centric research design. See Bilgin (2000b, 2002).

13 For post-structuralist IR, see Ashley and Walker (1990), Walker (1990, 1993), George and Campbell (1990), Campbell (1992, 1993), Campbell and Dillon (1993), Edkins (1999), Der Derian and Shapiro (1989), Der Derian (1995).

14 This is not meant to single out social theory for criticism. On history, see Subrahmanyam (2005).

15 Also see Grovogui (2002, 2006a), Hobson (2007a, 2009), Jabri (2007a, 2013).

16 It is important to note here that Edward Said was among Bourdieu's anti-Eurocentric critics. Whereas Said looked at one, relatively later work of Bourdieu, Go looked at earlier works to excavate his early thoughts. See Go (2013).

17 The following draws upon Bilgin (2007).

18 Both the Frankfurt School inspired critical security theorising and Copenhagen School securitisation theory rest on social constructivist notions of security. Differences between the two rest on their understanding of what Wæver refers to as 'politics of theorising'. I have elsewhere compared the 'ethico-political' arguments of the two schools with reference to the case of Turkey vis-à-vis the Cyprus conflict (Bilgin, 2007).

19 This is not to suggest that feminist IR has not come under criticism but that these criticisms have been acknowledged if not always addressed by some feminist IR scholars. Consider, by way of illustration, Michael Brecher and Frank Harvey's edited volume *Millennial Reflections on International Studies*. Contributions to this 703-page volume are composed of 10 theme panels organised by the editors in their capacity as ISA president and conference chair in 1999–2000. Of the eight sections in the book, the one on feminist IR most explicitly and frequently engages with issues related to multiple facets of difference. See Brecher and Harvey (2002).

20 More extensive treatment of feminist IR and its critics is beyond the mandate of this chapter. For feminist IR, also see Sylvester (2002), O'Gorman and Jabri (1999), Youngs (2004), Murphy (1996), *Alternatives* (1993), *Millennium* (1988, 1998), Zalewski (1995), Chowdhry and Nair (2002), Tickner (1997).

72 *Critical IR theorising*

21 For a brief discussion on parallels between feminist and postcolonial IR, see Hutchings (2001, 2011).
22 The method of 'worlding' as proposed by Pettman was later taken up by Arlene Tickner and Ole Wæver in designing 'Worlding IR'.

Bibliography

Acharya, A. 2000. Ethnocentrism and Emancipatory IR Theory. In: Arnold, S. & Bier, J. M. (eds.) *Displacing Security*, Toronto, Centre for International and Security Studies, York University.

Acharya, A. 2014. Global International Relations (IR) and Regional Worlds. *International Studies Quarterly*, 58, 647–659.

Acharya, A. & Buzan, B. 2007. Why is There No Non-Western International Relations Theory? An Introduction. *International Relations of the Asia-Pacific*, 7, 287–312.

Agathangelou, A. M. 2004. *The Global Political Economy of Sex: Desire, Violence, and Insecurity in Mediterranean Nation States*, New York, Palgrave Macmillan.

Agathangelou, A. & Ling, L. H. M. 2003. Desire Industries: Sex Trafficking, UN Peacekeeping, and the Neo-Liberal World Order. *Brown Journal of World Affairs*, 10, 133.

Agathangelou, A.. & Ling, L. H. M. 2004. Power, Borders, Security, Wealth: Lessons of Violence and Desire from September 11. *International Studies Quarterly*, 48, 517–538.

Agathangelou, A. M. & Ling, L. 2009a. *Transforming World Politics: From Empire to Multiple Worlds*, London, Taylor & Francis.

Agathangelou, A. M. & Ling, L. H. M. 2009b. Postcolonial Dissidence within Dissident IR: Transforming Master Narratives of Sovereignty in Greco-Turkish Cyprus. *Studies in Political Economy*, 54, 7–38.

Ahluwalia, P. 2005. Out of Africa: Post-structuralism's Colonial Roots. *Postcolonial Studies*, 8, 137–154.

Alker, H. 2005. Emancipation in the Critical Security Studies Project. In: Booth, K. (ed.) *Critical Security Studies and World Politics*, Boulder, CO, Lynne Rienner.

Alternatives 1993. Special Issue: Feminists Write International Relations. *Alternatives: Global, Local, Political*, 18.

Aradau, C. 2004. Security and the Democratic Scene: Desecuritization and Emancipation. *Journal of International Relations & Development*, 7, 388–413.

Aras, B. & Polat, R. K. 2008. From Conflict to Cooperation: Desecuritization of Turkey's Relations with Syria and Turkey. *Security Dialogue*, 39, 495–515.

Ashley, R. 1984. The Poverty of Neorealism. *International Organization*, 38, 225–286.

Ashley, R. & Walker, R. B. J. 1990. Reading Dissidence/Writing the Discipline: Crisis and the Question of Sovereignty in International Studies. *International Studies Quarterly*, 34, 367–416.

Azar, E. E. & Moon, C.-I. 1988. Rethinking Third World National Security. In: Azar, E. E. & Moon, C.-I. (eds.) *National Security in the Third World: The Management of Internal and External Threats*, Aldershot, Edward Elgar.

Banks, M. 1986. The International Relations Discipline: Asset or Liability for Conflict Resolution? In: Azar, E. E. & Burton, J. (eds.) *International Conflict Resolution: Theory and Practice*, Boulder, CO, Lynne Rienner.

Barkawi, T. & Laffey, M. 2006. The Postcolonial Moment in Security Studies. *Review of International Studies*, 32, 329–352.

Critical IR theorising   73

Bhambra, G. K. 2007a. Multiple Modernities or Global Interconnections: Understanding the Global Post the Colonial. In: Karagiannis, N. & Wagner, P. (eds.) *Varieties of World-Making: Beyond Globalization*, Liverpool, Liverpool University Press.

Bhambra, G. K. 2007b. *Rethinking Modernity: Postcolonialism and the Sociological Imagination*, New York, Palgrave.

Bhambra, G. K. & Shilliam, R. 2009a. 'Silence' and Human Rights: Introduction. In: Bhambra, G. K. & Shilliam, R. (eds.) *Silencing Human Rights: Critical Engagements with a Contested Project*, New York, Palgrave Macmillan.

Bhambra, G. K. & Shilliam, R. 2009b. *Silencing Human Rights: Critical Engagements with a Contested Project*, New York, Palgrave Macmillan.

Biersteker, T. J. 1989. Critical Reflections on Post-positivism in International Relations. *International Studies Quarterly*, 33, 263–267.

Bigo, D. 2000. When Two Become One: Internal and External Securitisations in Europe. In: Keltsrup, M. & Williams, M. C. (eds.) *International Relations Theory and the Politics of European Integration: Power, Security, and Community*, London & New York: Routledge.

Bigo, D. 2001. The Möbius Ribbon of Internal and External Securit(ies). In: Albert, M. E. A. (ed.) *Identities Borders Orders: Rethinking International Relations Theory*. Minneapolis, University of Minnesota Press.

Bigo, D. 2002. Security and Immigration: Toward a Critique of the Governmentality of Unease. *Alternatives: Global, Local, Political*, 27, 63–92.

Bigo, D. & Guild, E. (eds.) 2005. *Controlling Frontiers: Free Movement into and within Europe*, Aldershot, Ashgate Pub Ltd.

Bilgin, P. 2000a. Inventing Middle East? The Making of Regions through Security Discourses. In: Vikor, K. (ed.) *The Middle East in Globalizing World*, Oslo, Nordic Society for Middle Eastern Studies.

Bilgin, P. 2000b. Regional Security in the Middle East: A Critical Security Studies Perspective. Ph.D., University of Wales, Aberystwyth.

Bilgin, P. 2002. Beyond Statism in Security Studies? Human Agency and Security in the Middle East. *Review of International Affairs*, 2, 100.

Bilgin, P. 2004a. *Regional Security in the Middle East: A Critical Perspective*, London, Routledge.

Bilgin, P. 2004b. Whose Middle East? Geopolitical Inventions and Practices of Security. *International Relations*, 18, 17–33.

Bilgin, P. 2007. Making Turkey's Transformation Possible: Claiming 'Security-Speak' – Not Desecuritization! *Journal of Southeast European and Black Sea Studies*, 7, 555–571.

Bilgin, P. 2011. The Politics of Studying Securitization? The Copenhagen School in Turkey. *Security Dialogue*, 42, 399–412.

Bilgin, P. 2012. Continuing Appeal of Critical Security Studies. In: Brincat, S., Lima, L. & Nunes, J. (eds.) *Critical Theory in International Relations and Security Studies: Interviews and Reflections*, London, Routledge.

Bilgin, P., Booth, K. & Jones, R. W. 1998. Security Studies: The Next Stage. *Naçao e Defesa*, 82, 131–157.

Blaney, D. L. & Inayatullah, N. 2008. International Relations from Below. In: Reus-Smit, C. & Snidal, D. (eds.) *The Oxford Handbook of International Relations*, Oxford, Oxford University Press.

Bleiker, R. 2007. Postmodernism. In: Devetak, R., Burke, A. & George, J. (eds.) *Introduction to International Relations: Australian Perspectives*, Cambridge, UK & New York, Cambridge University Press.

74 Critical IR theorising

Blumi, I. 2011. *Foundations of Modernity: Human Agency and the Imperial State*, London, Routledge.

Booth, K. (ed.) 1991a. *New Thinking about Strategy and International Security*, London, Harper Collins.

Booth, K. 1991b. Security and Emancipation. *Review of International Studies*, 17, 313–326.

Booth, K. 1991c. Security in Anarchy: Utopian Realism in Theory and Practice. *International Affairs*, 67, 527–545.

Booth, K. 1995. Human Wrongs and International Relations. *International Affairs*, 71, 103.

Booth, K. 1997a. Discussion: A Reply to Wallace. *Review of International Studies*, 23, 371–377.

Booth, K. 1997b. Security and Self: Reflections of a Fallen Realist. In: Krause, K. & Williams, M. C. (eds.) *Critical Security Studies: Concepts and Cases*, Minneapolis, University of Minnesota Press.

Booth, K. (ed.) 1998. *Statecraft and Security: The Cold War and Beyond*, Cambridge, UK & New York, Cambridge University Press.

Booth, K. 2005a. Beyond Critical Security Studies. In: Booth, K. (ed.) *Critical Security Studies and World Politics*, Boulder, CO, Lynne Rienner Publishers.

Booth, K. (ed.) 2005b. *Critical Security Studies and World Politics*, Boulder, CO, Lynne Rienner Publishers.

Booth, K. 2005c. Emancipation. In: Booth, K. (ed.) *Critical Security Studies and World Politics*. Boulder, CO, Lynne Rienner Publishers.

Booth, K. 2007. *Theory of World Security*, Cambridge, Cambridge University Press.

Booth, K. & Vale, P. 1995. Security in Southern Africa: After Apartheid, Beyond Realism. *International Affairs*, 71, 285.

Bourbeau, P. 2011. *The Securitization of Migration: A Study of Movement and Order*, London, Routledge.

Brecher, M. & Harvey, F. P. (eds.) 2002. *Millennial Reflections on International Studies*, Ann Arbor, The University of Michigan Press.

Brincat, S., Lima, L. & Nunes, J. (eds.) 2012. *Critical Theory in International Relations and Security Studies*, London, Routledge.

Brown, C. 1988. The Modern Requirement? Reflections on Normative International Theory in a Post-Western World. *Millennium – Journal of International Studies*, 17, 339–348.

Buck-Morss, S. 2003. *Thinking Past Terror: Islamism and Critical Theory on the Left*, New York, Verso.

Burke, A. 2001. *Fear of Security: Australia's Invasion Anxiety*, Annandale, Pluto Press.

Burke, A. 2007. *Beyond Security, Ethics and Violence: War against the Other*, New York, Routledge.

Burke, A. 2013. Post-structural Security Studies. In: Shepherd, L. J. (ed.) *Critical Approaches to Security: An Introduction to Theories and Methods*, London, Routledge.

Buzan, B. 1991. *People, States, and Fear: An Agenda for International Security Studies in the Post-cold War Era*, 2nd ed. New York, Harvester Wheatsheaf.

Buzan, B. 1997. Rethinking Security after the Cold War. *Cooperation and Conflict*, 32, 5.

Buzan, B. 2001. The English School: An Underexploited Resource in IR. *Review of International Studies*, 27, 471–488.

Buzan, B. 2004. *From International to World Society? English School Theory and the Social Structure of Globalisation*, Cambridge, UK & New York, Cambridge University Press.

Critical IR theorising 75

Buzan, B., Wæver, O. & De Wilde, J. 1998. *Security: A New Framework of Analysis*, Boulder, CO, Lynne Rienner.

Caballero-Anthony, M. & Emmers, R. 2006a. The Dynamics of Securitization in Asia. In: Emmers, R., Caballero-Anthony, M. & Acharya, A. (eds.) *Studying Non-traditional Security in Asia: Trends and Issues*, London, Marshall Cavendish Academic.

Caballero-Anthony, M. & Emmers, R. 2006b. Understanding the Dynamics of Securitizing Non-traditional Security. In: Caballero-Anthony, M., Emmers, R. & Acharya, A. (eds.) *Non-Traditional Security in Asia: Dilemmas in Securitisation*, Aldershot, Ashgate.

Caballero-Anthony, M., Emmers, R. & Acharya, A. (eds.) 2006. *Non-Traditional Security in Asia: Dilemmas in Securitisation*, Aldershot, Ashgate.

Campbell, D. 1992. *Writing Security: United States Foreign Policy and the Politics of Identity*, Manchester, Manchester University Press.

Campbell, D. 1993. *Politics without Principle: Sovereignty, Ethics and the Narratives the Gulf War*, Boulder, CO, Lynne Rienner Publishers.

Campbell, D. 1998. *National Deconstruction: Violence, Identity, and Justice in Bosnia*, Minneapolis, University of Minnesota Press.

Campbell, D. & Dillon, M. (eds.) 1993. *The Political Subject of Violence*, Manchester & New York, Manchester University Press.

Chan, S. 1997. Seven Types of Ambiguity in Western International Relations Theory and Painful Steps Towards Right Ethics. *Theoria: A Journal of Social and Political Theory*, 106–115.

Chowdhry, G. & Nair, S. (eds.) 2002. *Power, Postcolonialism, and International Relations: Reading Race, Gender, and Class*, London, Routledge.

Cohn, C. 1987a. Sex and Death in the Rational World of Defense Intellectuals. *Signs: Journal of Women in Culture and Society*, 12, 687–718.

Cohn, C. 1987b. Slick'ems, Glick'ems, Christmas Trees, and Cookie Cutters: Nuclear Language and How We Learned to Pat the Bomb. *Bulletin of the Atomic Scientists*, 43, 17–24.

Cohn, C. 1993. Wars, Wimps, and Women: Talking Gender and Thinking War. *Gendering War Talk*, 37, 233–235.

Constantinou, C. 2000. Diplomacy, Grotesque Realism, and Ottoman Historiography. *Postcolonial Studies*, 3, 213–226.

Cox, R. W. 1981. Social Forces, States and World Orders: Beyond International Relations Theory. *Millennium – Journal of International Studies*, 10, 126–155.

Cox, R. W. 1987. *Production, Power, and World Order: Social Forces in the Making of History*, New York, Columbia University Press.

Curley, M. G. & Wong, S. (eds.) 2008. *Security and Migration in Asia: The Dynamics of Securitisation*, London, Taylor & Francis.

Der Derian, J. (ed.) 1995. *International Theory: Critical Investigations*, New York, New York University Press.

Der Derian, J. & Shapiro, M. J. (eds.) 1989. *International/Intertextual Relations: Postmodern Readings of World Politics*, Lexington, MA, Lexington Books.

Deudney, D. 1983. *Whole Earth Security: A Geopolitics of Peace*, Washington, DC, Worldwatch Institute.

Dirlik, A. 2011. Culture in Contemporary IR Theory: The Chinese Provocation. In: Shilliam, R. (ed.) *International Relations and Non-Western Thought: Imperialism, Colonialism and Investigations of Global Modernity*, London, Routledge.

76 Critical IR theorising

Dunne, T. 1998. *Inventing International Society: A History of the English School*, New York, St. Martin's Press.

Dussel, E. 1993. Eurocentrism and Modernity (Introduction to the Frankfurt Lectures). *boundary 2*, 20, 65–76.

Duvall, R. & Varadarajan, L. 2003. On the Practical Significance of Critical International Relations Theory. *Asian Journal of Political Science*, 11, 75–88.

Edkins, J. 1999. *Poststructuralism and International Relations: Bringing the Political Back In*, Boulder, CO, Lynne Rienner Publishers.

Elbe, S. 2006. Should HIV/AIDS Be Securitized? The Ethical Dilemmas of Linking HIV/AIDS and Security. *International Studies Quarterly*, 50, 119–144.

Emmers, R., Caballero-Anthony, M. & Acharya, A. (eds.) 2006. *Studying Non-traditional Security in Asia: Trends and Issues*, London, Marshall Cavendish Academic.

Enloe, C. 1990. *Bananas, Beaches and Bases: Making Feminist Sense of International Politics*, Berkeley, University of California Press.

Enloe, C. 1993. *The Morning After: Sexual Politics at the End of the Cold War*, Berkeley, University of California Press.

Enloe, C. 1996. Margins, Silences and Bottom Rungs: How to Overcome the Underestimation of Power in the Study of International Relations. In: Booth, K., Smith, S. & Zalewski, M. (eds.) *International Theory: Positivism and Beyond*, Cambridge, Cambridge University Press.

Enloe, C. 2000. *Maneuvers: The International Politics of Militarizing Women's Lives*, Berkeley, University of California Press.

Enloe, C. 2012. Militarization, Feminism and the International Politics of Banana Boats [Online]. Theory Talks. Available: http://www.theory-talks.org/2013/08/theory-talk-57.html [Accessed 30 January 2014].

Epp, R. 1998. The English School on the Frontiers of International Society: A Hermeneutic Recollection. *Review of International Studies*, 24, 47–63.

George, J. 1994. *Discourses of Global Politics: Critical (Re)Introduction to International Relations*, Boulder, CO, Lynne Rienner Publishers.

George, J. & Campbell, D. 1990. Patterns of Dissent and the Celebration of Difference: Critical Social Theory and International Relations. *International Studies Quarterly*, 34, 3, 269–293.

Go, J. 2013. Decolonizing Bourdieu: Colonial and Postcolonial Theory in Pierre Bourdieu's Early Work. *Sociological Theory*, 31, 49–74.

Grovogui, S. N. 2002. Postcolonial Criticism: International Reality and Modes of Inquiry. In: Chowdhry, G. & Nair, S. (eds.) *Power, Postcolonialism, and International Relations: Reading Race, Gender and Class*, London, Routledge.

Grovogui, S. N. 2005. The New Cosmopolitanisms: Subtexts, Pretexts and Context of Ethics. *International Relations*, 19, 103–113.

Grovogui, S. N. 2006a. *Beyond Eurocentrism and Anarchy: Memories of International Order and Institutions*, New York, Palgrave Macmillan.

Grovogui, S. N. 2006b. Mind, Body, and Gut! Elements of a Postcolonial Human Rights Discourse. In: Jones, B. G. (ed.) *Decolonizing International Relations*, London, Routledge.

Grovogui, S. N. 2011. To the Orphaned, Dispossessed, and Illegitimate Children: Human Rights Beyond Republican and Liberal Traditions. *Indiana Journal of Global Legal Studies* 18, 41–63.

Gurtaudon, V. 2012. Citizenship: Bourdieu, Migration and the International. In: Adler-Nissen, R. (ed.) *Bourdieu in International Relations: Rethinking Key Concepts in IR*, London, Routledge.

Guzzini, S. 2001. The Significance and Roles of Teaching Theory in International Relations. *Journal of International Relations and Development*, 4, 98–117.

Guzzini, S. 2015. The Dual History of 'Securitisation'. *DIIS working paper*. Copenhagen, Danish Institute for International Studies.

Haacke, J. 1996. Theory and Praxis in International Relations: Habermas, Self-reflection, Rational Argumentation. *Millennium – Journal of International Studies*, 25, 255–289.

Haacke, J. 2005. The Frankfurt School and International Relations on the Centrality of Recognition. *Review of International Studies*, 31, 181–194.

Hall, S. 1996. When was 'the Post-colonial'? Thinking at the Limit. In: Chambers, I. & Curti, L. (eds.) *The Post-colonial Question: Common Skies, Divided Horizons*, London, Routledge.

Halliday, F. 1994. *Rethinking International Relations*, Basingstoke, Palgrave Macmillan.

Halperin, S. 2006. International Relations Theory and the hegemony of Western Conceptions of Modernity. In: Jones, B. G. (ed.) *Decolonizing International Relations*, Lanham, MD, Rowman & Littlefield.

Hansen, L. 2000. The Little Mermaid's Silent Security Dilemma and the Absence of Gender in the Copenhagen School. *Millennium – Journal of International Studies*, 29, 285–306.

Hobson, J. M. 2007a. Deconstructing the Eurocentric Clash of Civilizations: De-Westernizing the West by Acknowledging the Dialogue of Civilizations. In: Hall, M. & Jackson, P. T. (eds.) *Civilizational Identity: The Production and Reproduction of 'Civilizations' in International Relations*, New York, Palgrave Macmillan.

Hobson, J. M. 2007b. Is Critical Theory Always for the White West and Western Imperialism? Beyond Westphilian towards a Post-Racist Critical IR. *Review of International Studies*, 33, 91–116.

Hobson, J. M. 2009. The Myth of the Clash of Civilizations in Dialogical-Historical Context. In: Bilgin, P. & Williams, P. D. (eds.) *Global Security, in Encyclopedia of Life Support Systems (EOLSS)*, Oxford, UNESCO, EoLSS Publishers.

Holsti, K. J. 1985. *The Dividing Discipline: Hegemony and Diversity in International Theory*, Boston, Allen & Unwin.

Hutchings, K. 1999. *International Political Theory: Rethinking Ethics in a Global Era*, London, Sage Publications Limited.

Hutchings, K. 2001. The Nature of Critique in Critical International Relations Theory. In: Jones, R. W. (ed.) *Critical Theory and World Politics*, Boulder, CO, Lynne Rienner.

Hutchings, K. 2011. Dialogue between Whom? The Role of the West/Non-West Distinction in Promoting Global Dialogue in IR. *Millennium – Journal of International Studies*, 39, 639–647.

Hutchings, K. 2012. Turning Towards the World: Practicing Critique in IR. In: Brincat, S., Lima, L. & Nunes, J. (eds.) *Critical Theory in International Relations and Security Studies*, London, Routledge.

Huysmans, J. 1995. Migrants as a Security Problem: Dangers of 'Securitizing' Societal Issues. In: Thränhardt, D. & Miles, R. (eds.) *Migration and European Integration: The Dynamics of Inclusion and Exclusion*, London, Pinternair.

Huysmans, J. 1998. Security! What Do You Mean? From Concept to Thick Signifier. *European Journal of International Relations*, 4, 226–255.

Huysmans, J. 2006a. International Politics of Insecurity: Normativity, Inwardness and the Exception. *Security Dialogue*, 37, 11–29.

78 Critical IR theorising

Huysmans, J. 2006b. *The Politics of Insecurity: Fear, Migration, and Asylum in the EU*, New York, Routledge.

Huysmans, J., Dobson, A. & Prokhovnik, R. (eds.) 2006. *The Politics of Protection: Sites of Insecurity and Political Agency*, New York, Routledge.

Hyun, T., Kim, S.-H. & Lee, G. 2006. Bringing Politics Back. In: Globalization, Pluralism and Securitization in East Asia. In: Emmers, R., Caballero-Anthony, M. & Acharya, A. (eds.) *Studying Non-traditional Security in Asia: Trends and Issues*, London, Marshall Cavendish Academic.

International Relations 2004. Special Issue: Critical Security Studies. *International Relations*, 18, 5–143.

Jabri, V. 2007a. Michel Foucault's Analytics of War: The Social, the International, and the Racial. *International Political Sociology*, 1, 67–81.

Jabri, V. 2007b. Solidarity and Spheres of Culture: The Cosmopolitan and the Postcolonial. *Review of International Studies*, 33, 715–728.

Jabri, V. 2012. Cosmopolitan Politics, Security, Political Subjectivity. *European Journal of International Relations*, 18, 625–644.

Jabri, V. 2013. *The Postcolonial Subject: Claiming Politics/Governing Others in Late Modernity*, London, Routledge.

Jabri, V. 2014. Disarming Norms: Postcolonial Agency and the Constitution of the International. *International Theory*, 6, 372–390.

Jabri, V. & O'Gorman, E. (eds.) 1999. *Women, Culture, and International Relations*, Boulder, CO, Lynne Rienner Publishers.

Jahn, B. 1998. One Step Forward, Two Steps Back: Critical Theory as the Latest Edition of Liberal Idealism. *Millennium – Journal of International Studies*, 27, 613–641.

Kaliber, A. 2005. Securing the Ground through Securitized 'Foreign' Policy: The Cyprus Case. *Security Dialogue*, 36, 319–337.

Kaliber, A. & Tocci, N. 2010. Civil Society and the Transformation of Turkey's Kurdish Question. *Security Dialogue*, 41, 191–215.

Kandiyoti, D. 1988. Bargaining with Patriarchy. *Gender & Society*, 2, 274–290.

Karakaya Polat, R. 2008. The 2007 Parliamentary Elections in Turkey: Between Securitisation and Desecuritisation. *Parliamentary Affairs*, 62, 129–148.

Keohane, R. O. 1988. International Institutions: Two Approaches. *International Studies Quarterly*, 32, 379–396.

Klein, B. S. 1990. How the West Was One: Representational Politics of NATO. *International Studies Quarterly*, 34, 311–325.

Klein, B. S. 1994. *Strategic Studies and World Order*, Cambridge, Cambridge University Press.

Knudsen, O. F. 2001. Post-Copenhagen Security Studies: Desecuritizing Securitization. *Security Dialogue*, 32, 355.

Krishna, S. 1993. The Importance of Being Ironic: A Postcolonial View on Critical International Relations Theory. *Alternatives*, 18, 385–417.

Kristensen, P. M. 2015. Revisiting the 'American Social Science'—Mapping the Geography of International Relations. *International Studies Perspectives*, 16, 246–269.

Lapid, Y. 1989. The Third Debate: On the Prospects of International Theory in a Post-Positivist Era. *International Studies Quarterly*, 33, 235–254.

Lapid, Y. 2002. En Route to Knowledge: Is There a 'Third Path' (in the Third Debate)? In: Brecher, M. & Harvey, F. P. (eds.) *Millennial Reflections on International Studies*, Ann Arbor, The University of Michigan Press.

Critical IR theorising   79

Lee-Koo, K. 2007. Security as Enslavement, Security as Emancipation: Gendered Legacies and Feminist Futures in the Asia-Pacific. In: Burke, A. & McDonald, M. (eds.) *Critical Security in the Asia-Pacific*, Manchester, Manchester University Press.

Levine, D. 2012. *Recovering International Relations: The Promise of Sustainable Critique*, New York, Oxford University Press.

Ling, L. H. M. 2002. *Postcolonial International Relations: Conquest and Desire between Asia and the West*, New York, Palgrave.

Ling, L. H. M. 2014. *The Dao of World Politics: Towards a Post-Westphalian, Worldist International Relations*, London, Routledge.

Linklater, A. 1982. *Men and Citizens in the Theory of International Relations*, New York, St. Martin's Press.

Linklater, A. 1990. *Beyond Realism and Marxism: Critical Theory and International Relations*, Basingstoke, Macmillan.

Linklater, A. 1992. The Question of the Next Stage in International Relations Theory: A Critical-theoretical Point of View. *Millennium – Journal of International Studies*, 21, 77–98.

Linklater, A. 1998. *The Transformation of Political Community: Ethical Foundations of the Post-Westphalian Era*, Columbia, University of South Carolina Press.

Linklater, A. 2005. Political Community and Human Security. In: Booth, K. (ed.) *Critical Security Studies and World Politics*, Boulder, CO, Lynne Rienner.

Linklater, A. 2007. Torture and Civilisation. *International Relations*, 21, 111–118.

Liow, J. 2006. Malaysia's Approach to Indonesian Migrant Labor: Securitization, Politics, or Catharsis? In: Emmers, R. & Acharya, A. (eds.) *Non-traditional Security in Asia: Dilemmas in Securitization*, London, Marshall Cavendish Academic.

Lo Yuk-ping, C. & Thomas, N. 2010. How is Health a Security Issue? Politics, Responses and Issues. *Health Policy and Planning*, 25, 447–453.

Maghroori, R. & Ramberg, B. (eds.) 1982. *Globalism versus Realism: International Relations' Third Debate*, Boulder, CO, Westview.

Mak, J. 2006. Securitizing Piracy in Southeast Asia: Malaysia, the International Maritime Bureau and Singapore. In: Caballero-Anthony, M., Emmers, R. & Acharya, A. (eds.) *Non-Traditional Security in Asia: Dilemmas in Securitisation*, Aldershot, Ashgate.

Mathews, J. T. 1989. Redefining security. *Foreign Affairs*, 68, 2, 162–177.

McSweeney, B. 1996. Identity and Security: Buzan and the Copenhagen School. *Review of International Studies*, 22, 81–94.

Millennium 1988. Special Issue: Women and International Relations. *Millennium – Journal of International Studies*, 17.

Millennium 1998. Special Issue: Gender and International Relations. *Millennium – Journal of International Studies*, 27, 4.

Milliken, J. 2001. *The Social Construction of the Korean War: Conflict and its Possibilities*, Manchester, New York, Manchester University Press.

Mohanty, C. T. 1984. Under Western eyes: Feminist Scholarship and Colonial Discourses. *boundary 2*, 12, 333–358.

Murphy, C. N. 1994. *International Organization and Industrial Change: Global Governance Since 1850*, Oxford, Polity.

Murphy, C. N. 1996. Seeing Women, Recognizing Gender, Recasting International Relations. *International Organization*, 50, 513–538.

Murphy, C. N. 2001. Critical Theory and the Democratic Impulse: Understanding a Century-Old Tradition. In: Wyn Jones, R. (ed.) *Critical Theory and World Politics*. Boulder, CO, Lynne Rienner.

80   Critical IR theorising

Murphy, C. N. 2006. *The United Nations Development Programme: A Better Way?*, Cambridge, Cambridge University Press.

Murphy, C. N. 2007. The Promise of Critical IR, Partially Kept. *Review of International Studies*, 33, 117.

Neufeld, M. A. 1995. *The Restructuring of International Relations Theory*, Cambridge, UK & New York, Cambridge University Press.

Neufeld, M. 2004. Pitfalls of Emancipation and Discourses of Security: Reflections on Canada's 'Security With a Human Face'. *International Relations*, 18, 109–123.

Neufeld, M. 2012. Beyond (Western) IR Theory: The Post-colonial Tradition and the Restructuring of (Critical) IR Theory. In: Brincat, S., Lima, L. & Nunes, J. (eds.) *Critical Theory in International Relations and Security Studies*, London, Routledge.

Nyers, P. (ed.) 2009. *Securitizations of Citizenship*, London, Routledge.

O'Gorman, E. & Jabri, V. 1999. Locating Difference in Feminist International Relations. In: Jabri, V. & O'Gorman, E. (eds.) *Women, Culture, and International Relations*, Boulder, CO, Lynne Rienner Publishers.

Panggabean, S. R. 2006. Securitizing Health in Violence Affected Areas of Indonesia. In: Cabellero-Anthony, M., Emmers, R. & Acharya, A. (eds.) *Non-Traditional Security in Asia: Dilemmas in Securitisation*, Aldershot, Ashgate.

Pasha, M. K. 1996. Security as Hegemony. *Alternatives*, 21, 283–302.

Peterson, V. S. (ed.) 1992. *Gendered States: Feminist (Re)visions of International Relations Theory*, Boulder, CO, Lynne Rienner Publishers.

Pettman, J. J. 1996. *Worlding Women: A Feminist International Politics*, London, Routledge.

Pettman, J. J. 2005. Questions of Identity: Australia and Asia. In: Booth, K. (ed.) *Critical Security Studies and World Politics*. Boulder, CO, Lynne Rienner.

Pieterse, J. N. 1992. Emancipations, Modern and Postmodern. *Development and Change*, 23, 5–41.

Price, R. & Reus-Smit, C. 1998. Dangerous Liaisons?: Critical International Theory and Constructivism. *European Journal of International Relations*, 4, 259.

Rao, R. 2010. *Third World Protest: Between Home and the World*, Oxford, Oxford University Press.

Rasmussen, M. V. 2004. 'It Sounds like a Riddle': Security Studies, the War on Terror and Risk. *Millennium – Journal of International Studies*, 33, 381–395.

Rengger, N. J. 2001. Negative Dialectic? The Two Modes of Critical Theory in World Politics. In: Jones, R. W. (ed.) *Critical Theory and World Politics*, Boulder, CO, Lynne Rienner.

Rosenberg, J. 2006. Why is there No International Historical Sociology? *European Journal of International Relations*, 12, 307–340.

Ruane, J. & Todd, J. 1996. *The Dynamics of Conflict in Northern Ireland: Power, Conflict and Emancipation*, Cambridge, Cambridge University Press.

Sabaratnam, M. 2013. Avatars of Eurocentrism in the Critique of the Liberal Peace. *Security Dialogue*, 44, 259–278.

Security Dialogue 2011. Special Issue: The Politics of Securitization. *Security Diaogue*, 42.

Seth, S. 2013. Introduction. In: Seth, S. (ed.) *Postcolonial Theory and International Relations: A Critical Introduction*, London, Routledge.

Shani, G. 2007. 'Provincializing' Critical Theory: Islam, Sikhism and International Relations Theory. *Cambridge Review of International Affairs*, 20, 417–433.

Shani, G. 2008. Toward a Post-Western IR: The Umma, Khalsa Panth, and Critical International Relations Theory. *International Studies Review*, 10, 722–734.

Critical IR theorising 81

Shapiro, M. J. 1990. Strategic Discourse/Discursive Strategy: The Representation of 'Security Policy' in the Video Age. *International Studies Quarterly*, 34, 327–340.

Sharoni, S. 1993. Middle East Politics Through Feminist Lenses: Toward Theorizing International Relations from Women's Struggles. *Alternatives: Global, Local, Political*, 18, 5–28.

Sharoni, S. 1996. Gender and the Israeli-Palestinian Accord: Feminist Approaches to International Politics. In: Kandiyoti, D. (ed.) *Gendering the Middle East: Emerging Perspectives*, Syracuse, NY, Syracuse University Press.

Sharoni, S. 1998. Gendering Conflict and Peace in Israel/Palestine and the North of Ireland. *Millennium – Journal of International Studies*, 27, 1061–1090.

Shilliam, R. 2009. The Enigmatic Figure of the Non-Western Thinker in International Relations. *Antepodium* [Online]. Available: http://www.victoria.ac.nz/atp/articles/pdf/Shilliam-2009.pdf Accessed 27 January 2014.

Shilliam, R. (ed.) 2011. *International Relations and Non-Western Thought: Imperialism, Colonialism, and Investigations of Global Modernity*, New York, Routledge.

Siddiqui, T. 2006. Securitization of Irregular Migration: The South Asian Case. In: Emmers, R., Caballero-Anthony, M. & Acharya, A. (eds.) *Studying Non-traditional Security in Asia: Trends and Issues*, London, Marshall Cavendish Academic.

Smith, S. 1996. Positivism and Beyond. In: Booth, K., Smith, S. & Zalewski, M. (eds.) *International Theory: Positivism and Beyond*, Cambridge, Cambridge University Press.

Smith, S. 1997. Power and Truth: A Reply to William Wallace. *Review of International Studies*, 23, 507–516.

Smith, S. 2002a. Alternative and Critical Perspectives. In: Brecher, M. & Harvey, F. P. (eds.) *Millennial Reflections on International Studies*, Ann Arbor, The University of Michigan Press.

Smith, S. 2002b. The United States and the Discipline of International Relations: 'Hegemonic Country, Hegemonic Discipline'. *International Studies Review*, 4, 67–85.

Smith, S. 2004. Singing our World into Existence: International Relations Theory and September 11. *International Studies Quarterly*, 48, 499–515.

Smith, S. 2005. The Contested Concept of Security. In: Booth, K. (ed.) *Critical Security Studies and World Politics*, Boulder, CO, Lynne Rienner.

Spivak, G. C. 1995. Can the Subaltern Speak? In: Ashcroft, B., Griffiths, G. & Tiffin, H. (eds.) *The Postcolonial Studies Reader*, London, Routledge.

Spivak, G. C. 1998. Gender and International Studies. *Millennium – Journal of International Studies*, 27, 809–831.

Stamnes, E. 2004. Critical Security Studies and the United Nations Preventive Deployment in Macedonia. *International Peacekeeping*, 11, 161–181.

Stamnes, E. & Wyn Jones, R. 2000. Burundi: A Critical Security Perspective. *Peace and Conflict Studies*, 7, 37–55.

Subrahmanyam, S. 2005. On World Historians in the Sixteenth Century. *Representations*, 91, 26–57.

Suzuki, S., Zhang, Y. & Quirk, J. (eds.) 2014. *International Orders in the Early Modern World: Before the Rise of the West*, London: Routledge.

Sylvester, C. 1994. *Feminist Theory and International Relations in a Postmodern Era*, Cambridge, Cambridge University Press.

Sylvester, C. 2002. *Feminist International Relations: An Unfinished Journey*, New York, Cambridge University Press.

Tickner, A. B. & Wæver, O. 2009. Introduction: Geocultural Epistemologies. In: Tickner, A. B. & Wæver, O. (eds.) *International Relations Scholarship Around the World*, London, Routledge.

82   Critical IR theorising

Tickner, J. A. 1992. *Gender in International Relations: Feminist Perspectives on Achieving Global Security*, New York, Columbia University Press.

Tickner, J. A. 1995. Re-visioning Security. In: Booth, K. & Smith, S. (eds.) *International Relations Theory Today*, Oxford, Polity.

Tickner, J. A. 1997. You Just Don't Understand: Troubled Engagements between Feminists and IR Theorists. *International Studies Quarterly*, 41, 611–632.

Tooze, R. & Murphy, C. N. 1996. The Epistemology of Poverty and the Poverty of Epistemology in IPE: Mystery, Blindness, and Invisibility. *Millennium – Journal of International Studies*, 25, 681–707.

Upadhyaya, P. 2006. Securitization Matrix in South Asia: Bangladeshi Migrants as Enemy Alien. In: Caballero-Anthony, M., Emmers, R. & Acharya, A. (eds.) *Non-Traditional Security in Asia: Dilemmas in Securitisation*, Aldershot, Ashgate.

Vale, P. 2003. *Security and Politics in South Africa: The Regional Dimension*, Boulder, CO, Lynne Rienner Publishers.

Wæver, O. 1987. Conflicts of Vision: Visions of Conflict. *European Polyphony: Perspectives beyond East-West Confrontation*, London, Macmillan.

Wæver, O. 1989. Security, the Speech Act: Analysing the Politics of a Word. *COPRI Working Paper*. Copenhagen, Copenhagen Peace Research Institute.

Wæver, O. 1990. Three Competing Europes: German, French, Russian. *International Affairs*, 66, 477.

Wæver, O. 1993. Societal Security: The Concept. In: Wæver, O., Buzan, B., Kelstrup, M. & Lemaitre, P. (eds.) *Identity, Migration, and the New Security Agenda in Europe*, London, Pinter.

Wæver, O. 1995. Securitization and Desecuritization. In: Lipschutz, R. D. (ed.) *On Security*, New York, Columbia University Press.

Wæver, O. 1998a. Insecurity, Security, and Asecurity in the West European Non-war Community. In: Adler, E. & Barnett, M. N. (eds.) *Security Communities*, Cambridge, Cambridge University Press.

Wæver, O. 1998b. The Sociology of a Not So International Discipline: American and European Developments in International Relations. *International Organization*, 52, 687–727.

Wæver, O. 1999. Securitizing Sectors?: Reply to Eriksson *Cooperation and Conflict*, 34, 334–340.

Wæver, O. 2004. Aberystwyth, Paris, Copenhagen – New 'Schools' in Security Theory and their Origins between Core and Periphery. Paper presented at the annual conference of the International Studies Association, Montreal, Canada.

Wæver, O. 2011. Politics, Security, Theory. *Security Dialogue*, 42, 465–480.

Walker, R. B. J. 1990. Security, Sovereignty and the Challenge of World Politics. *Alternatives*, 15, 3–28.

Walker, R. B. J. 1993. *Inside/outside: International Relations as Political Theory*, Cambridge, Cambridge University Press.

Walker, R. B. J. 1997. The Subject of Security. In: Krause, K. & Williams, M. C. (eds.) *Critical Security Studies: Concepts and Cases*, Minneapolis, MN, University of Minnesota Press.

Walker, R. B. J. 2002. Alternative, Critical, Political. In: Brecher, M. & Harvey, F. P. (eds.) *Millennial Reflections on International Studies*, Ann Arbor, The University of Michigan Press.

Walker, R. B. J. 2006. Lines of Insecurity: International, Imperial, Exceptional. *Security Dialogue*, 37, 65–82.

Critical IR theorising 83

Walt, S. M. 1991. The Renaissance of Security Studies. *International Studies Quarterly*, 35, 211–239.

Weber, C. 1995. *Simulating Sovereignty: Intervention, the State and Symbolic Exchange*, Cambridge, Cambridge University Press.

Weldes, J. 1996. Constructing National Interests. *European Journal of International Relations*, 2, 275–318.

Weldes, J. 1999. The Cultural Production of Crises: US Identity and Missiles In Cuba. In: Weldes, J., Laffey, M., Gusterson, H. & Duvall, R. (eds.) *Cultures of Insecurity: States, Communities, and the Production of Danger*, Minneapolis, University of Minnesota Press.

Weldes, J., Laffey, M., Gusterson, H. & Duvall, R. (eds.) 1999. *Cultures of Insecurity: States, Communities and the Production of Danger*, Minneapolis, University of Minnesota Press.

Wendt, A. 1992. Anarchy is What States Make of it: The Social Construction of Power Politics. *International Organization*, 46, 391–425.

Wendt, A. 1999. *Social Theory of International Politics*, Cambridge, Cambridge University Press.

White, S. C. 1999. Gender and Development: Working with Difference. In: Jabri, V. & O'Gorman, E. (eds.) *Women, Culture, and International Relations*, Boulder, CO, Lynne Rienner Publishers.

Wilkinson, C. 2007. The Copenhagen School on Tour in Kyrgyzstan: Is Securitization Theory Useable Outside Europe? *Security Dialogue*, 38, 5.

Williams, M. C. 1992. Rethinking the 'Logic' of Deterrence. *Alternatives: Global, Local, Political*, 17, 67–93.

Williams, M. C. & Neumann, I. B. 2000. From Alliance to Security Community: NATO, Russia, and the Power of Identity. *Millennium – Journal of International Studies*, 29, 357–387.

Williams, P. D. 2000. South African Foreign Policy: Getting Critical? *Politikon: South African Journal of Political Studies*, 27, 73–91.

Williams, P. D. 2007. Thinking about Security in Africa. *International Affairs*, 83, 1021–1038.

Wyn Jones, R. 1999. *Security, Strategy and Critical Theory*, Boulder, CO, Lynne Rienner Publishers.

Wyn Jones, R. (ed.) 2001a. *Critical Theory and World Politics*, Boulder, C, Lynne Rienner Publishers.

Wyn Jones, R. 2001b. Introduction: Locating Critical International Relations Theory. In: Jones, R. W. (ed.) *Critical Theory and World Politics*, Boulder, CO, Lynne Rienner.

Wyn Jones, R. 2005. On Emancipation: Necessity, Capacity and Concrete Utopias. In: Booth, K. (ed.) *Critical Security Studies and World Politics*, Boulder, CO, Lynne Rienner.

Youngs, G. 2004. Feminist International Relations: A Contradiction in Terms? Or: Why Women and Gender are Essential to Understanding the World 'We' Live in. *International Affairs*, 80, 75–87.

Zalewski, M. 1995. Well, What is the Feminist Perspective on Bosnia? *International Affairs*, 71, 339–356.

3 How to access others' conceptions of the international

The previous chapter considered the contributions of critical theorising in identifying and addressing IR's limits. Arguably, it was the very accomplishments of critical IR scholarship in fulfilling this task that has rendered more visible those limits that remain to be addressed (as with Eurocentrism). I suggested that this eventuality could be viewed as a consequence of the manner in which the students of critical IR sought to address IR's limits, that is, by asking 'who does the theorising?' and endeavouring to reflect on the geo-cultural situatedness of IR scholars – those who 'founded' the discipline and those who were apparently 'absent'. As such, what was left out of the discussions was IR's 'constitutive outside', that is, the ways in which the ideas and experiences of 'others' have shaped IR even as they were not always visible in debates. It is this very contradiction (that others' ideas and experiences have shaped IR and yet these contributions and contestations have not been acknowledged explicitly in the literature) that has rendered more complicated the task of addressing IR's limits.

Chapter 3 further develops this point by considering the efforts of those scholars who sought to understand how 'others' approach the international. Here I look at two sets of efforts in two parts: (1) those studies that focused on IR scholarship around the world to see how 'others' do IR; (2) those studies that inquired into conceptions of the international as found in texts and contexts outside IR and/or North America and Western Europe. Where the latter set of efforts pointed to a rich potential for thinking differently about the international, the former revealed the persistence of 'standard' concepts and theories of IR outside North America and Western Europe.

IR scholarship outside North America and Western Europe

Research into IR scholarship outside North America and Western Europe had two thwarted beginnings during the 1980s and early 1990s. These were the 1987 special issue of the *Millennium – Journal of International Studies*, which was later turned into an edited volume by Hugh Dyer and Leon Mangasarian (1989), and A.J.R. Groom and Margot Light's survey of IR scholarship entitled *Contemporary International Relations: A Guide to Theory* (1994). If I characterise

Others' conceptions of the international 85

these efforts as thwarted beginnings, this is because they were not followed up by sustained efforts to interpret their otherwise noteworthy findings.

In the mid-2000s the launch of two new sets of studies revived research into IR scholarship around the world. This time around efforts were more focused in that while Amitav Acharya and Barry Buzan (2007, 2009) inquired into the apparent 'absence' of IR theorising outside North America and Western Europe, Arlene Tickner and Ole Wæver (2009b) explored how IR is studied around the world. Arguably, these efforts into finding out about what 'others' do and how they do it were conditioned by pre-existing definitions as to what counts as 'IR theory', and expectations of 'difference'.

The 1980s and early 1990s: Two thwarted beginnings of inquiring into IR scholarship around the world

Stanley Hoffmann's 1977 observation about International Relations as an 'American Social Science' was followed by soul searching in others parts of the world with scholars seeking to take stock of IR scholarship in their own locale and beyond. The contributors to the 1987 survey by the *Millennium* journal and the 1994 volume by Groom and Light cited the Hoffman article, and framed their findings as a response to his arguments.

The 1989 volume by Hugh Dyer and Leon Mangasarian was based on the 1987 *Millennium* special issue and covered 14 countries and regions of the world. While not explicitly discussed by the editors, there emerged one common characteristic of IR scholarship in the countries and regions surveyed. The beginnings of IR studies in many of these countries/regions were marked by their international encounters and the perceived need to 'catch up' with the rest of the world. For Japan (Inoguchi, 1989), this was the post-World War II encounter with the United States; for South Africa (Vale, 1989) it was encounters with colonial powers and particularly Britain from the early twentieth century onwards; for Brazil (Fonseca, 1989), China (Yahuda, 1989) and Hispanic America (Simpson and Wrobel, 1989) it was a search for greater activism in international affairs; for Nigeria (Olajide, 1989) and Israel (Klieman, 1989) it was the need for training diplomats following independence. As such, the 1987 *Millennium* survey found the beginnings of IR in many contexts around the world to be tied up with the international outlook of that particular country's leaders, and where in the world they sought to (re)locate their country ('East', 'West', 'non-aligned', 'developed', 'developing').

Less comprehensive than the *Millennium* survey, Groom and Light's 1994 edited volume focused mostly on the differences between US and British contributions to IR scholarship, devoting only one chapter each to 'continental Europe' and 'the rest of the world'. Six years later, the organisation of the volume and the amount of space devoted to 'continental Europe' was met with Knud Erik Jorgensen's reproach in the following manner:

> in John Groom and Margot Light's guide to theory, we do not arrive at Groom's chapter 'The World *Beyond*: The European Dimension' until

86 Others' conceptions of the international

Chapter 16 (characteristically and faithful to dear old British tradition, the European dimension is regarded as being beyond the British); and Chris Brown has naturally chosen the irresistible title *Fog in the Channel: Continental IR Theory Isolated.*

(Jorgensen, 2000: 9)

What Jorgensen did not note was that there was a bigger world beyond 'The World Beyond'. This bigger world was covered by a single chapter, authored by Stephen Chan (1994) and entitled 'Beyond the North-West: Africa and the East'. The point being, it was not only (Continental) European IR, but also a large part of the globe that remained somewhat 'marginal' to Groom and Light's survey of IR scholarship around the world.

Stephen Chan's (1994) contribution to Groom and Light's volume was singular in offering a discussion on the differences, similarities and promises of IR scholarship in a wide range of settings across 'Africa and the east'. Two of the observations proffered by Chan are helpful in making sense of both survey volumes and worth reproducing here.

First, Chan pointed to how

theoretical IR accompanies other modernisations. It cannot precede it. It can stand alongside culturally based rejections of the West, as in Iran and, to a tentative extent, China, provided certain levels of modernisation have been reached in other sectors.

(Chan, 1994: 248)

As noted above, this was also one of the unarticulated findings of the *Millennium* survey where the beginnings of IR studies around the world emerged to be related to the international encounters of individual countries and their attempts to (re)locate themselves in the world. Chan's observation regarding 'theoretical IR [accompanying] other modernisations' was later affirmed by Stefano Guzzini's (2001, 2007) reflections on his experiences at the (then newly established) Central European University after the end of the Cold War (also see Drulák, 2009). For many of these IR newcomers in post-Communist Central and Eastern Europe, IR was about managing international encounters through training diplomats and (re)locating their countries in the world.

Chan's second observation was on (what he termed) 'the question of culture'. Chan noted how such survey efforts pointed to 'some non-Western IR without articulating the theoretical problems that accompany the erosion of IR's universalism' (Chan, 1994: 238). Surveys such as that of the *Millennium* journal or Groom and Light, wrote Chan, 'helped expose the ontological bases for other epistemologies, as well as explain why it is that each different ontology can advance a different primary world view' (Chan, 1993a: 441). Yet, at the time, Chan's observations found relatively little echo in critical IR debates.[1]

Indeed, as noted in the beginning, these two surveys from the late 1980s and early 1990s were not followed up by sustained efforts to interpret their findings

Others' conceptions of the international 87

(but see Dunn and Shaw, 2001). It is difficult to know whether the radical challenge posed by these findings as articulated by Chan was downplayed or merely overlooked. During the 1990s, critical IR was already under challenge by the mainstream on grounds of 'incommensurability' (see, for example, Lapid, 1989, Biersteker, 1989, Wight, 1996, Wæver, 1996, Guzzini, 1998). Acknowledging not only the 'erosion of IR's universalism' but also the 'ontological bases for other epistemologies', as Chan suggested, might have further complicated an already complex debate. It took another decade for scholarly interest in this subject to be revived.

The mid-2000s onwards: assumptions of 'absence' and expectations of 'difference'

From the mid-2000s onwards, students of IR observed another bout of interest in IR scholarship around the world. I will focus on two major sets of efforts: Amitav Acharya and Barry Buzan's edited special issue and volume on IR thinking in Asia, and the 'geocultural epistemologies' project initiated by Arlene Tickner and Ole Wæver. As will be suggested below, these efforts were conditioned by pre-existing definitions as to what counts as 'IR theory', and expectations of 'difference'.

Amitav Acharya and Barry Buzan's 2007 special issue of the journal *International Relations of the Asia-Pacific* was provocatively titled: 'Why is There No Non-Western IR Theory? Reflections on and from Asia' (2007). The 2009 edited volume based on the special issue had a less provocative title: *Non-Western IR Theory: Perspectives on and Beyond Asia* (2009). Notwithstanding the change in title, both the 2007 special issue and the 2009 volume were shaped by an understanding as to what counts as 'IR' and observations regarding its 'absence' in Asia. In their introductory paper, the editors Acharya and Buzan rephrased Martin Wight's (1960) question ('why is there no international theory?') and asked: 'why is there no non-Western international theory?' More specifically, Acharya and Buzan inquired into possible reasons as to why it is that scholars in Asia, notwithstanding (what they characterised as) a misfit between 'Western' IR theory and 'non-Western experiences', did not seem to pursue theory building.[2]

The contributors to Acharya and Buzan's edited volume affirmed widespread portrayals of IR in Asia as 'pre-theoretical' (Pasha, 2011) while recording a recent increase in theory testing. They also noted that interest in offering a so-called 'non-Western IR theory' was almost non-existent in Asia except for China.[3] Building on these findings, editors Acharya and Buzan observed the limits of IR in Asia as twofold. First, in many Asian contexts there was little interest in theoretical explorations of the international. The second aspect of the problem was that Asian scholars' theoretical explorations seldom got recognised as 'IR theory' (also see Acharya, 2000).

Acharya and Buzan did not point to the tension between these two observations. What was it that is 'absent'? Scholarship that engages with theoretical

88   *Others' conceptions of the international*

explorations of the international? Or recognising existing theoretical explorations as 'IR theory'? Following Dirlik (see Chapter 2), we could also ask why it is that 'we' look for IR theory (as 'we' know it) in other parts of the world. Such a question would then highlight how our inquiries into IR scholarship around the world are conditioned by pre-existing definitions as to what counts as 'IR theory'. The point being, identifying the issue as one of 'absence' of IR theory (as 'we' know it) outside North America and Western Europe misplaces the problem and diverts attention away from inquiring into Acharya and Buzan's second observation regarding theoretical explorations produced in Asia not being recognised as 'IR theory' (but see Acharya, 2014).

The second set of studies into IR scholarship in other parts of the world explicitly cautioned against assumptions of 'absence' as such. The 'geocultural epistemologies and IR project' was designed by Ole Wæver and Arlene Tickner and launched at a workshop organised as a part of the 2004 convention of the International Studies Association.[4] In their introduction to the survey study that came out in 2009, Tickner and Wæver highlighted how inquiries into IR outside North America and Western Europe risked depicting 'the centre as normal and the periphery as a projected "other" through which the disciplinary core is reinforced'. Having cautioned against starting from pre-existing definitions as to what counts as IR, they suggested the following course of action:

> In order to transcend this state of affairs, it is necessary to actually know about the ways in which IR is practiced around the world, and to identify the concrete mechanisms shaping the field in distinct geocultural sites, a knowledge effort which must use theories drawn from sociology (and history) of science, postcolonialism, and several other fields.
>
> (Tickner and Wæver, 2009c: 1)

It is as part of this project that Tickner and Wæver (2009c: 10) called for 'worlding IR', arguing that efforts should be directed at exploring the ways in which 'the field is constituted by numerous intersecting academic practices that are all about the world and all making their own worlds'.[5]

While Tickner and Wæver sought to avoid depicting 'the centre as normal and the periphery as a projected "other"', expectations of 'difference' nevertheless shaped their project. As they noted in the introduction to their survey volume, when they initially embarked upon this project, the editors did expect others' thinking about the international to be shaped by their differences (Tickner and Wæver, 2009c). Through surveying IR scholarship around the world, Tickner and Wæver expected to gain some insight into how others' 'strong cosmologies, distinct religious-philosophical traditions' shaped their scholarship (Tickner and Wæver, 2009c: 20). This is in no way surprising; as with many others frustrated with the limits of IR (see below), Tickner and Wæver expected to find out about others' 'different' ways of approaching the international.

Others' conceptions of the international 89

What, then, do we learn from Tickner and Wæver's survey of IR scholarship around the world? To begin with, we have a series of extremely rich case studies by scholars who were invited to reflect on their geo-cultural situatedness. From these studies we learn that IR scholarship outside North America and Western Europe is shaped around familiar concepts such as 'nation-state' and 'national security'; that these concepts seem to be conceptualised not very differently in these geo-cultural settings; and that there is little engagement with theoretical exploration, beyond 'testing' received hypotheses. In the words of the editors,

> Scholarly communities in IR throughout the world share a state-centric ontology that in most cases is manifest in the internalisation of realist-based ideas concerning concepts such as power, security, and the national interest.
>
> More than a problem of ontology, however, the centrality of the state to IR thinking around the globe reminds us of the importance of episte-mology…the epistemological base of IR is anchored in the idea of the Westphalian state. Not only is this actor the point of departure for most inquiries into international politics, but it is also viewed in ahistorical and unproblematic terms.
>
> (Tickner and Wæver, 2009a: 334–335)

Describing the implications of these observations as 'problematic', Tickner and Wæver (2009a: 337–338) called for further research, writing that 'the prevalent notion that non-core, non-Western readings of International Relations are essentially "different" needs to be thought through'.

To recap, those who surveyed IR scholarship around the world found that notwithstanding well-known limits of IR (Neuman, 1998, Dunn and Shaw, 2001, Korany, 1986, Korany et al., 1993, Thomas, 1987, 1989) 'standard' concepts and theories of the discipline continue to prevail in IR scholarship outside North America and Western Europe where there is very little theoretical exploration of these limits. As will be seen below, this is not for lack of alternative approaches to the international, as found in texts and contexts outside IR and/or North America and Western Europe. How can one make sense of this eventuality – that IR scholars outside North America and Western Europe seem to hold on to 'standard' concepts and theories whose limits are so well-known? That alternatives are available but remain untapped? Let me discuss the second set of efforts before offering my answer.

Conceptions of the international in texts and contexts outside IR and/or North America and Western Europe

Those scholars who focused on texts and contexts outside IR and/or North America and Western Europe in search for others' conceptions of the international can be analysed in three groups. One group of authors focused on texts from outside IR to tease out their implications for thinking about the

90 *Others' conceptions of the international*

international. A second group of authors looked at practices in contexts beyond North America and Western Europe. A third group of authors looked at theoretical explorations of politics and the international as found in contexts outside North America and Western Europe – a body of work that they termed 'non-Western thought'. What follows looks at each group of studies in turn.

Texts outside IR and/or North America and Western Europe

In the early 2000s, a group of authors diagnosed the source of IR's limits to be its 'social scientific' foundations (as practised in North America and Western Europe) and turned to texts from outside IR so as to be able to '(re)consider the political wisdom hidden in sources outside the orthodox parameters of the discipline' (Jones, 2003: 107) and 'rewrite the foundations of IR' (Chan and Mandaville, 2001: 9). I will look at three prominent examples of this group of studies: Roland Bleiker's 'Forget IR theory' (1997); the edited volume entitled *The Zen of International Relations: International Theory from East to West* by Stephen Chan, Roland Bleiker and Peter Mandaville (which reproduced, in extended form, Bleiker's 1997 article); and the 2003 special issue of *Global Society*, edited by Christopher S. Jones (to which both Chan and Mandaville contributed). While sharing a common concern regarding IR's limits, Bleiker, Chan and Jones emphasised three related but different rationales for turning to texts from outside IR. Whereas Chan was frustrated with IR's limits in incorporating 'non-Western' perspectives, Bleiker expressed his exasperation with critical IR for getting bogged down in (what he considered to be) futile debates with the mainstream. Jones, in turn, considered stepping outside IR texts to be one way of gaining a new perspective into IR. What follows considers each scholar's rationale.

Chan formulated his rationale for turning to texts from outside IR in a series of essays that came out in the early 1990s. Some of these texts were later collected in a volume entitled *Towards a Multicultural Roshamon* [sic] *Paradigm in International Relations* (Chan, 1996). The book's title invokes Akira Kurosawa's celebrated film *Rashomon*, which tells its story by juxtaposing several protagonists' different perspectives on a violent episode that they all witnessed. In the film, Kurosawa highlights the differences between these multiple perspectives without privileging any one of their stories or questioning their truthfulness. Invoking Kurosawa's portrayal of the human condition, Chan (1993a: 442) suggested that the 'Rashomon condition' characterises present-day IR insofar as different ontologies condition different ways of knowing.

> The Rashomon condition is the true condition which IR faces. It is not the post-war Western condition, with its modernist paradigm and textual posturing, which spoke in the name of Enlightenment universality and did so by means of an imperial practice of its own export, and an alternative sense of what it excluded.
>
> (Chan, 1993a: 442)

Others' conceptions of the international 91

IR did not allow incorporating other ways of knowing, by way of privileging a particular epistemology, noted Chan, without considering how epistemological choices are not independent of ontology. Notwithstanding his insistence on the significance of beginning one's inquiries with ontology (and not epistemology)[6] Chan considered IR's privileging of positivism to be due to its social science envy. As such, Chan's rationale for turning to texts from outside IR was based on his conviction that IR, 'in its fetish to catch up with the social sciences, might have chosen the wrong bond-group. Perhaps it should catch up with literature' (Chan, 1993b: 88).[7]

Roland Bleiker's rationale for turning to texts outside IR was based on his frustration with critical scholars getting bogged down in debates with the mainstream as opposed to directly addressing IR's limits. The most effective way of addressing IR's limits, Bleiker suggested, was not to engage with the mainstream 'but to forget them, to tell new stories about world politics – stories that are not constrained by the boundaries of the established and objectified IR narratives' (Bleiker, 2001b: 38). Only by telling 'different stories', argued Bleiker, it would be possible to move beyond IR as 'we' know it; 'for once these stories have become validated, they may well open up spaces for a more inclusive and less violence-prone practice of world politics' (Bleiker, 2001b: 39). The way to do this, Bleiker wrote, was to step outside of IR texts and produce knowledge in forms that mainstream IR does not recognise (or approve of).[8]

Christopher Jones's rationale for looking at texts outside IR was different from Bleiker insofar as Jones sought to address IR's limits. By 'getting outside of IR', Jones argued, one would be able to 'see' the field's limits anew. Jones used the field of mathematics to draw a contrast with IR. In mathematics, he noted, the discipline 'grows' as new generations of scholars 'internalise the achievements of the last before making a contribution of its own' (Jones, 2003: 108).

> Hence, if IR were a discipline on the model of mathematics, scholars from 'India and postwar Japan' would have to learn its rules before they could play – dissent would be filtered out during the rite of passage.
>
> (Jones, 2003: 108)

However, in the case of IR, Jones reminded, the newcomers are not a new generation *per se*, but those scholars whose ways of thinking about the international have thus far not been considered. Since IR 'is a normative or ideological construct as well as a set of intellectual tools', a solution different than the one used in mathematics was needed. Accordingly, Jones favoured stepping outside of IR

> and then look back – in an echo of the returnee travelogue. The rite of passage is thus compounded: learn the tools of the discipline and then reconsider the tools. Hence, this is not a call for the abandonment of the rites of passage that define IR; rather, it is a call for IR to embrace further rites which negate (or at least challenge) those at its foundations.
>
> (Jones, 2003: 108)

92   *Others' conceptions of the international*

To recapitulate, notwithstanding their different rationales, Chan, Bleiker and Jones shared similar concerns regarding IR's limits. They also joined in calling for turning to texts from outside IR to identify the limits of the field. Where they differed was the way to address these limits. Yet, as with the 'geocultural epistemologies and IR' project that surveyed IR scholarship around the world with expectations of 'difference' (Tickner and Wæver, 2009c), this group of studies went outside IR texts also expecting to find 'difference'.

Practices outside North America and Western Europe

In the attempt to access others' approaches to the international, another group of authors studied practices outside North America and Western Europe. I will look at two studies: Marshall J. Beier's (2005) study of the practices of the Lakota people of the Northern Great Plains of North America[9] and Arlene Tickner's (2003b, 2008) research on 'everyday life'. While both authors focused on the study of practices, they offered different rationales in choosing to do so.

To start with Marshall Beier's study on the Lakota people, Beier maintained that his focus on indigenous ways of knowing allowed him to move beyond not only different ways of being in the world but also different ways of knowing, which promise 'new (to International Relations) and potentially counter-hegemonic bases for theory' (Beier, 2005: 4). In particular, Beier noted, the Lakota people's cosmology would allow students of IR to view differences not as obstacles to peace, and/or equate the absence of an over-arching authority with 'anarchy'. Managing conflict and searching for peace need not involve seeking to erase or transcend differences, argued Beier, but approaching the international as akin to the Lakota idea of the 'sacred hoop of the nation', which

> is a metaphor, derived from the camp circle, for the holistic unity of the Lakota people. Like the tipis that make up the camp circle, the nation is seen in terms of a hoop wherein no one constituent part is logically or implicitly prior to any other and such that all are equally necessary to complete the unity of the circle. The significance of the circle, then, is rooted in the assumption of an essential continuity from individual, through nation, to all elements of the cosmos, and back again. In fact, no one of these can be separated out from the others, since together they constitute a single totality encompassing all of Creation.
>
> (Beier, 2005: 105)

Approaching the international through the metaphor of the sacred hoop, suggested Beier, would allow doing away with hierarchies between peoples. It would also allow doing away with entrenched hierarchies between humans and nature, wrote Beier.

It is significant to highlight that Beier resisted 'appropriating' indigenous knowledges into IR theory, for, he thought, this would

Others' conceptions of the international   93

[signal] a prior assumption of a hierarchical ordering of authoritative voices, reconfirming that of the scholar while once again reducing Indigenous people themselves to ethnographic subjects-cum-objects.

(Beier, 2005: 221)

What Beier proposed instead was to

[recognise] that Indigenous people(s) and their knowledges should be of interest not because we might suppose that they can inform our theories, but because what they have to tell us is bona fide international theory in its own right.

(Beier, 2005: 221)

The point being, Beier was cautious of Spivak's caution regarding treating peoples from the global South as 'native informants'. Indeed, throughout his analysis, Beier remained cognisant of the difficulties involved in the use of ethnographic methods, difficulties that include 'interpretive problems, ethical considerations, and the danger of "colonizing" informants' knowledges' (Beier, 2005: 56, also see Vrasti, 2008).

Arlene Tickner's rationale for focusing on practices was different from Beier insofar as she viewed focusing on 'everyday life' a good way of accessing others' conceptions of the international against the background of the apparent 'invisibility' of 'third world scholarship' (Tickner, 2003b: 297). Consider the following quote:

For those scholars for whom a colonial legacy, war, chronic instability and insecurity, and acute poverty form part of their concrete working conditions, the ways in which reality is reflected upon and problematised is no doubt influenced by the intrusive nature of everyday life.

(Tickner, 2003b: 307)

Hence the need for focusing on 'everyday life' as experienced by peoples outside North America and Western Europe, Tickner concluded.

Turning to study 'everyday life' in the attempt to access others' conceptions of the international is not uncontroversial. On the one hand, there is no denying that scholars in some parts of the world have to face different conditions when producing their studies, including the 'destruction of meagre technological facilities' during times of violent conflict, disruption of power supply, banning of alternative sources of fuel (thereby preventing the use of oil lamps and communication facilities such as telephone, fax or e-mail), interruption in mail deliveries (due to roadblocks as well as screening or censoring), shortages of stationery, travel restrictions, and banning of 'foreign language' materials (Canagarajah, 1996: 438). That not all of us have to face such 'non-discursive requirements' (Canagarajah, 1996: 46) in our everyday lives, was also the point Tickner underscored in explaining her turn to studying 'everyday life' in the global South.

94   *Others' conceptions of the international*

On the other hand, many of those 'non-discursive requirements'

> are applicable as well to the periphery within the center: the marginalised communities and poorly facilitated institutions in the technologically advanced notions that might also face the disadvantages suggested here.
>
> (Canagarajah, 1996: 447)

Indeed, while chronic insecurity and instability may characterise peripheries within North America and Western Europe, some areas in Asia or Africa may remain relatively immune to such insecurities. The point being that portraying 'everyday life' outside North America and Western Europe in terms of 'colonial legacy, war, chronic instability and insecurity' (Tickner, 2003b) may come across as reducing life in those parts of the world to these elements. At the same time, it may result in overlooking the ways in which 'everyday life' in other parts of the world is also shaped by insecurity, instability and poverty.[10]

The point being that while many authors would agree with Tickner's observation that IR scholarship originating from outside North America and Western Europe has been marginal to IR debates, some would nevertheless take issue with the utilisation of ethnographic methods to study 'everyday life' as a way of accessing others' conceptions of the international. The critics offered three reasons. First, utilising ethnographic methods to access others' perspectives, they argued, amounts to treating them as 'blank, though generative of a text of cultural identity that only the West (or a Western-model discipline) could inscribe' (Spivak quoted in Jabri, 2013: 123). The second and related reason is that the problem may reside less with the ethnographic methods, and more with the way in which they may be being incorporated into IR, i.e. without always paying attention to the 1980s' 'great disciplinary turbulence in cultural anthropology' (Vrasti, 2008: 281). Indeed, studies that focused on the practices of others proved to be of significant value in accessing the ideas of peoples who do not produce written accounts and/or when the author critically reflects on his/her use of ethnographic methods (see, for example, Beier, 2005, Smith, 2009, 2012a, 2013). Third, the critics asked, why not engage with 'non-Western' thought and explore IR's 'constitutive outside'? In the following section, I turn to a body of studies that asked precisely this question.

'Non-Western' thought

Here, I will focus on Robbie Shilliam's (2011a) edited volume *International Relations and Non-Western Thought: Imperialism, Colonialism, and Investigations of Global Modernity* and Karen Smith's (2012a, 2012b, 2013) writings on the African notion of *ubuntu*. The emphasis of this third group of studies was different from the previous two in that whereas the first focused on texts from outside IR to tease out other conceptions of the international, Smith and Shilliam focused on 'non-Western' thought about politics and the international.

Others' conceptions of the international 95

Shilliam's concern in particular was challenging those who turn to study others' practices of 'everyday life'. Shilliam asked:

> Why is it that the non-Western world has been a defining presence for IR scholarship and yet said scholarship has consistently balked at placing non-Western thought at the heart of its debates?
>
> (Shilliam, 2011b: 1)

Invoking Acharya and Buzan's question ('Why is there no non-Western IR theory?') as well as Tickner's observation about 'invisibility' of 'third world scholarship', Shilliam maintained that the question is less about an 'absence' or 'invisibility' of 'non-Western' thought, and more about mainstream IR's obliviousness to others' theoretical explorations about the international (Shilliam, 2011c).[11] Such obliviousness, argued Shilliam (2011b: 2), was rooted in widely held assumptions that IR shares with some other social sciences as to 'who can "think" and produce valid knowledge of human existence' (Shilliam, 2009) or who decides what counts as 'IR' (Acharya, 2000, 2014). What follows identifies the key contributions of Shilliam and Smith's studies on 'non-Western' thought and then contrasts their approach with Donald Puchala's (1997, 1998) engagement with 'non-Western' thought. My aim here is to highlight that there is more than one way of approaching 'non-Western' thought.

To begin with Shilliam's analysis of 'non-Western' political thought, Shilliam argued against the 'marginalisation' of 'non-Western' political thought by virtue of treating IR as, 'effectively, the domain of Anglo-American culture' (Shilliam, 2009: 2). Undeniably, a major difficulty with considering 'non-Western' thought is that such writings do not always take forms that are immediately recognisable to students of IR whose training is based on standard textbooks. According to Mustapha Kamal Pasha (2011: 218), this proclivity is a consequence of the 'naturalisation of Western IR *as* IR'. Shilliam and the contributors to his edited volume took up this challenge and presented 'non-Western' theoretical explorations on politics and the international. According to Shilliam, 'the potential pay-off for IR from investigations that grapple with the enigma of the non-Western subject as thinker rather than as object' would be no less than transformative for IR insofar as a 'global, rather than narrowly European or Western context' would be retrieved as the context for the beginnings of 'the modern experience' (Shilliam, 2009: 10–11).

Shilliam and his collaborators also highlighted 'non-Western' thought as IR's 'constitutive outside'. Shilliam identified two aspects. On the one hand, he reminded, 'the content of the modern social sciences and humanities was at least in part cultivated by reference to non-European bodies of knowledge and culture' (Shilliam, 2011b: 2). Next to this 'borrowing' aspect was the self/other dialectics and the making of 'European' (and/or 'Western') identity: 'non-European culture was a crucial resource deployed within that most enduring battle amongst European thinkers over the form and content of modernity, namely rationalism versus romanticism' (Shilliam, 2011b: 2). Accordingly,

96 Others' conceptions of the international

Shilliam called for orientating scholarly efforts towards '[undermining] the security of an epistemological cartography that quarantines legitimate knowledge production of modernity to one (idealized) geocultural site' (Shilliam, 2011c: 24). Others also picked up this thread, following Edward Said's lead to study 'intertwined and overlapping histories' of humankind.

Somewhat differently from Shilliam and his collaborators, Karen Smith focused on African thought as well as diplomatic practices to tease out an alternative conception of the international as found in *ubuntu* (Smith, 2012a, 2012b). Retrieving and utilising *ubuntu* would be useful for students of IR in two ways, argued Smith. On the one hand, the notion of *ubuntu* would help students of IR to appreciate the dynamics of relations between African states in a way that was not possible if one relied on 'standard' concepts and theories. *Ubuntu*, in this sense, could be viewed as a guide into 'how southern Africans view the international community, and the responsibilities of citizens and states towards one another', she wrote (Smith, 2012b: 312). On the other hand, noted Smith, *ubuntu* as a conception of the international was not confined to the existing diplomatic practices of states but also *praxis*. For, as conceptualised by African authors, *ubuntu* pointed to

> the possibility of a different kind of relationship from the friend/enemy dichotomy so prevalent in IR. It could inform the notion of 'responsibility to protect' and underline the role of morality in international affairs (that many Western theories dismiss as insignificant).
>
> (Smith, 2012b: 312)

Accordingly, suggested Smith, *ubuntu*

> [c]an also help refocus attention in IR towards important principles such as shared humanity, given that it places emphasis on cooperation, mutual understanding and a greater sense of responsibility towards a collective well-being.
>
> (Smith, 2012b: 313)

Finally, while presenting *ubuntu* as an 'African' conception of the international, Smith also highlighted instances of give-and-take between Africans and others. Citing approvingly Ali Mazrui's point about 'the paradox of counterpenetration and the cyclic boomerang effect in Africa's interaction with other civilisations' (Mazrui cited in Smith, 2012b: 315, also see Mazrui, 2008), Smith noted that *ubuntu* may not be unique to Africa. As such, research into 'intertwined and overlapping histories' of *ubuntu* may allow approaching the international differently – both in ethics and in epistemology – while avoiding 'culturalism' in outlook (see Chapter 1).

I now turn to Puchala who also looked at 'non-Western' thought, echoing Shilliam in reproaching mainstream approaches to IR. However, having decided to look at 'non-Western' political thought, Puchala (1997: 129) made a second

Others' conceptions of the international 97

decision: to look at 'radical, non-Western thinking' as opposed to, that is, 'non-radical, Third-World views – those of the moderates, modernists, secularists, and globalists, and of the westernised and social-science socialized products of American and European graduate schools'. It is the former that should be looked at, he argued, because 'it is these rather extreme perspectives that are most at variance with Western formulations' (Puchala, 1997: 129). Puchala (1997: 129) further maintained that these 'radical' perspectives were the 'themes [that] resonate among young people, poor people and angry people, of which there are many in the non-Western world'.

Be that as it may, the rest of Puchala's analysis did not present his findings as portraying *some* aspects of 'non-Western' thought but 'non-Western World-views', without any qualifiers (or any references to the so-called 'moderates'). Consider, for instance, how the author explained why he did not consider the 'non-radicals' to be representative of 'non-Western' perspectives. This is because, he argued,

> [i]n the non-Western world-view the only centrally significant subdivision of humanity and its constituent social units is the bifurcation 'non-West/West'.
>
> (Puchala, 1997: 130)

Having reduced 'non-Western' perspectives to its 'radical' dimension, the author then reified the 'Western'/'non-Western' binary. Also consider the following quote:

> Any conventional, Western, analytical scheme constructed to illuminate non-Western thinking about what we in the West call 'international relations' must be artificial, because non-Western theorists do not organize their world-views in terms of familiar Western categories.
>
> (Puchala, 1997: 130)

The point being that the implications of conflating 'non-Western' thought with 'radical non-Western thinking' cannot be underestimated. As such, Puchala's analysis comes across as an instance of reinscribing the difference/s between 'West' and 'non-West' rather than merely inquiring into others' conceptions of the international.

It is worth highlighting here that some of the issues and concerns that Puchala pointed to as being 'important' for 'non-Western' thought are those phenomena the significance of which IR scholars around the world have come to recognise over the years. Consider what Puchala had to say about the notion of 'state' in non-Western thinking:

> 'States', for example, are not very important in non-Western thinking about world affairs, but, 'forces', 'movements', 'parties', 'peoples', 'cultures', and 'civilizations' are important...Similarly, in non-Western thinking, state-to-state interactions constitute far less of the substance of world affairs

98 *Others' conceptions of the international*

than other kinds of interactions, such as those that arise from the activities of transnational social and ideological movements. Also significant are intra-state interactions that are actually inter-national because they are intercultural or intercommunal.

(Puchala, 1997: 130)

When Puchala was writing these texts during the 1990s, some IR scholars interested in 'transnational relations' were also pointing to dynamics inside and beyond states (Czempiel and Rosenau, 1989, Rosenau and Czempiel, 1992, Rosenau, 1969, 1997). The irony here is that, Since then, such so-called 'radical' thinking has become prevalent in IR in North America and Western Europe as well.

The broader point being that there is no one way of addressing the apparent 'absence' of 'non-Western' thought. Whereas Puchala introduced some aspects of 'non-Western' thought in a way that further reinforced the 'West'/'non-West' binary, Shilliam and his collaborators introduced some other aspects that highlighted 'non-Western' thought as IR's 'constitutive outside'.

One final note: I recognise that my way of distinguishing between these studies may come across as artificial. For, they were produced by a body of scholars who share similar concerns. In some cases the same scholars contributed to more than one effort. I nevertheless consider this categorisation to be useful for two reasons. First, it allows me to underscore the rationale shared by scholars contributing to the first group of studies who focused on texts outside IR, i.e. that the humanities (rather than IR as a social science) may be a better place to search for others' conceptions of the international. Second, I would like to highlight the significance of the point advanced by the scholars who explored 'non-Western thought'. The point being that there *is* a body of theoretical explorations about the international outside North America and Western Europe that often does not get recognised as 'IR'.[12]

The second set of efforts discussed here went outside of IR texts and contexts and/or North America and Western Europe in search of others' conceptions of the international and found them, be it in 'traditional' texts of Chinese philosophy, daily practices of Lakota people or 'non-Western' political thought about politics and the international. As such, they highlighted heretofore untapped ideas about the international. In doing so, they rendered only more apparent the puzzle I identified in the Introduction: that 'standard' concepts and theories persist in IR scholarship around the world notwithstanding their well-known limits and the availability of alternatives.

Conclusion

Chapter 3 considered the efforts of those scholars who sought to access others' conceptions of the international by way of looking outside IR texts and contexts and/or North America and Western Europe. I looked at two sets of efforts: (1) those studies that focused on IR scholarship around the world to see how 'others' do IR; (2) those studies that inquired into conceptions of the

Others' conceptions of the international 99

international as found in texts and contexts outside IR and/or North America and Western Europe. Viewed together, the findings of these studies seem to indicate that notwithstanding the availability of resources for thinking differently about the international, we are no closer to understanding, let alone moving beyond, the persistence of 'standard' concepts and theories in IR (the question that I began with in the Introduction). Are we, then, back at where we started?

If these otherwise informative and inspiring studies do not seem to have brought us closer to answering the question I began with, I suggest, this may have to do with two factors. First, none of the contributors explicitly inquired into our question. Some like Puchala, who recognised the persistence of the 'standard' concepts and theories in others' IR scholarship, explained it away as a consequence of the graduate training received by scholars, before turning to so-called 'radicals' who presumably received no similar training.[13] Mandaville and Jones concurred, noting that those who have 'thoroughly digested' IR's 'standard' concepts and theories should not be expected to produce anything other than what they are taught. Hence the need to look beyond IR, they argued. Tickner and Wæver differed, identifying the persistence of 'standard' concepts and theories as a puzzle that required further inquiries.

A second reason may have to do with the starting point many of these studies share: expectations of 'difference'. Why is it that we presume others' conceptions of the international to be 'different'? As Uma Narayan (2000: 83) has argued, 'projection of imaginary "differences"' onto others is problematic insofar as it helps 'constitute one's Others as Other'. Furthermore, approaching others with expectations of 'difference' may result in papering over the emergence and persistence of what Narayan called 'sad similarities' that limit our scholarship, including

> ethnocentrism, androcentrism, classism, heterosexism, and other objectionable 'centrisms' that often pervaded both sides of this 'reiterated' contrast between 'Western culture' and its several 'Others'.
>
> (Narayan, 2000: 95)

Put differently, inquiring into others' conceptions of the international through research frameworks that are shaped by expectations of 'difference' may not allow making sense of the ways in which IR scholarship in other parts of the world comes across as 'similar' *and* the ways in which the production of similarities may belie other differences.

To recap, what we learn from this body of studies is that seeking to address IR's limits by considering the ideas and 'everyday life' of those who are differently situated gets us only thus far. Unless, that is, we couple such analysis with research into IR's 'constitutive outside' by worlding IR in the second sense ('worlding-as-constitutive'). As with students of Critical IR who sought to address IR's limitations by focusing on worlding-as-situatedness, scholars who went outside IR texts and contexts and/or North America and Western Europe also focused on geo-cultural situatedness. That said, there was one difference here. Shilliam

100 *Others' conceptions of the international*

and the contributors to his edited volume highlighted the ideas and experiences of those who were apparently 'absent' from IR debates. By way of studying 'non-Western thought' as such, they highlighted IR's 'constitutive outside' in a way that was not done before.

The point being that 'others' are not 'out there' to be discovered by travelling elsewhere; they are 'in here', to be excavated for the purposes of self-discovery. Self-discovery through excavation is what Chapters 4 and 5 aim for. As will be argued in Chapter 4, 'worlding' is not only about studying the geo-cultural situatedness of IR scholars (worlding-as-situatedness) but also about IR's worlding of the world (worlding-as-constitutive). Through worlding IR in its twofold sense, we learn to inquire into others' conceptions of the international by studying 'connections'. More specifically, in Chapter 4, I suggest that we read IR scholarship outside North America and Western Europe not only as an attempt to understand or explain world politics, but also as an aspect of world politics. Such a reading, I suggest, would allow understanding how others' insecurities, experienced in a world that is already worlded, have shaped (and been shaped by) their conceptions of the international.

Notes

1 The exception here is a series of exchanges between Martin Hollis and Steve Smith, and Vivienne Jabri and Stephen Chan. See Hollis and Smith (1994, 1996), Jabri and Chan (1996), Chan (1998).
2 For previous explorations of such 'misfit', see Neuman (1998).
3 In China these debates have a longer history (Wang, 1994) and have begun to produce some results, however controversial (Song, 2001) (see Chapter 4).
4 I was one of the participants of the 2004 workshop and the follow-up panels that were convened in later years (see Bilgin, 2004). My chapter published in the second volume of the project is a revised version of the paper I presented at that workshop (Bilgin, 2012). My article 'Thinking Past "Western" IR?' was written in response to the 2004 workshop (Bilgin, 2008).
5 Tickner and Wæver were later joined by Blaney to produce three introductory volumes as part of the 'geocultural epistemologies and IR' project. The first one edited by Tickner and Wæver (2009b) offered a comprehensive mapping effort of the study of IR in different parts of the world. This survey volume offered accounts on IR scholarship in Latin America, South Africa, Africa, Japan, Korea and Taiwan, China, Southeast Asia, Iran, Arab world, Israel, Turkey, Russia, Central and Eastern Europe, Western Europe, the Anglo world, and the US. The contributors writing on and from these regions offered their surveys of IR scholarship in their own geo-cultural context as well as their reflections on their situatedness. The second volume edited by Tickner and Blaney (2012) focused on key IR concepts and their conceptualisation in different parts of the world. The third one looked at alternative conceptions of the international by scholars who do not always think through IR (Tickner and Blaney, 2013).
6 See the 1990s debate between Chan and Jabri (Jabri and Chan, 1996, Chan, 1998) and Hollis and Smith (Hollis and Smith, 1994, 1996).
7 Many of Chan's works on this issue (some of which were included in the volume he co-edited with Mandaville and Bleiker and the *Global Society* special issue) turned to texts from outside IR (Chan, 2001a, 2001b, 2001c, 2003a, 2003b, 2009). While some of these texts were decidedly 'non-Western', others were 'Western' texts that he revisited in a way that IR had not done before (Chan, 2001b, 2001c).

Others' conceptions of the international   101

8 In his work since then Bleiker indeed focused on aesthetics and art. See Bleiker (2001a, 2003, 2006, 2012).
9 In this particular case, North America is defined not in terms of physical geography, but geo-culturally.
10 Focusing on 'everyday life' was only one of the approaches Tickner utilised in her studies. Also see Tickner (2003a, 2003b, 2013).
11 Acharya also emphasised this point in his later writings, particularly in his 2014 ISA Presidential address (Acharya, 2014).
12 As noted in the first part of the chapter, this is an observation also made by Acharya and Buzan (2007, also see Acharya, 2000) but not pursued further in the said volume (but see Acharya, 2014).
13 Needless to say, this assumption does not always hold.

Bibliography

Acharya, A. 2000. Ethnocentrism and Emancipatory IR Theory. In: Arnold, S. & Bier, J. M. (eds.) *Displacing Security*, Toronto, Centre for International and Security Studies, York University.

Acharya, A. 2014. Global International Relations (IR) and Regional Worlds. *International Studies Quarterly*, 58, 647–659.

Acharya, A. & Buzan, B. 2007. Why is there No Non-Western International Relations Theory? An Introduction. *International Relations of the Asia-Pacific*, 7, 287–312.

Acharya, A. & Buzan, B. (eds.) 2009. *Non-Western International Relations Theory: Perspectives on and Beyond Asia*, London, Routledge.

Beier, J. M. 2005. *International Relations in Uncommon Places: Indigeneity, Cosmology, and the Limits of International Theory*, Palgrave Macmillan.

Biersteker, T. J. 1989. Critical Reflections on Post-positivism in International Relations. *International Studies Quarterly*, 33, 263–267.

Bilgin, P. 2004. Os estudos de segurança na Turquia: situando a Turquia no 'ocidente' por meio de 'escrever a segurança' (The study of security in Turkey: locating Turkey in the 'West' through 'writing security'). *Contexto Internacional*, 26, 149–185.

Bilgin, P. 2008. Thinking Past 'Western' IR? *Third World Quarterly*, 29, 5–23.

Bilgin, P. 2012. Security in the Arab World and Turkey: Differently Different. In: Tickner, A. & Blaney, D. (eds.) *Thinking International Relations Differently*, London, Routledge.

Bleiker, R. 1997. Forget IR theory. *Alternatives: Global, Local, Political*, 22, 57–85.

Bleiker, R. 2001a. The Aesthetic Turn in International Political Theory. *Millennium – Journal of International Studies*, 30, 509–533.

Bleiker, R. 2001b. Forget IR Theory. In: Chan, S., Mandaville, P. G. & Bleiker, R. (eds.) *The Zen of International Relations: IR Theory From East to West*, London: Palgrave Macmillan. (37–66)

Bleiker, R. 2003. Aestheticising Terrorism: Alternative Approaches to 11 September. *Australian Journal of Politics and History*, 49, 430–445.

Bleiker, R. 2006. Art after 9/11. *Alternatives: Global, Local, Political*, 31, 77–99.

Bleiker, R. 2012. *Aesthetics and World Politics*, Palgrave Macmillan.

Canagarajah, A. S. 1996. 'Nondiscursive' Requirements in Academic Publishing, Material Resources of Periphery Scholars, and the Politics of Knowledge Production. *Written Communication*, 13, 435–472.

Chan, S. 1993a. Cultural and Linguistic Reductionisms and a New Historical Sociology for International Relations. *Millennium – Journal of International Studies*, 22, 423–442.

102 *Others' conceptions of the international*

Chan, S. 1993b. A Summer Polemic: Revolution, Rebellion and Romance. Some Notes Towards the Resacralisation of I.R. *Paradigms*, 7, 85–100.

Chan, S. 1994. Beyond the North-West: Africa and the East. In: Groom, A. J. R. & Light, M. (eds.) *Contemporary International Relations: A Guide to Theory*, London, Pinter.

Chan, S. 1996. *Towards a Multicultural Roshamon Paradigm in International Relations: Collected Essays*, Tampere, Tampere Peace Research Institute.

Chan, S. 1998. An Ontologist Strikes Back: A Further Reply to Hollis and Smith. *Review of International Studies*, 24, 441–442.

Chan, S. 2001a. Seven Types of Ambiguity in Western International Relations Theory and Painful Steps Towards Right Ethics. In: Chan, S., Mandaville, P. G. & Bleiker, R. (eds.) *The Zen of International Relations: IR Theory from East to West*, London, Palgrave Macmillan.

Chan, S. 2001b. Stories of Priam and Job, the Slaughter of Their Families, and Twenty Theses on the Suggestiveness of Good for the Person of IR. In: Chan, S., Mandaville, P. G. & Bleiker, R. (eds.) *The Zen of International Relations: IR Theory from East to West*, London, Palgrave Macmillan.

Chan, S. 2001c. A Story Beyond Telos: Redeeming the Shield of Achilles for a Realism of Rights in IR. In: Chan, S., Mandaville, P. G. & Bleiker, R. (eds.) *The Zen of International Relations: IR Theory from East to West*, London, Palgrave Macmillan.

Chan, S. 2003a. A New Triptych for International Relations in the 21st Century: Beyond Waltz and Beyond Lacan's Antigone, with a Note on the Falun Gong of China. *Global Society*, 17, 187–208.

Chan, S. 2003b. A Problem for IR: How Shall We Narrate the Saga of the Bestial Man? *Global Society*, 17, 385–413.

Chan, S. 2009. A Chinese Political Sociology in Our Times. *International Political Sociology*, 3, 332–334.

Chan, S. & Mandaville, P. G. 2001. Introduction: Within International Relations Itself, a New Culture Rises Up. In: Chan, S., Mandaville, P. G. & Bleiker, R. (eds.) *The Zen of International Relations: IR Theory from East to West*, London, Palgrave Macmillan.

Chan, S., Mandaville, P. G. & Bleiker, R. (eds.) 2001. *The Zen of International Relations: IR Theory from East to West*, London, Palgrave Macmillan.

Czempiel, E. O. & Rosenau, J. N. (eds.) 1989. *Global Changes and Theoretical Challenges: Approaches to World Politics for the 1990s*, Lexington, MA, Lexington Books.

Drulák, P. (ed.) 2009. Special Forum Section: International Relations (IR) in Central and Eastern Europe. *Journal of International Relations and Development*, 12, 2, 168–173.

Dunn, K. C. & Shaw, T. M. 2001. *Africa's Challenge to International Relations Theory*, New York, Palgrave.

Dyer, H. C. & Mangasarian, L. (eds.) 1989. *The Study of International Relations: The State of the Art*, Basingstoke, Macmillan.

Fonseca, Jr., G. 1989. Studies on International Relations in Brazil: Recent Times. In: Dyer, H. C. & Mangasarian, L. (eds.) *The Study of International Relations: The State of the Art*, London, Macmillan.

Global Society. 2003. Special Issue: Locating the 'I' in 'IR': Dislocating Euro-American Theories. *Global Society*, 17.

Groom, A. J. R. & Light, M. (eds.) 1994. *Contemporary International Relations: A Guide to Theory*, London, Pinter Publishers.

Guzzini, S. 1998. *Realism in International Relations and International Political Economy: The Continuing Story of a Death Foretold*, London, Routledge.

Guzzini, S. 2001. The Significance and Roles of Teaching Theory in International Relations. *Journal of International Relations and Development*, 4, 98–117.

Others' conceptions of the international   103

Guzzini, S. 2007. Theorising International Relations: Lessons from Europe's Periphery. DIIS Working Paper.

Hoffmann, S. 1977. An American social science: international relations. *Daedalus*, Summer, 41–60.

Hollis, M. & Smith, S. 1994. Two Stories about Structure and Agency. *Review of International Studies*, 20, 241–251.

Hollis, M. & Smith, S. 1996. A Response: Why Epistemology Matters in International Theory. *Review of International Studies*, 22, 111–116.

Inoguchi, T. 1989. The Study of International Relations in Japan. In: Dyer, H. C. & Mangasarian, L. (eds.) *The Study of International Relations: The State of the Art*, London, Macmillan.

International Relations of the Asia-Pacific. 2007. Special Issue: Why is there no Non-Western IR Theory? Reflections on and from Asia. *International Relations of the Asia-Pacific*, 7.

Jabri, V. 2013. *The Postcolonial Subject: Claiming Politics/Governing Others in Late Modernity*, London, Routledge.

Jabri, V. & Chan, S. 1996. The Ontologist Always Rings Twice: Two More Stories about Structure and Agency in Reply to Hollis and Smith. *Review of International Studies*, 22, 107–110.

Jones, C. S. 2003. Locating the 'I' in IR – Disclocating Euro-American Theories. *Global Society*, 17, 107–110.

Jorgensen, K. E. 2000. Continental IR Theory: The Best Kept Secret. *European Journal of International Relations*, 6, 9–42.

Klieman, A. 1989. The Study of International Relations in Israel. In: Dyer, H. C. & Mangasarian, L. (eds.) *The Study of International Relations: The State of the Art*, London, Macmillan.

Korany, B. 1986. Strategic Studies and the Third World: A Critical Evaluation. *International Social Science Journal*, 38, 547–562.

Korany, B., Noble, P. & Brynen, R. (eds.) 1993. *The Many Faces of National Security in the Arab World*, London, Macmillan.

Lapid, Y. 1989. The Third Debate: On the Prospects of International Theory in a Post-positivist Era. *International Studies Quarterly*, 33, 3, 235–254.

Mazrui, A. A. 2008. Africa and Other Civilizations: Conquest and Counter-Conquest. In: Harbeson, J. W. & Rothchild, D. (eds.) *Africa in World Politics: Reforming Political Order*, Boulder, CO, Westview.

Narayan, U. 2000. Essence of Culture and a Sense of History: A Feminist Critique of Cultural Essentialism. In: Narayan, U. & Harding, S. (eds.) *Decentering the Center: Philosophy for a Multicultural, Postcolonial, and Feminist World*, Bloomington, Indiana University Press.

Neuman, S. G. (ed.) 1998. *International Relations Theory and the Third World*, London, Macmillan.

Olajide, A. 1989. The Study of International Relations in Nigeria. In: Dyer, H. C. & Mangasarian, L. (eds.) *The Study of International Relations: The State of the Art*, London, Macmillan.

Pasha, M. K. 2011. Untimely Reflections. In: Shilliam, R. (ed.) *International Relations and Non-Western Thought: Imperialism, Colonialism, and Investigations of Global Modernity*, Milton Park, Abingdon, Oxon, UK & New York, Routledge.

Puchala, D. 1997. Non-Western Perspectives on International Relations. *Journal of Peace Research*, 34, 129–134.

Puchala, D. 1998. Third World Thinking and Contemporary International Relations. In: Neuman, S. G. (ed.) *International Relations Theory and the Third World*, London, Macmillan.

104 *Others' conceptions of the international*

Rosenau, J. N. 1969. *Linkage Politics: Essays on the Convergence of National and International Systems*, New York, Free Press.

Rosenau, J. N. 1997. *Along the Domestic-Foreign Frontier: Exploring Governance in a Turbulent World*, Cambridge, UK & New York, Cambridge University Press.

Rosenau, J. N. & Czempiel, E. O. 1992. *Governance without Government: Order and Change in World Politics*, Cambridge, Cambridge University Press.

Shilliam, R. 2009. The Enigmatic Figure of the Non-Western Thinker in International Relations. *Antepodium* [Online]. Available: http://www.victoria.ac.nz/atp/articles/pdf/Shilliam-2009.pdf [Accessed 27 January 2014].

Shilliam, R. (ed.) 2011a. *International Relations and Non-Western thought: Imperialism, Colonialism, and Investigations of Global Modernity*, New York, Routledge.

Shilliam, R. 2011b. Non-Western Thought and International Relations. In: Shilliam, R. (ed.) *International Relations and Non-Western Thought: Imperialism, Colonialism, and Investigations of Global Modernity*, New York, Routledge.

Shilliam, R. 2011c. The Perilous but Unavoidable Terrain of the Non-West. In: Shilliam, R. (ed.) *International Relations and Non-Western Thought: Imperialism, Colonialism, and Investigations of Global Modernity*, New York, Routledge.

Simpson, M. S. C. & Wrobel, P. 1989. The Study of International Relations in Hispanic America. In: Dyer, H. C. & Mangasarian, L. (eds.) *The Study of International Relations: The State of the Art*, London, Macmillan.

Smith, K. 2009. Has Africa Got Anything to Say? African Contributions to the Theoretical Development of International Relations. *The Round Table*, 98, 269–284.

Smith, K. 2012a. Africa as an Agent of International Relations Knowledge. In: Cornelissen, S., Cheru, F. & Shaw, T. M. (eds.) *Africa and International Relations in the 21st Century*, New York, Palgrave Macmillan.

Smith, K. 2012b. Contrived Boundaries, Kinship and Ubuntu: A (South) African View of the 'International'. In: Tickner, A. B. & Blaney, D. (eds.) *Thinking International Relations Differently*, London, Routledge.

Smith, K. 2013. International Relations in South Africa: A Case of 'Add Africa and Stir'? *Politikon*, 40, 533–544.

Song, X. 2001. Building International Relations Theory with Chinese Characteristics. *Journal of Contemporary China*, 10, 61–74.

Thomas, C. 1987. *In Search of Security: The Third World in International Relations*, Boulder, CO, Wheatsheaf Books.

Thomas, C. 1989. Southern Instability, Security and Western Concepts: On an Unhappy Marriage and the Need for a Divorce. In: Thomas, C. & Saravanamuttu, P. (eds.) *The State and Instability in the South*, Basingstoke, Macmillan.

Tickner, A. 2003a. Hearing Latin American Voices in International Relations Studies. *International Studies Perspectives*, 4, 325–350.

Tickner, A. 2003b. Seeing IR Differently: Notes from the Third World. *Millennium – Journal of International Studies*, 32, 295–324.

Tickner, A. B. 2008. Aquí en el Ghetto: Hip-Hop in Colombia, Cuba, and Mexico. *Latin American Politics and Society*, 50, 121–146.

Tickner, A. 2013. Core, Periphery and (Neo)imperialist International Relations. *European Journal of International Relations*, 19, 627–646.

Tickner, A. B. & Blaney, D. (eds.) 2012. *Thinking International Relations Differently*, London, Routledge.

Tickner, A. B. & Blaney, D. (eds.) 2013. *Claiming the International*, London, Routledge.

Tickner, A. B. & Wæver, O. 2009a. Conclusion: Worlding where the West Once Was. In: Tickner, A. B. & Wæver, O. (eds.) *International Relations Scholarship Around the World*, London, Routledge.

Tickner, A. B. & Wæver, O. (eds.) 2009b. *International Relations Scholarship Around the World*, London, Routledge.

Tickner, A. B. & Wæver, O. 2009c. Introduction: Geocultural epistemologies. In: Tickner, A. B. & Wæver, O. (eds.) *International Relations Scholarship Around the World*, London, Routledge.

Vale, P. 1989. 'Whose World is it Anyway?' International Relations in South Africa. In: Dyer, H. C. & Mangasarian, L. (eds.) *The Study of International Relations: The State of the Art*, London, Macmillan.

Vrasti, W. 2008. The Strange Case of Ethnography and International Relations. *Millennium – Journal of International Studies*, 37, 279–301.

Wæver, O. 1996. The Rise and Fall of the Inter-paradigm Debate. In: Booth, K. & Smith, S. (eds.) *International Theory: Positivism and Beyond*, Oxford, Polity.

Wang, J. 1994. International Relations Theory and the Study of Chinese Foreign Policy: A Chinese Perspective. In: Robinson, T. W. & Shambaugh, D. (eds.) *Chinese Foreign Policy: Theory and Practice*, Oxford, Clarendon Press.

Wight, M. 1960. Why is there no International Theory? *International Relations*, 2, 1, 35–48.

Wight, C. 1996. Incommensurability and Cross-Paradigm Communication in International Relations Theory: 'What's the Frequency Kenneth?' *Millennium – Journal of International Studies*, 25, 291–319.

Yahuda, M. B. 1989. International Relations Scholarship in the People's Republic of China. In: Dyer, H. C. & Mangasarian, L. (eds.) *The Study of International Relations: The State of the Art*, London, Macmillan.

4 Inquiring into security in the international

What do I mean by inquiring into security in the international? Is not the conception of the international in mainstream approaches already about security – more precisely about anarchy as the condition, and constant vigilance against threats to 'national security' as the solution? Yes and no. Yes, mainstream IR's conception of the international is shaped around a particular conception of security. No, because this is a *particular* conception of security. As laid out in Chapters 1 and 2, students of IR and Security Studies have seldom inquired into others' conceptions of the international and security, or reflected on the particularity of their own conceptions. Yet, as discussed in Chapter 3, notwithstanding the well-known limits of our theorising about IR and security and the availability of alternatives, 'standard' concepts such as 'state' and 'national security' persist in IR scholarship around the world.

Chapter 4 suggests that if others' IR scholarship does not reflect the 'differences' as found in texts and contexts found outside North America and Western Europe, we could take this as the beginning of our analysis and inquire into security in the international. Rather than, that is, explaining away such 'similarity' as a confirmation of the claim to 'universality' on the part of mainstream IR, or as evidence of the periphery's 'unthinking emulation' of the core. More specifically, I propose that we begin by reading others' IR scholarship as responding to a world that is already worlded. Worlding IR would allow us to understand how others' insecurities, experienced in a world that is already worlded, have shaped (and have been shaped by) their conceptions of the international.

Before offering my own answer, in the first section I discuss two other explanations as to why 'standard' concepts and theories of IR may have persisted outside North America and Western Europe. In the second section, I begin building my own answer by highlighting two different understandings of 'worlding', and call for worlding IR in its twofold meaning – that is, reflecting on the geo-cultural situatedness of IR scholarship (worlding-as-situatedness) *and* inquiring into how IR has worlded the world (worlding-as-constitutive). The third section submits that the persistence of 'standard' concepts and theories of IR outside North America and Western Europe (notwithstanding their well-known limits and the availability of alternatives) could be understood as a way of doing IR in a seemingly 'similar' but unexpectedly 'different' way. Where worlding IR outside North America and Western Europe reveals it to be 'almost the same but not quite' (to invoke Homi K. Bhabha's turn of phrase), a close reading of IR scholarship produced in such contexts offers insight into insecurities that have shaped (and are being shaped by) others' conceptions of the international.

'We already understand', don't we?

Chapter 1 began by considering the challenge of the 'what limit?' question. Those students of mainstream IR and security studies who ask that question, I suggested, presume that 'we already understand' others' behaviour and that there is no need to consider IR's limits. Arguably, some explain away the persistence of 'standard' concepts and theories in IR scholarship around the world in a similar fashion, presuming that 'we already understand' the reasons behind such persistence and that there is no need for further inquiry. To the students of mainstream IR and security, the persistence of 'standard' concepts and theories outside North America and Western Europe does not need explaining. For them, it is only to be expected that scholars around the world turn to 'standard' concepts and theories. They have universal relevance! For students of critical IR who problematise claims to 'universal relevance' as such, there is also not that much that deserves inquiring into. This is because the latter view the persistence of 'standard' concepts and theories of IR outside North America and Western Europe as an instance of 'unthinking emulation'. Put differently, they presume that peripheral scholars are products of the training they receive in the graduate schools of the 'core' and that once they return home, they emulate their mentors in an unthinking manner. Let us consider each explanation in turn.

Universal relevance

It is argued that if 'standard' concepts and theories of IR prevail outside North America and Western Europe, this proves their 'universal relevance'. From this perspective, there is no need for worlding IR; if concepts such as 'state' and 'national security' are being adopted and utilised by IR scholars here, there and everywhere, it is because they 'make sense' given predominant understandings of the 'international' as billiard balls clashing with one another, to pick one prevalent metaphor.

Be that as it may, those who favour the 'universal relevance' answer overlook one question: how is it that 'we' have come to think of the international as billiard balls clashing with one another? If the 'billiard ball' model of the international has become predominant in IR scholarship around the world (see Chapter 3), this may be because students of IR have learned world history through accounts shaped by such 'standard' concepts and categories. Our understanding of world history is conditioned by this very model insofar as 'we' look at the past through (1) state-centric lenses; (2) often without being aware

108   *Inquiring into security in the international*

of the particularity of the notion of state that is adopted (Milliken and Krause, 2002, Bilgin and Morton, 2002); and (3) by overlooking relationships of mutual constitution between peoples, states, empires and civilisations throughout history (Halperin, 2006) (see the discussion in Chapter 1).

In offering this argument, I follow the anthropologist Eric Wolf (1982: 4–5) who noted that if we tend to think of contemporary dynamics through particular concepts and categories, this is because that is 'the way we have learned our own history'. In *Europe and the People Without History*, Wolf argued that we read notions such as 'state', 'nation' and 'the West' back into history as 'things', which, in turn, impedes our understanding of the fluid and undetermined nature of the history of humankind. He wrote:

> By turning names into things we create false models of reality. By endowing nations, societies, or culture with the qualities of internally homogeneous and externally distinctive and bounded objects, we create a model of the world as a global pool hall in which the enemies spin off each other like so many hard and round coloured balls, to declare that 'East is East, and West is West, and never the twain shall meet'.
>
> (Wolf, 1982: 6)

Then, if IR scholars outside North America and Western Europe seem to share the so-called 'standard' concepts and theories of IR, this may be because they, too, do not see the fluid, undetermined and intertwined character of world history.

The point being that, addressing the limits of IR involves addressing the Eurocentric historical accounts that students of IR draw upon (Halperin, 1997, 2006, Grovogui, 2002, Hobson, 2004). The need to underscore the fluid, undetermined and intertwined character of world history is also one of the reasons why Barry Buzan and George Lawson (2015) engaged in writing a history of the 'great transformation' of the nineteenth century. Existing accounts, many of which read contemporary ('standard') concepts back into history end up reinforcing Eurocentrism in IR. Understanding how it is that students of IR around the world have come to learn world history through accounts shaped by 'standard' concepts and theories entails worlding IR (see below).

Unthinking emulation

Those students of critical IR who problematise the mainstream's claims to 'universal relevance' suggest that if IR scholarship outside North America and Western Europe is shaped by the 'standard' concepts and theories, this is because it is produced by scholars who were trained at US graduate schools and went on to emulate their professors in an unthinking manner. Put differently, this answer views IR scholars as 'social science socialised products of American graduate schools' (Puchala, 1998: 139) that presumably cannot become anything other than what they were taught by their professors.

Inquiring into security in the international 109

Indeed, IR is but one example of the emulation of US 'ways of doing things' in other parts of the world. Since the United States emerged to be the 'dominant producer of both ideas *and* things' (original emphasis) (Bell, 1991: 97) in the post-World War II era, US practices in all fields including the academia were adopted by elites in other parts of the world (albeit in different ways in different contexts). In the early decades of the post-World War II era, governments in the global South made scholarships available in view of their perceived need for a 'transfer of knowledge' from the 'core' to the 'periphery'. During the Cold War, philanthropic and governmental actors in the United States and elsewhere made funds available in the attempt to shape 'hearts and minds' elsewhere around the world. Sending students to postgraduate schools in the United States (and/or United Kingdom, Germany, France, depending on the context) has been a well-established practice in many parts of the global South.[1] Over the years, seeking a Ph.D. in North America and Western Europe has become a part of individual scholars' strategy of pursuing better job prospects when they return home.

Be that as it may, those who favour the 'unthinking emulation' answer have paid surprisingly little attention to scholars' own thinking in producing the kind of work that they do. Where research into IR scholars in the core has under-scored their agency by way of suggesting how they may be read as responding to the context that they live in (see, for example, Murphy, 2001, Williams, 2009), research into non-core scholars' agency has not been inquired into (but see Bilgin, 2011). This is perhaps because, until recently, very limited information was available on this subject. However, latest research into the sociology of IR in different parts of the world (see Chapter 3) has offered us the wherewithal to reconsider the 'unthinking emulation' answer.

I have recently surveyed these recent additions to the literature on IR the sociology of IR around the world. Arguably, doing IR 'as it is done in the United States' has emerged as a way of signalling a break with the past and embracing a 'modern-day' way of doing things in some parts of the world. Consider Turkey, where during the late 1950s, scholars embraced IR as it is taught in the United States as part of the overall attempt to locate Turkey in the 'West' (Bilgin, 2005, Bilgin and Tanrisever, 2009).[2] Also consider the examples of Central and East Europe and Taiwan. In the post-Cold War era, Central and East European scholars who wanted to put some distance between themselves and the Soviet Bloc past (Drulák 2009) and Taiwanese scholars that sought to distinguish their approaches from China have exhibited similar dynamics (Chen, 2011: 12, on China, see Wang, 2009). The point being that the 'unthinking emulation' answer falls short of responding to our question when scholarly agency is taken into account – albeit as responding to structures that condition such agency.

To conclude this section, notwithstanding their differences, both of these explanations understate the role played by scholars as reflexive agents who shape their own research agendas (albeit within structural constraints) as they participate in the production of knowledge about world politics. In the

110 *Inquiring into security in the international*

'unthinking emulation' explanation, while the agency of the US is recognised (IR travelled to other parts of the world through scholarships and grants provided by the US in an environment shaped by Cold War concerns), the agency of the global South goes under-examined. However, what IR offered at the time (a state-focused approach to world politics, and 'national security' as language of state action) also served the purposes of elites concerned with state-building and/or consolidation in the global South. This latter point also goes unacknowledged by those who favour the 'universal relevance' answer, as they fail to inquire into scholars' own agency in producing the kind of work that they do. As will be discussed below in the third section, worlding IR would allow considering the agency of scholars in responding to a world that is already worlded by IR. The second section highlights two different approaches to 'worlding', and calls for worlding IR in its twofold meaning.

Worlding IR – twofold meaning

In IR scholarship, 'worlding' is typically used to refer to reflecting on the geocultural situatedness of knowing. However, there is another, equally important aspect to 'worlding', which is about reflecting on the constitutive effects of knowing. These two understandings were introduced to the students of IR at around the same time. Yet, it has been the first one that has shaped the debates on IR's limits.

The notion of worlding was initially introduced to IR through feminist scholarship. Jan Jindy Pettman's (1996) book entitled *Worlding Women* was one of the first feminist IR monographs, exploring the ways in which IR is gendered. For Pettman (1996: vii), worlding women meant 'taking women's experiences of the international seriously'. Pettman (1996: vi) called for adopting 'worlding' as a strategy so that 'the different worlds of those outside the powerful centres and classes be included in our understanding of international politics'. Put differently, for Pettman, worlding IR was meant to address the field's limits, including the apparent 'absence' of women, gendered nature of knowledge, and IR's narrow understanding of 'difference', including gendered difference.

Different from Pettman's feminist standpoint approach to 'worlding-as-situatedness', postcolonial studies discussions introduced another understanding, 'worlding-as-constitutive'. Presenting Edward Said's notion of 'worldliness' to IR audiences, Pal Ahluwalia and Michael Sullivan (2001: 363) defined it as 'the un- or non- neglect of other ideologies and experiences'. Understanding texts, underscored Said, involved becoming aware how they are 'worldly', that is, how they respond to and reflect their context. Accordingly, Ahluwalia and Sullivan invited IR scholars to reflect on the ways in which scholarship is shaped by scholars' ideologies and experiences, as they seek to respond to their context. The authors suggested that raising scholars' awareness of 'the effects that researchers and their knowledge have on the objects of their study' would offer 'the beginning of a solution' to IR's problems (Ahluwalia and Sullivan, 2001: 363).

Inquiring into security in the international 111

In a later study on the links between post-structuralist and postcolonial thinking, Pal Ahluwalia (2005) stressed the need for understanding IR's 'constitutive outside'. Noting how postcolonial scholars are sometimes criticised for their debts to post-structuralist thought, Ahluwalia highlighted that the reverse is also true. Where worlding postcolonial studies points postcolonial scholars' situatedness, worlding post-structuralist thought reveals its beginnings in colonial encounters and the ways in which the colonial roots of post-structuralism is overlooked by those who critique postcolonial scholars for their indebtedness to post-structuralism (Ahluwalia, 2005, also see Go, 2013). Hence the need for exploring our 'connected histories' and taking care so as not to decouple the two understandings of 'worlding'.

The notion of 'worlding' came to the attention of a broader group of IR students in the 2000s through the 'geocultural epistemologies and IR' project. In calling for worlding IR, Tickner and Wæver's concern was that although critical scholars' 'critique or lament' regarding IR being 'not so international' was acknowledged, it was not always considered as valid due to lack of evidence. Finding out about the study of IR and conceptions of the international in other parts of the world was crucial, argued Tickner and Wæver, not only because there was a need for evidence beyond the anecdotal, but also because

> when this is done without a concrete study of non-dominant and non-privileged parts of the world, it becomes yet another way of speaking from the centre about the whole, and of depicting the centre as normal and the periphery as a projected 'other' through which the disciplinary core is reinforced.
>
> (Tickner and Wæver, 2009b: 1)

Accordingly, Tickner and Wæver designed their project around the notion of worlding. Yet, where Tickner and Wæver discussed 'worlding' in both senses of the term, the rest of the volume emphasised geo-cultural situatedness. Arguably, it was the 'comparative structure' (Pasha, 2011) of the volume that conditioned the contributors to look into the situatedness of IR scholarship in different parts of the world (Bilgin, 2010). As with the latest literature on the sociology of IR,[3] in the 2009 volume, too, the second understanding of 'worlding-as-constitutive' all but disappeared from the discussions.[4]

Let me make a brief detour here to say more on 'worlding-as-constitutive'. Edward Said's 1983 book, *The World, the Text and the Critic* offered his initial elaboration on the 'worldliness' of texts. Arguing against then-prevalent views of the role of the critic as apolitical and interest-free, Said maintained that

> Criticism…is always situated; it is sceptical, secular, reflectively open to its own failings. This is by no means to say that it is value-free. Quite the contrary, for the inevitable trajectory of critical consciousness is to arrive at some acute sense of what political, social and human values are entailed in the reading, production, and transmission of every text.
>
> (Said, 1983: 26)

112 *Inquiring into security in the international*

For Said, texts were 'worldly'. He proposed studying the 'worldliness' of texts through scholarly reflection on the 'concrete reality about which political, moral, and social judgements have to be made and, if not only made, then exposed and demystified' (Said, 1983: 26). The critic's situation demanded reflecting on the 'worldliness' of texts wrote Said. When offering criticism, the critic should reflect on how texts as well as their authors *and* their critics are 'worldly', he wrote. As opposed to, that is, pretending that the author, the text and the critic exist outside of history and politics. In offering this argument, Said was not seeking to encourage the critic to 'discover' a/the truth about history and politics. He wrote:

> My position is that texts are worldly, to some degree they are events, and, even when they appear to deny it, they are nevertheless a part of the social world, human life, and of course the historical moments in which they are located and interpreted.
>
> (Said, 1983: 4)

Accordingly, Said's was a plea for worlding texts so that their 'worldliness', understood as their situatedness *and* their constitutive effects, could be studied by the critic.

Another postcolonial scholar who elaborated on worlding-as-constitutive is Gayatri Spivak. In her conceptualisation, 'worlding' refers to representing something or someone by locating them in one's own world of known things – that is, on one's own terms, using one's own categories and frames of reference. Understood as such, 'worlding' is a process of 'epistemic violence' for Spivak, involving inscription of one's own notions and discourse upon those of others, and without due regard for the possibility that others already have their own worlding of the world (Connery, 2007).

This second understanding of worlding crystallises in postcolonial studies' discussions on the 'Third World'. Among others, Spivak highlighted how the literature on the subject has worlded the "Third World" 'on a supposedly uninscribed earth' (Spivak, 1985: 253). Inquiring into constitutive effects of writings on the 'Third World' helps to uncover how colonised space is 'brought into the "world", that is, made to exist as part of a world essentially constructed by a Euro-centrism' (Ashcroft et al., 2009: 225). Worlding the scholarship on the 'Third World', then, highlights how focusing on 'worlding-as-situatedness' alone, may result in overlooking the constitutive effects of the 'colonial encounter' in the making of the world – both the 'First World' and the 'Third World'.

By way of illustration, consider Peter Vale's discussion on the relationship between theorising about IR and security in/on South Africa. Well until the emergence of critical thinking about IR and security, argued Vale, 'understanding the historical location of the idea of security in southern Africa has been totally absent from debates around the region, its ways, its future' (Vale, 2003: 9). This was because, wrote Vale, it was a particular 'way of knowing' that came to shape thinking about South Africa. This particular 'way of knowing' was viewed as the only way of knowing South Africa. 'And these ways

Inquiring into security in the international   113

of knowing were successively protected by the routines of their late-modern manifestations: strategic studies, military science, and, now, realist security studies', wrote Vale (2003: 175). As such, Vale's analysis of South Africa's relationship with mainstream theorising about IR and security highlights the ways in which South Africa was worlded by IR – not only IR scholarship, but also practices of world politics shaped by this particular 'way of knowing'. It was only after the post-positivist turn in IR, noted Vale, that it became possible to begin to understand 'the historical location of the idea of security in southern Africa', or the ways in which South Africa has been worlded by IR.

Echoing Vale, worlding writings on security in South Africa would allow us to: (1) inquire into how these writings are constitutive of a particular under-standing of South Africa; and (2) how South Africans were 'brought into the world' in security studies literature 'not in their own terms, but in the newly dominant ones, and not in their own right, but as *different* from European forms' (Pieter Boele Van Hesbroek, quoted in Vale, 2003: 176). Hence the significance of worlding IR in its twofold meaning.

Worlding IR, inquiring into security in the international

Worlding IR scholarship originating from outside North America and Western Europe allows us to begin to understand how others' insecurities, experienced in a world that is already worlded, shape (as they are shaped by) their conceptions of the international. In reading others' IR scholarship as an aspect of world politics, I follow R.B.J. Walker (1993) and approach the writings of IR scholars from outside North America and Western Europe not (only) as explanations of world politics, but (also) as aspects of world politics that need explaining. This is not to downplay the significance of inquiring into the sociology of IR, but to underscore how IR outside North America and Western Europe has developed in a world that is already worlded.

In this section, I begin by worlding IR scholarship in China, highlighting that a close reading of the reflections of China's IR scholars reveals how they view IR scholarship as serving to help to locate China in a world that is already worlded by IR. Here, I invoke Homi K. Bhabha's phrase 'almost the same but not quite', and suggest that China's IR scholars' writings could be read as an instance of responding to insecurities in a world that is already worlded. Put differently, the 'similarity' of the concepts and theories adopted by China's IR scholars mask (unacknowledged and understudied) 'differences' (Bilgin, 2008). It is in this sense that others' IR scholarship could be read as doing IR in a seemingly 'similar' but unexpectedly 'different' way. I conclude this section by further illustrating this point by looking at the example of Cold War scholarship on security in Turkey.

Worlding IR scholarship in China

China comes across as an instance of the second of the two questions that I began with in the Introduction: *How is it that IR scholarship in other parts of the*

114 *Inquiring into security in the international*

world does not reflect the kind of 'difference' found in texts and contexts outside IR and/ or North America and Western Europe, but adopts the 'standard' concepts and theories of the field, notwithstanding their well-known limits? For, given the prevalence of 'strong cosmologies' in China (see Tickner and Wæver, 2009b), and the availability of alternative conceptions of the international as revealed by critical readings (see Chapter 3) one would expect its IR scholarship to be 'different'. Yet, since the early 1980s, 'standard' concepts and theories have been predominant in China's IR (Wang, 1994, Wang, 2013, Chan, 1993, 1994, Yee, 1983, Qin, 2011b). Indeed, throughout the 2000s, IR scholars in China made important strides in locating themselves on the map of IR, as measured by the metric standards (the same standards that are utilised in the United States and parts of Western Europe).[5] This was done through sending students abroad (mostly to the United States), inviting international scholars (mostly from the US) for high-level seminars and/or to teach intensive courses, and through offering incentives and rewards to scholars who get published in international peer-reviewed journals (Qin, 2011b).

Yet at the same time, China is also the place where the drive for 'non-Western IR' is by far the strongest. Debates on 'IR theory with Chinese characteristics' have been ongoing since the late 1990s with scholars arguing for and against such an undertaking (Shoude, 1997, Song, 2001, Qin, 2011b, 2013, Wang, 2013). That said, close observers of China have noted that even those studies that sought to build an 'IR theory with Chinese characteristics' do not seem to have deviated from the aforementioned pattern of 'emulation'. Where some scholars sought to replicate the example of the 'English school' tradition, they did not offer a critique of 'standard' IR concepts (Kristensen and Nielsen, 2013). Nor did they drop 'standard' concepts of IR in favour of alternatives that were offered in the body of studies discussed in Chapter 3. Hence William Callahan's characterisation of this body of thinking as 'Realism with Chinese characteristics' (cited in Dirlik, 2011: 149). A long-time observer of China, Arif Dirlik (2011) concurred, noting that this group of scholars' effort is better understood as an attempt to find their ostensibly 'authentic' voice in the world of IR, and not as a challenge to mainstream IR theorising.

Before rushing to judgement about IR scholarship in China as an instance of 'unthinking emulation', it is important to remind ourselves that IR scholars in China did not always seek to locate their scholarship in the world of IR in this manner. Indeed, this trend has been visible only since the early 1980s. Hence the need to consider changing trends in IR studies in China as responses to a world that is already worlded.

To begin from the beginning, IR scholars in China relate the story of the development of IR studies in China in four main periods: (1) during the 1950s when scholars' approach to the world was shaped by the division between the 'two camps', capitalism and communism; (2) during the 1960s when 'opposing imperialism' took precedence, distancing China from both the US-led capitalist 'camp' and the USSR-led communist 'camp'; (3) from the early 1970s until the early 1980s, when China's scholars proposed a different approach to

Inquiring into security in the international   115

understanding the world, the so-called 'Three World Theory', which underscored the independent stance of the previous eras but also proposed a leadership position for China as the leader of the 'Third World'; (4) from the early 1980s onwards when the so-called 'peace and development' approach was adopted, pursuing China's integration into world politics and the world of IR (Wang, 1994).

The third period ('Three World Theory') is particularly relevant for our purposes here. During the early 1970s China's scholars offered a 'different' conception of the international, the so-called 'Three World Theory', which was credited to Mao Zedong but was integrated into China's global strategy by Chairman Deng Xiaoping:

> The sense of Mao's Three World theory was to unite the 'progressive' Third World states, to win over the 'middle' Second World and to isolate the two 'reactionary' superpowers.
>
> At the outset, Beijing thus engaged the two superpowers, especially the Soviet Union, in a war of nerves. Identifying China as a member of the Third World that formed the strategic base of the united front, Beijing had apparently assigned itself a leadership role in the forefront of 'defence' against superpower expansion.
>
> (Yee, 1983: 241)

The 'Three World Theory' was inspired by 'antique Chinese theory', Stephen Chan noted, to portray the international as 'a battle for alliances, in which the proletariat sought to win over the bourgeoisie', whereby a 'Third World' composed of developing states including China struggled against the 'First World' of superpowers, the United States and Soviet Union (the so-called 'socialist–imperialist hegemonism') (Chan, 1998). The 'Second World' was composed of the 'developed' countries. What was different in China's approach to the 'Third World', when compared to those understandings that prevailed at the time (see, for example, Pletsch, 1981) was that the 'Third World' was accorded agency in the 'Three World Theory'. Yet this was a limited form of agency, which was expected to be exercised with some help from China (Yee, 1983).

There is no evidence of the 'Three World Theory' having resonated with IR scholars in other parts of the world. Chan (1993: 97) noted how it comes across as an 'utter failure of western i.r. to know about [the 'Three World Theory'] and, above all, to find theoretical space for it'. Yet, it is equally curious that IR scholars in China seldom find the theoretical space in their scholarship for the 'Three World Theory'. There is very little scholarly discussion on the 'Three World Theory' in Chinese scholars' accounts. It emerges at best as an afterthought in scholarly accounts on the development of IR studies in China (Wang, 1994, Song, 2001, but see Chan, 1993). Indeed, present-day discussions on IR studies in China usually focus on the fourth period that coincided with the adoption of the 'peace and development' approach in China's foreign policy (Song, 2001, Wang, 2009). Still, the fact that the 'Three World Theory' is all but forgotten

116   *Inquiring into security in the international*

in Chinese scholars' treatises on IR studies in China is also worth inquiring into. Put differently, the eventuality that a 'different' conception of the international was offered in China during the 1970s, and that IR scholars in China mostly focus on the trajectory of 'similarity' when they discuss IR studies in China, calls for an explanation.

My reading of China's IR scholars' reflections on the development of IR studies in China suggests that IR is portrayed as not only helping to explain or understand the world, but also helping to respond to China's insecurities. This may be partly to do with the prevailing understanding of 'theory' in China. Among others, Chan (1994: 245) noted that in China 'there is no pure knowledge, only theory which may be applied'. Wang Jisi concurred:

> international relations theory, as understood by the Chinese, is not only an explanatory tool or a prism through which world affairs are observed, but more importantly a guide for international action and foreign policy.
>
> (Wang, 1994: 243)

But then, this could be viewed as another reason for considering scholars' reflections on the state of IR studies in China. Let me focus on two texts by IR scholars Song Xinning and Wang Yiwei.

According to Song Xinning (2001), IR studies are treated differently by China's leadership compared to other social sciences. In the aftermath of the events of Tiananmen Square in 1989, wrote Song (2001: 62), the Chinese leadership sought to limit studies on Political Science, Sociology and Journalism, because of 'the ideological liberalism of Chinese scholars and the so-called peaceful evolution initiated by the West'. IR theorising, wrote Song (2001: 62), received a different treatment in that 'the teaching of Western IR theories continued at key universities, and academic exchanges with the West in IR studies became more active'. According to Song, this was because China's leadership viewed IR studies as serving a different purpose. He wrote:

> Chinese leaders worried more about China's isolation from the outside world than a 'peaceful evolution'. Since 1990 new exchange programs, especially faculty training programs, began at Renda. These were jointly sponsored by the Chinese Government and private foundations from the United States.
>
> (Song, 2001: 62)[6]

Put differently, China's leadership considered IR studies in general and IR theorising in particular as serving a purpose beyond explaining and understanding the world or advising policy. As told by Song, then, China's leadership considered IR studies as serving the purpose of responding to a world already worlded (Song, 2001). IR scholarship was expected to not only help make sense of the world and/or inform China's policies, but also locate China and its scholars in the world of IR.

Inquiring into security in the international 117

Elaborations on China's IR as responding to a world that is already worlded can be found most explicitly in Wang Yiwei's words, quoted below:

> With China's defeat in the Opium War, China was unable to sustain her traditional identity as the central dynasty, or middle kingdom. The first challenge for Chinese thinkers of the nineteenth and early twentieth century was to open their eyes and see the world. Later, after successive revolutions, China's elites sought to establish a new Chinese identity in the world, finally succeeding with the founding of the Republic of China (in 1912) and the People's Republic of China (in 1949). After asserting its status as an independent country, Mao Zedong declared that China should make her own contributions to the world. At this point, relations between China and the world entered the stage of 'constructing the world'.
>
> (Wang, 2009: 103)

Wang's text is one of those studies that trace the beginning of IR scholarship to the fourth period, when the 'peace and development' in foreign policy approach was adopted. As such, Wang's story about IR studies in China is about China's entry into a world that was already worlded by IR. And not, for instance, the story of the 'Three World Theory' that constituted an attempt to resist IR's worlding of the world. Indeed, what is significant about Wang's text is that he frames the choices made by China's scholars as '[opening] their eyes and [seeing] the world' (Wang, 2009: 103). This is a world that is not considered to be China's making, according to Wang, who views China's scholars as 'entering' into this world and eventually seeking to make a 'contribution' – the assumption being that this particular world is not one of China's making.

Before proceeding, a caveat is in order. The principle or practice of academic freedom was not paramount in China during the period under consideration. Accordingly, the choices made by scholars could be viewed as determined elsewhere insofar as China's leadership defines the broad categories through which scholars are expected to approach the world.[7] Yet, the fact that scholars in China may not be as 'free' as their colleagues in some other parts of the world need not render China's IR scholars' reflections on their scholarship less illuminating for our purposes here. As will be seen below in the discussion on the study of security in Turkey, similar dynamics can be observed in other contexts where academia may be less constrained by regime security concerns. That said, it is important that our research design allows for IR scholarship outside North America and Western Europe to be 'differently different' (Bilgin, 2012a).

Doing IR in an unexpectedly 'different' way

Building on the analysis above, here I argue that IR scholarship in China comes across as 'similar' insofar as 'standard' concepts and categories are adopted and utilised by China's scholars. Yet it is 'different' in an unexpected way in that IR

118 *Inquiring into security in the international*

scholarship is viewed as serving a purpose in addition to its 'day job' of explaining and understanding the world, and that scholarship is also considered as helping to locate China in a world that is already worlded. My call for inquiring into security in the international is a plea for inquiring into the ways in which IR scholarship outside North America and Western Europe is 'seemingly similar but unexpectedly different' (Bilgin, 2008).

In offering this argument, I invoke Homi Bhabha's (1984, 1994) phrase 'almost the same but not quite' where he underscored how the postcolonial may come across as 'similar', but a different line of thinking and code of behaviour may belie such similarity. If the postcolonial comes across as 'almost the same but not quite', noted Bhabha, this should be taken as the beginning and not the endpoint of our inquiry into the dynamics between the coloniser and the colonised (also see Ling, 2002). By way of restoring the agency of the postcolonial as such, Bhabha's analysis repudiated the critics who suggested that postcolonialism reduces the 'colonised' to 'mimic men' (see Ben Beya, 1998). This is because the 'colonised' becoming 'almost the same but not quite' as the 'coloniser' is not for lack of 'authentic'[8] grounds upon which modernity can be erected. Rather, in a context of insecurities experienced in a world that is already worlded by IR that such behaviour is observed.

The point being that, while China's IR scholarship outside North America and Western Europe seems to share the assumption of 'anarchy as the condition' in the international realm, the texts that discuss this very condition highlight their authors' responses to the international as 'hierarchical'. If, as John Hobson (2014: 559) argued, mainstream IR rests upon unacknowledged and under-analysed inequalities between states that are 'derived from various *a priori* Eurocentric-hierarchic conceptions of the "standard of civilisation"', China's IR scholarship that persists in utilising 'standard' concepts of anarchy could be read as responding to hierarchy as such also see Chapter 5.

To recapitulate, the apparent 'similarity' of IR studies outside North America and Western Europe could be understood as an instance of doing IR in a seemingly 'similar' but unexpectedly 'different' way. It is 'similar' in the sense that IR scholarship comes across as adopting the same 'standard' concepts and theories as IR scholarship in some other parts of the world. It is 'different' in the sense that such search for 'similarity' is shaped in responding to insecurities experienced in a world that is already worlded by IR. Having laid out my argument, the following sub-section offers an illustration by focusing on the case of security scholarship in Turkey during the Cold War.

Security scholarship in Turkey – unexpectedly 'different'

IR was introduced to Turkey in the aftermath of World War II, when Turkey was struggling with internal and external insecurities. At the time, Turkey's leaders were intent on locating their country in the 'West' via NATO member-ship and accession to European integration (Bilgin, 2009). At its founding, Turkey's scholars modelled IR studies in Turkey after the US example, because

Inquiring into security in the international   119

this is how the United States made sense of 'the international'. This intention is recorded in the minutes of the first meeting convened to discuss the design of IR studies in Turkey (see Ataöv, 1961, 1967). As such, the study of IR in Turkey comes across as an instance of responding to IR's worlding of the world.

That having been said, Turkey's IR scholars do not come across as reflective as their Chinese counterparts in their statements on the state-of-the-art of IR in Turkey. Accordingly, we do not know whether they considered their IR scholarship as part of the attempts to locate Turkey in the world. What follows draws upon my survey of security scholarship in Turkey in the Cold War period,[9] and suggests that Turkey's scholars' persistence in portraying Turkey's insecurities through the 'standard' concepts and theories of IR could be read as an instance of responding to IR's worlding of the world.

All throughout the Cold War, studies on security in Turkey (as with IR scholarship in general) adopted 'standard' concepts in the analysis of Turkey's insecurities. During most of this period, Turkey's IR scholars' studies on security portrayed Turkey as a 'junior partner' of the United States in the 'fight against communism' while its security concerns were understood as derivative of the security interests and policies of the United States and other NATO allies and framed in terms of 'Western security'. Needless to say, these were the very concepts scholars specialising in security in the 'Third World' were critical of (see Chapter 2). In contrast, Turkey's IR scholars focused on those insecurities shared by other NATO members, thereby overlooking those problems stemming from inside the state boundaries as per other countries located in the global South.[10]

Consider, for example, Metin Tamkoç's 1961 article entitled 'Turkey's Quest for Security through Defensive Alliances', in which the author defined security in explicitly state-based, outward-directed and military-focused terms. At the same time, however, his analysis gave away an inward-directed conception of security especially when Tamkoç (1961: 2) discussed the policy priorities of the early Republican period in terms of the search for security and peace through relying 'mainly on its own strength in order to consolidate the homeland'. Once this was achieved, he argued, the governing elite's goal became one of 'preserving and defending [Turkey's] territorial integrity and political independence against possible encroachments by the great powers to overthrow the status quo in the Middle East' (Tamkoç, 1961: 13–14). In other words, although Tamkoç explicitly adopted a 'standard' definition of 'national security' that emphasised threats originating from outside the state, his analysis of Turkey's insecurities revealed an internally focused conception of security, including establishing the idea of the state in the minds of the populace and strengthening its institutions.

Needless to say, aforementioned are the very concerns that the students of security in the 'Third World' underscored as they called for analysing the 'software' side of security (Azar and Moon, 1988a). Neither Tamkoç nor his contemporaries chose to frame Turkey's insecurities in terms similarly sceptical of the relevance of 'standard' concepts and theories. What is particularly interesting about Tamkoç's writings is that where his analysis revealed a mismatch

120 *Inquiring into security in the international*

between Turkey's insecurities and the 'standard' concepts he was using, the author did not explicitly identify or elaborate on such a mismatch.

Not until the 1960s and 1970s, when Turkey's foreign policy underwent a period of re-thinking and re-adjustment, do we see any evidence of scholars questioning the relevance of the 'Western' alliance in seeking security for Turkey. This period witnessed relatively widespread public debate on Turkey's foreign policy in which IR scholars also contributed. The country's Western orientation in general and membership in NATO in particular were the most popular topics of discussion.

That said the terms of the debate were still narrowly defined in that Turkey's security was considered solely in terms of threats stemming from outside the national boundaries. While the appropriateness of the 'Western' framework was questioned, the main concerns that were raised had to do with the implications of the 'Western' alliance for the country's foreign policies. Turkey's insecurities stemming from inside the boundaries, the interaction between the 'internal' and 'external' dynamics, and the appropriateness of 'standard' concepts in accounting for these insecurities were still not a part of scholarly debates.

Consider Haluk Ülman's 1966 study, titled 'Thoughts on Turkey's National Defense', which constitutes an example of studies that pointed to the discrepancy between Turkey's insecurities and those of its NATO allies. Where the author did not reflect upon the roots of such differences, he did call for re-thinking Turkey's national security interests with a view to the economic costs of investments into the military sector.[11] As such, while adopting a comprehensive notion of security by integrating the economic dimension, Ülman did not reflect upon insecurities stemming from developing statehood. Rather, he explained away Turkey's 'different' insecurities as consequences of the country's ostensibly 'unique' characteristics, such as its geographical position and historical background (Ülman, 1966). In doing so, Ülman was not adopting a unique stance but displaying a trend, long visible in Turkey's IR scholarship, of relying on geopolitics as opposed to IR theories in explaining how the world works (Bilgin, 2012b).

Duygu Sezer's 1981 *Adelphi Paper*, 'Turkey's Security Policies', constitutes the first comprehensive study that did not shy away from pointing to aforementioned incongruities between Turkey's insecurities and 'standard' concepts and theories of IR. Contrary to many authors who preceded her, Sezer's study moved away from state-centred and military-focused understandings of security and analysed those vulnerabilities generated by the socio-economic transformation that Turkey experienced during the Republican era. She wrote:

> Despite the absence of obvious military threats, the very precariousness of Turkey's domestic situation exposes her to precisely the kind of internal and external pressures which may dangerously undermine her ability to stand on her own feet and to formulate a coherent security policy. This internal instability is currently the major source of Turkey's insecurity.
>
> (Sezer, 1981: 39)

Inquiring into security in the international 121

Domestic vulnerabilities included the rising socio-economic expectations and demands of Turkish youth, political instability, systemic economic difficulties, resource scarcity, and the role of the military in Turkish politics. Hence the need for focusing on the 'internal' aspects of Turkey's insecurities, argued Sezer (1981: 39): 'external security cannot be achieved without a stable internal environment and a large degree of consensus'. On the issue of Turkey's differences from its Western allies, Sezer introduced underdevelopment as a factor, which had until then remained unexamined in the literature on Turkey's security. That said, Sezer discussed underdevelopment primarily as a factor that impeded cooperation in arms procurement, by emphasising the 'wide gap in the level of development between Turkey and the other European members' (Sezer, 1981: 28). Put differently, while considering domestic dimensions of security in Turkey, Sezer nevertheless prioritised those factors that were likely to impact the external dimension.

How can one make sense of Turkey's IR scholars' reliance on 'standard' concepts and theories throughout the Cold War? Throughout the twentieth century Turkey experienced challenges similar to many others in the global South. Yet, the similarity ended there. Whereas scholars in some other parts of the global South sought to come to terms, in their analyses, with developing statehood, trans-state identity and superpower interventionism as discussed by scholars specialising in 'security in the Third World' (see, for example, Ayoob, 1980, Azar and Moon, 1986, 1988b, Korany, 1986, Al-Mashat, 1985), in Turkey scholars focused almost exclusively on those insecurities the country shared with the 'West' (for notable exceptions, see Sezer, 1981, Bölükbaşı, 1988). The same was true for Turkey's scholars' analyses of the global South. For instance, Middle East dynamics were analysed from the perspective of NATO security (Karaosmanoglu, 1983, Taşhan, 1987, Dış Politika Enstitüsü, 1982) and not necessarily Turkey's perspective, or that of regional states. Indeed, even as they wrote about security in the Middle East, Turkey's scholars focused on Turkey's insecurities in the Middle East as viewed from the 'West'. While it is possible to explain Turkey's scholars' emphasis on 'similarity' as mere by-products of the international context (i.e. alliance with NATO) and the domestic difficulties related to registering dissent, given Turkey's foreign policy orientation (anti-Soviet) and domestic political environment (anti-communist), worlding IR in Turkey would allow further insight here.

To begin with 'worlding-as-situatedness', sociological inquiries into IR scholarship in Turkey have revealed IR studies in Turkey as resting on 'standard' concepts and theories (Tickner and Wæver, 2009a, Aydin and Yazgan, 2010, but see Bilgin, 2012a). This could partly be explained reflecting on the training many scholars received in the United States. All throughout the Cold War, students who were sent abroad by the government for training in Political Science and IR went to the United States. This began to change since the 1990s when Western Europe also became a destination for IR studies (Bilgin and Tanrisever, 2009). There is no denying the formative influence their training in the United States has had on Turkey's IR scholars.

122   *Inquiring into security in the international*

Worlding IR in Turkey by focusing on its constitutive effects, in turn, allows us to read the persistence of 'standard' concepts in Turkey's IR as scholars' responses to IR's worlding of the world. The study of security in Turkey during the Cold War could be read as an instance of studying security in a seemingly 'similar' but unexpectedly 'different' way. As discussed above, what characterised the scholarship on security in Turkey was a somewhat surprising lack of reflection on the limits of 'standard' notions of security in understanding and explaining Turkey's insecurities. Throughout the Cold War, Turkey's IR scholars studied security through utilising 'standard' concepts as developed by their 'Western' ally, the United States. In doing so, scholars did not touch upon those insecurities shared by others in the global South (as with state-building, discussed in other aspects of social science scholarship in Turkey). Furthermore, the issue of the mismatch that some scholars observed between Turkey's insecurities and the 'standard' concepts and theories of IR and security was not elaborated upon. In those times when there arose the need to explain the mismatch between Turkey's insecurities and the 'standard' concepts of IR and security, scholars summoned geopolitical concepts and theories to the rescue (Bilgin, 2012b).

To recap, security scholarship in Turkey located the country in a world that was already worlded by IR. Utilising 'standard' concepts and theories in the study of Turkey's security and highlighting how Turkey shares the same insecurities as the 'Western' allies, these studies served to: (1) underscore the appropriateness of Western-oriented foreign policies; (2) locate Turkey in the 'West'. Reliance on geopolitical discourse regarding Turkey's 'unique' position, in turn, could be viewed as having allowed explaining away the mismatch between Turkey's insecurities as observed by scholars and what the 'standard' concepts allowed them to analyse, thereby leaving untouched the dominance of 'standard' concepts and theories in Turkey (Bilgin, 2012b).

Conclusion

Chapter 4 offered my response to the second of the two questions that the book began with: *How is it that IR scholarship in other parts of the world does not reflect the kind of 'difference' found in texts and contexts outside IR and/or North America and Western Europe, but adopts the 'standard' concepts and theories of the field, notwithstanding their well-known limits?* After considering two alternative explanations, I suggested the following: If IR scholarship outside North America and Western Europe seems to persist in offering analyses shaped by 'standard' concepts and theories of IR, this need not be explained away with reference to US-trained scholars becoming 'unthinking emulators'; or by assuming that 'standard' IR concepts are 'universally relevant'. Building upon China's IR scholars' reflections on the development of IR in China, and Turkey's IR scholars' studies on security in Turkey, I echoed Bhabha and suggested that the persistence of 'standard' concepts and theories outside North America and Western Europe may transpire to be a seemingly 'similar' but unexpectedly 'different' way of doing IR. It is through

Inquiring into security in the international   123

worlding IR in its twofold meaning that we make sense of such 'similarity' as a response to a world that is already worlded by IR, I suggested.

Inquiring into security in the international involves becoming curious about others' apparent 'similarity' in the IR scholarship they produce. As opposed to explaining away such 'similarity', worlding IR in its twofold meaning points to 'differences' that have heretofore gone unacknowledged and under-analysed. These differences could be read as responses to insecurities experienced in a world that is already worlded by IR. In Chapter 5, I build on the argument here and answer the first of our two questions (*How to think about security in a world characterised by a multiplicity of inequalities and differences?*) by suggesting one way of reflecting on others' conceptions of the international in the study of security.

Notes

1 See several contributions to Tickner and Wæver (2009a).
2 During the 2000s 'securitisation theory' was utilised in a context characterised by Turkey's European Union membership bid (Bilgin, 2011).
3 See, *inter alia*, Friedrichs (2001, 2004), Hagmann and Biersteker (2014), Chen (2011), Behera (2008), Guzzini (2007), Wang (2009), Qin (2011a), Kristensen and Nielsen (2013), Breitenbauch and Wivel (2004), Drulák (2009), Morozov (2009), Lucarelli and Menotti (2002), Drulák and Druláková (2000).
4 It was in the third volume of the project entitled *Claiming the International*, that the 'Worlding Beyond the West' book series returned to the second meaning of worlding, noting (albeit briefly) that we are 'at once worlded and worlding' (Tickner and Blaney, 2014: ix).
5 Communication during the workshop 'IR Studies in Europe and China', organised by Standing Group on International Relations, Nordic Centre for International Studies, Fudan University, Shanghai, 26–27 November 2012. Also see Qin (2011b).
6 This account was corroborated by Chinese scholars who participated in the workshop 'IR Studies in Europe and China'. See note 5.
7 This is acknowledged and described in the aforementioned studies (Wang, 1994, Wang, 2013, Chan, 1993, 1994, Yee, 1983, Qin, 2011b).
8 Spivak warned against the search for authenticity (Spivak, 1995). Also see Loomba (2005).
9 Based on a survey of *Milletlerarası Münasebetler Türk Yıllığı* (The Turkish Yearbook of International Relations), *Siyasal Bilgiler Fakültesi Dergisi* (both published by the Faculty of Political Science, Ankara University) and *Dış Politika/Foreign Policy* (published by the Foreign Policy Institute, Ankara). Previously published in Bilgin (2004). Also see Bilgin (2012a).
10 This is not to deny the ways in which foreign and security policy serves to address 'internal' insecurities in developed as well as developing countries but to emphasise the latter's concern with prioritising 'internal' over the 'external' for reasons of state-building.
11 Ülman's study constitutes an exception to the generalisation made above about the dearth of studies addressing the relationships between economic and military dimensions of Turkey's insecurities.

Bibliography

Ahluwalia, P. 2005. Out of Africa: Post-structuralism's Colonial Roots. *Postcolonial Studies*, 8, 137–154.

124 *Inquiring into security in the international*

Ahluwalia, P. & Sullivan, M. 2001. Beyond International Relations: Edward Said and the World. In: Crawford, R. A. & Jarvis, D. S. (eds.) *International Relations – Still an American Social Science?: Toward Diversity in International Thought*, Albany, NY, State University of New York Press.

Al-Mashat, A. M. M. 1985. *National Security in the Third World*, Boulder, CO, Westview Press.

Ashcroft, B., Griffiths, G., Tiffin, H. & Ashcroft, B. 2009. *Post-colonial Studies: The Key Concepts*, London & New York, Routledge.

Ataöv, T. 1961. Symposium on the Teaching of International Politics in Turkey. *Milletlerarası Münasebetler Türk Yıllığı*, 2, 188–196.

Ataöv, T. 1967. The Teaching of International Relations in Turkey. *Siyasal Bilgiler Fakültesi Dergisi*, 22, 373–383.

Aydin, M. & Yazgan, K. 2010. Survey of International Relations Faculty in Turkey: Research, Teaching and Views on the Discipline-2009. *Uluslararasi Iliskiler-International Relations*, 7, 3–41.

Ayoob, M. 1980. *Conflict and Intervention in the Third World*, New York, St. Martin's Press.

Azar, E. E. & Moon, C. I. 1986. Managing Protracted Social Conflicts in the Third-World – Facilitation and Development Diplomacy. *Millennium – Journal of International Studies*, 15, 393–406.

Azar, E. E. & Moon, C.-I. 1988a. Legitimacy, Integration and Policy Capacity: The 'Software' Side of Third World National Security. In: Azar, E. E. & Moon, C.-I. (eds.) *National Security in the Third World: The Management of Internal and External Threats*, Aldershot, Edward Elgar.

Azar, E. E. & Moon, C.-I. (eds.) 1988b. *National Security in the Third World: The Management of Internal and External Threats*, Aldershot, Edward Elgar

Behera, N. C. 2008. *International Relations in South Asia: Search for an Alternative Paradigm*, UK, US, India & Singapore, Sage.

Bell, P. F. 1991. The Impact of the United States on the Development of Social Sciences in Thailand. *Social Science Models and Their Impact on the Third World* 10, 95–116.

Ben Beya, A. 1998. *Mimicry, Ambivalence, and Hybridity* [Online]. Available: https://scholarblogs.emory.edu/postcolonialstudies/2014/06/21/mimicry-ambivalence-and-hybridity/ Accessed 17 January 2015.

Bhabha, H. K. 1984. Of Mimicry and Man: The Ambivalence of Colonial Discourse. *October*, 28, 125–133.

Bhabha, H. K. 1994. *The Location of Culture*, London, Routledge.

Bilgin, P. 2004. Os estudos de segurança na Turquia: situando a Turquia no 'ocidente' por meio de 'escrever a segurança' (The study of security in Turkey: locating Turkey in the 'West' through 'writing security'). *Contexto Internacional*, 26, 149–185.

Bilgin, P. 2005. Uluslararası İlişkilerde 'Merkez-Çevre': Türkiye Nerede? *Uluslararasi Iliskiler-International Relations*, 2, 3–14.

Bilgin, P. 2008. Thinking Past 'Western' IR? *Third World Quarterly*, 29, 5–23.

Bilgin, P. 2009. Securing Turkey through Western-Oriented Foreign Policy. *New Perspectives on Turkey*, 40, 105–125.

Bilgin, P. 2010. Looking for 'the International' beyond the West. *Third World Quarterly*, 31, 817–828.

Bilgin, P. 2011. The Politics of Studying Securitization? The Copenhagen School in Turkey. *Security Dialogue*, 42, 399–412.

Bilgin, P. 2012a. Security in the Arab World and Turkey: Differently Different. In: Tickner, A. & Blaney, D. (eds.) *Thinking International Relations Differently*, London, Routledge.

Inquiring into security in the international   125

Bilgin, P. 2012b. Turkey's 'Geopolitics Dogma'. In: Guzzini, S. (ed.) *Fixing Foreign Policy Identity: 1989 and the Uneven Revival of Geopolitical Thought in Europe*, Cambridge, Cambridge University Press.

Bilgin, P. & Morton, A. D. 2002. Historicising Representations of 'Failed States': Beyond the Cold-War Annexation of the Social Sciences? *Third World Quarterly*, 23, 55–80.

Bilgin, P. & Tanrisever, O. F. 2009. A Telling Story of IR in the Periphery: Telling Turkey about the World, Telling the World about Turkey. *Journal of International Relations and Development*, 12, 174–179.

Bölükbaşı, S. H. 1988. *The Superpowers and the Third World: Turkish-American Relations and Cyprus*, Lanham, MD, University Press of America.

Breitenbauch, H. O. & Wivel, A. 2004. Understanding National IR Disciplines Outside the United States: Political Culture and the Construction of International Relations in Denmark. *Journal of International Relations and Development*, 7, 414–443.

Buzan, B. & Lawson, G. 2015. *The Global Transformation: History, Modernity and the Making of International Relations*, Cambridge, Cambridge University Press.

Chan, S. 1993. A Summer Polemic: Revolution, Rebellion and Romance. Some Notes Towards the Resacralisation of I.R. *Paradigms*, 7, 85–100.

Chan, S. 1994. Beyond the North-West: Africa and the East. In: Groom, A. J. R. & Light, M. (eds.) *Contemporary International Relations: A Guide to Theory*, London, Pinter.

Chan, S. 1998. Redefining the Third World for a New Milennium: An Aching Toward Subjectivity. In: Poku, N. & Pettiford, L. (eds.) *Redefining the Third World*, London, Macmillan.

Chen, C.-C. 2011. The Absence of Non-Western IR Theory in Asia Reconsidered. *International Relations of the Asia-Pacific*, 11, 1–23.

Connery, C. L. 2007. Introduction: Worlded Pedagogy in Santa Cruz. In: Wilson, R. & Connery, C. L. (eds.) *The Worlding Project: Doing Cultural Studies in the Era of Globalization*, Berkeley, CA, New Pacific Press.

Dirlik, A. 2011. Culture in Contemporary IR Theory: The Chinese Provocation. In: Shilliam, R. (ed.) *International Relations and Non-Western Thought: Imperialism, Colonialism and Investigations of Global Modernity*, London, Routledge.

Dış Politika Enstitüsü 1982. *Türkiye ve Müttefiklerinin Güvenliği (Security of Turkey and its Allies)*, Ankara, Dış Politika Enstitüsü/Foreign Policy Institute.

Drulák, P. & Druláková, R. 2000. International Relations in the Czech Republic: A Review of the Discipline. *Journal of International Relations and Development*, 3, 256–282.

Drulák, P. (ed.) 2009. Forum: International Relations (IR) in Central and Eastern Europe. *Journal of International Relations and Development*, 12, 168–220.

Friedrichs, J. 2001. International Relations Theory in France. *Journal of International Relations and Development*, 4, 118–137.

Friedrichs, J. 2004. *European Approaches to International Relations Theory: A House with Many Mansions*, London, Routledge.

Go, J. 2013. Decolonizing Bourdieu: Colonial and Postcolonial Theory in Pierre Bourdieu's Early Work. *Sociological Theory*, 31, 49–74.

Grovogui, S. N. 2002. Postcolonial Criticism: International Reality and Modes of Inquiry. In: Chowdhry, G. & Nair, S. (eds.) *Power, Postcolonialsm, and International Relations: Reading Race, Gender and Class*, London, Routledge.

126 Inquiring into security in the international

Guzzini, S. 2007. Theorising International Relations: Lessons from Europe's Periphery. DIIS Working Paper.

Hagmann, J. & Biersteker, T. J. 2014. Beyond the Published Discipline: Toward a Critical Pedagogy of International Studies. *European Journal of International Relations*, 20, 2, 291–315.

Halperin, S. 1997. *In the Mirror of the Third World: Capitalist Development in Modern Europe*, Ithaca, NY, Cornell University Press.

Halperin, S. 2006. International Relations Theory and the hegemony of Western Conceptions of Modernity. In: Jones, B. G. (ed.) *Decolonizing International Relations*, Lanham, MD, Rowman & Littlefield.

Hobson, J. M. 2004. *The Eastern Origins of Western Civilization*, Cambridge, Cambridge University Press.

Hobson, J. M. 2014. The Twin Self-Delusions of IR: Why 'Hierarchy' and Not 'Anarchy' Is the Core Concept of IR. *Millennium – Journal of International Studies*, 42, 3, 557–575.

Karaosmanoglu, A. 1983. Turkey's Security and the Middle East. *Foreign Affairs*, 62, 1, 157–175.

Korany, B. 1986. Strategic Studies and the Third World: A Critical Evaluation. *International Social Science Journal*, 38, 547–562.

Kristensen, P. M. & Nielsen, R. T. 2013. Constructing a Chinese International Relations Theory: A Sociological Approach to Intellectual Innovation. *International Political Sociology*, 7, 19–40.

Ling, L. H. M. 2002. *Postcolonial International Relations: Conquest and Desire between Asia and the West*, New York, Palgrave.

Loomba, A. 2005. *Colonialism/Postcolonialism*, London, Routledge.

Lucarelli, S. & Menotti, R. 2002. No-constructivists' Land: International Relations in Italy in the 1990s. *Journal of International Relations and Development*, 5, 114–142.

Milliken, J. & Krause, K. 2002. State Failure, State Collapse, and State Reconstruction: Concepts, Lessons and Strategies. *Development & Change*, 33, 753.

Morozov, V. 2009. Obsessed with Identity: The IR in Post-Soviet Russia. *Journal of International Relations and Development*, 12, 200–205.

Murphy, C. N. 2001. Critical Theory and the Democratic Impulse: Understanding a Century-Old Tradition. In: Jones, R. W. (ed.) *Critical Theory and World Politics*, Boulder, CO, Lynne Rienner.

Pasha, M. K. 2011. Untimely Reflections. In: Shilliam, R. (ed.) *International Relations and Non-Western Thought: Imperialism, Colonialism, and Investigations of Global Modernity*, UK & New York, Routledge.

Pettman, J. 1996. *Worlding Women: A Feminist International Politics*, London, Routledge.

Pletsch, C. E. 1981. The Three Worlds, or the Division of Social Scientific Labor, Circa 1950–1975. *Comparative Studies in Society and History*, 23, 565–590.

Puchala, D. 1998. Third World Thinking and Contemporary International Relations. In: Neuman, S. G. (ed.) *International Relations Theory and the Third World*, London, Macmillan.

Qin, Y. 2011a. Development of International Relations Theory in China: Progress through Debates. *International Relations of the Asia-Pacific*, 11, 231–257.

Qin, Y. 2011b. Rules vs Relations, Drinking Coffee and Tea, and a Chinese Approach to Global Governance [Online]. Available: http://www.theory-talks.org/2011/11/theo ry-talk- 45.html Accessed 14 May 2014.

Qin, Y. 2013. An Accidental (Chinese) International Relations Theorist. In: Tickner, A. B. & Blaney, D. (eds.) *Claiming the International*, London, Routledge.

Said, E. W. 1983. *The World, the Text, and the Critic*, Cambridge, MA, Harvard University Press.

Sezer, D. 1981. Turkey's Security Policies. *Adelphi Papers*, 164.

Shoude, L. 1997. Constructing an International Relations Theory with 'Chinese Characteristics'. *Political Science*, 49, 23–39.

Song, X. 2001. Building International Relations Theory with Chinese Characteristics. *Journal of Contemporary China*, 10, 61–74.

Spivak, G. C. 1985. The Rani of Sirmur: An Essay in Reading the Archives. *History and Theory*, 24, 247–272.

Spivak, G. C. 1995. Can the Subaltern Speak? In: Ashcroft, B., Griffiths, G. & Tiffin, H. (eds.) *The Postcolonial Studies Reader*, London, Routledge.

Tamkoç, M. 1961. Turkey's Quest for Security Through Defensive Alliances. *Milletlerarası Münasebetler Türk Yıllığı*, 2, 1–39.

Taşhan, S. 1987. Türkiye'nin Tehdit Algılamaları (Turkey's Threat Perceptions). In: DPE (ed.) *Türkiye'nin Savunması (Turkey's Defence)*, Ankara, DPE.

Tickner, A. B. & Blaney, D. 2014. Claiming the International Beyond IR. In: Tickner, A. B. & Blaney, D. (eds.) *Claiming the International*, London, Routledge.

Tickner, A. B. & Wæver, O. (eds.) 2009a. *International Relations Scholarship Around the World*, London: Routledge.

Tickner, A. B. & Wæver, O. 2009b. Introduction: Geocultural Epistemologies. In: Tickner, A. B. & Wæver, O. (eds.) *International Relations Scholarship Around the World*, London, Routledge.

Ülman, H. 1966. Türk Ulusal Savunması Üzerine Düşünceler. *Siyasal Bilgiler Fakültesi Dergisi*, 21, 4, 197–226.

Vale, P. 2003. *Security and Politics in South Africa: The Regional Dimension*, Boulder, CO, Lynne Rienner Publishers.

Walker, R. B. J. 1993. *Inside/outside: International Relations as Political Theory*, Cambridge, Cambridge University Press.

Wang, H.-J. 2013. Being Uniquely Universal: Building Chinese International Relations Theory. *Journal of Contemporary China*, 22, 518–534.

Wang, J. 1994. International Relations Theory and the Study of Chinese Foreign Policy: A Chinese Perspective. In: Robinson, T. W. & Shambaugh, D. (eds.) *Chinese Foreign Policy: Theory and Practice*, Oxford, Clarendon Press.

Wang, Y. 2009. China: Between Copying and Constructing. In: Tickner, A. B. & Wæver, O. (eds.) *Global Scholarship in International Relations: Worlding Beyond the West*, London, Routledge.

Williams, M. 2009. Waltz, Realism and Democracy. *International Relations*, 23, 328.

Wolf, E. R. 1982. *Europe and the People Without History*, Berkeley, University of California Press.

Yee, H. S. 1983. The Three World Theory and Post-Mao China's Global Strategy. *International Affairs*, 59, 239–249.

5 Inquiring into the international in security

Studying security in a world characterised by multiple inequalities and differences entails reflecting on others' conceptions of the international. However, as we saw in Chapter 3, accessing others' conceptions of the international has turned out to be a challenge for students of International Relations. Those who sought to locate others' conceptions of the international in their IR scholarship found 'similarity' and were disenchanted in their efforts. Those who turned to texts and contexts outside IR and/or North America and Western Europe found 'difference', yet their findings have yet to be fully integrated into our theorising about IR and security. Chapter 4 offered one way of turning 'similarity' into a research agenda, by reading others' IR scholarship as an aspect of world politics (and not only as an attempt to explain or understand world politics). More specifically, I suggested that others' IR scholarship could be read as responding to insecurities experienced in a world that is already worlded by IR. This, I called, 'security in the international'. In doing so, I offered an answer to one of the two questions that the book set out to respond to: *How is it that IR scholarship in other parts of the world does not reflect the kind of 'difference' found in texts and contexts outside IR and/or the 'West', but adopts those 'standard' concepts of the field, notwithstanding their well-known limits?*

Chapter 5 responds to the other question that the book began with: *How to think about security in a world characterised by a multiplicity of inequalities and differences.* By reflecting on others' conceptions of the international as we study security, I answer. Inquiring into 'the international in security' is about locating others' conceptions of the international in their 'discourses of danger' (Campbell, 1992). As such, I do not search for others' conceptions of the international by travelling elsewhere (see Chapter 3) with a view to injecting that into the study of security afterwards. Rather, I draw upon postcolonial studies to gain insight into the insecurities of those who are caught up in hierarchies that were built and sustained during the age of colonialism and beyond.

The chapter proceeds in the following manner. In the first section, I draw on postcolonial scholarship on India's nuclear (weapons) programme to tease out India's leaders' conceptions of the international as reflected in their 'discourses of danger'. In the second section, I suggest that studying others' 'discourses of danger' as such allows the students of IR to go beyond surface understandings

Inquiring into the international in security 129

of the postcolonial becoming 'almost the same but not quite' as mere imitation, but consider it as a response to insecurities shaped by (and shaping) their conception of the international. I term this conception of the international as 'hierarchy in anarchical society', capturing the anarchical, societal and hierarchical aspects of the international. The third section offers an illustration in my reading of Turkey's secularisation as part of an attempt to address the insecurities the country's early twentieth-century leadership experienced in their encounters with the international society.

Others' insecurities – re-thinking what 'we already understand'

Chapter 1 underscored that even as 'we' (as students of IR) show awareness of the limits of our theorising about IR and security, we do not always recognise the implications of these limits for our understanding of specific instances of in/security. This is true for both mainstream and critical IR, as discussed in Chapter 2. For instance, frequent laments about Eurocentrism in theorising about IR and security seldom result in re-thinking the 'standard' concepts and theories of our field. This is because, Chapter 1 argued, we do not see a puzzle; (we presume that) 'we already understand'. In this section of the chapter, I look at an historical example that we presume 'we already understand', namely India's nuclear (weapons) programme, which is not treated as 'puzzling' by students of IR. However, drawing upon postcolonial studies, I suggest that India's behaviour could be read as responding to insecurities generated by their less-than-equal treatment by some other members of the international society even after they gained full independence and sovereignty.

In 1974 India exploded its first so-called 'peaceful' nuclear weapon. The nuclear (weapons) programme in India had been in the making since 1948 when the Atomic Energy Act was passed. From 1974 (when the bomb was first tested) until 1998 (when additional tests were conducted) India remained a nuclear weapons-capable state that did not conduct further tests but negotiated at various non-proliferation *fora* (Abraham, 1998). As students of IR and security studies (we presume that), 'we already understand' India's nuclear behaviour. Even its label as a 'peaceful weapon' is not a source of curiosity for many, who take such labelling as mere 'propaganda'. Be that as it may, it is worth inquiring into the discursive economy that renders it meaningful for India's leadership to portray an 'atomic bomb' as a 'peaceful weapon'.

Structural realist accounts see little to be puzzled about concerning India's 1974 or 1998 tests. These accounts portray India's tests as a search for security through military means as conditioned by anarchy (*India Review*, 2003–2004). Those who contest the structural realist explanation point to the absence of a direct military threat to India's security, which they argue could have justified the need for developing a nuclear response capacity. Instead, they marshal another realist notion, the 'urge for power' as driving India's policies (often without inquiring into what type of power is being sought or to what end). From a realist perspective, India's behaviour is explained as a search for the

130 *Inquiring into the international in security*

ability to 'influence others to behave as it wants them to and, conversely, to resist the unwelcome influence of others' (Perkovich, 1998: 3). Neither of these accounts, however, inquire into India's insecurities as viewed from India. Rather, they superimpose onto India's nuclear behaviour the ostensibly 'universal' assumptions regarding deterrence and/or search for power.

Students of area studies who doubt the explanatory power of such 'universal' explanations emphasise the 'particular'. More specifically, they emphasise the role of domestic leadership in the Indian context. The development of India's 'peaceful' bomb is explained with reference to Prime Minister Jawaharlal Nehru's national, regional and global leadership ambitions during the 1940s–1950s. The 1974 test, in turn, is understood in terms of Prime Minister Indira Ghandi's search for legitimacy at home. That said, what the area studies accounts leave unexplained is how it was that India's leaders sought to utilise nuclear weapons (and not some other tool) for domestic political purposes, and what kind of a discursive economy allowed them to do so.

Seeking answers to these questions, as opposed to explaining away India's nuclear dynamics with reference to either 'universal' strategic reasoning (realist IR's answer) or 'particular' domestic dynamics (area studies' answer) requires students of world politics to be puzzled by India's nuclear behaviour.

One scholar who has found India's behaviour puzzling is Itty Abraham (1998: 17), who has maintained that prevalent accounts of India's 'atomic bomb' do not suffice, and that understanding the 1948 (the beginning of the programme), 1974 (the first test) and 1998 (multiple tests) decisions requires inquiring into post-colonial insecurities in India (Abraham, 1998, 2006, 2009, also see Biswas, 2001).

What distinguishes Abraham's (1998, also see Abraham, 2009) analysis from (structural) realist IR or area studies accounts is the way in which he has rendered puzzling what (we presume that) 'we already understand'. He did this by asking the following two questions: 'why would a nuclear explosion be the means by which a leader seeks to bolster sagging support?' and 'what was so compelling about a nuclear explosion that would give a government the popular legitimacy it sought?'. In his study on India's nuclear (weapons) programme entitled *The Making of the Indian Atomic Bomb: Science, Secrecy and the Postcolonial State*, Abraham (1998) answered these questions by studying India's leaders' 'discourses of danger' (Campbell, 1992).

Abraham's finding was that the nuclear (weapons) programme was associated with security in the minds of India's leadership. However, this was not only due to (1) (regional and global) 'power politics' concerns, or (2) domestic struggles, but also due to (3) 'postcolonial insecurities'. Put differently, whereas answer 1 ('power politics concerns') emphasises a particular understanding of the international (which is presumed to be 'universal'), answer 2 ('domestic struggles') privileges the domestic (i.e. the 'particular') as if it is autonomous of the international. Answer 3 ('postcolonial insecurities'), in turn, focuses on the dynamic relationship between the domestic and the international.

According to Abraham, in the decades following independence, India's leaders' insecurities were shaped by their remembrances of colonisation and

Inquiring into the international in security 131

considerations of the international society as not (yet) accepting of India as a fully sovereign and equal member. For example, India's postcolonial insecurities rendered difficult the country's relations with the United States, with which it shared 'democratic' identity. On the other hand, relations with the Soviet Union (with which India shared relatively little) were relatively smooth. This difference was not because of material threats, argued Himadeep Muppidi (1999), but postcolonial insecurities. Where the Soviet Union made a point of its recognition of India's sovereignty and equality as a new member of the international society, the United States exhibited little awareness of and attentiveness towards Indian leadership's concerns.

According to Abraham, India's leaders found the recipe for addressing their postcolonial insecurities in proving India's prowess to the rest of the world. The nuclear (weapons) programme was one ingredient in this recipe. Abraham wrote:

> Establishing the base for an Indian atomic energy program was much more than a scheme for building weapons. The urgent political need for national development and state legitimation was intimately wrapped up in the technological success of atomic energy, defined in terms of national strength, uniqueness, and security. 'So what should our role be in this dangerous and fast changing world? It is obvious that the first thing is to make ourselves strong and better off to face any danger.' The constant iteration of themes of self-reliance, autonomy, independence make it impossible to separate atomic energy from a host of other techno-political projects also begun by the Indian state soon after independence.
>
> (Abraham, 2006: 63)

It is significant to note here that what distinguished India's nuclear (weapons) programme from the rest of the 'technopolitical projects' that also served a 'legitimation function for the postcolonial state' (Abraham, 2006: 63) was its relationship with 'national security' understood in 'standard' (state-centric and military-focused) terms. In the post-World War II context of India, two key concepts, 'national security' and 'development' 'came to set the conceptual limits to national "pathways to progress"' understood as becoming 'modern' (Abraham, 1998: 13). Consider the following remark by Nehru as highlighted by Abraham:

> Modern technology, especially in the postcolony, was always marked with the trace of the foreign. Yet true independence required self-reliance and indigeneity, especially in relation to technology. Seeking approval to set up an atomic energy commission in 1948, Nehru would remind the Constituent Assembly of India that in spite of 'its many virtues', India had become a 'backward' country and 'a slave country' because it had missed earlier technological revolutions, namely those of steam and electricity.
>
> (Abraham, 2006: 56)

132 *Inquiring into the international in security*

As such, the securityness of the atomic bomb for Nehru was not isolated to its use as a military instrument to deter (potential or actual) military threats. Nor was it (only) about proving to the world that India was capable of building its own nuclear (weapons) programme. It was also about portraying India as having 'arrived' at the world stage as a 'modern' state. India's leaders felt confident, Abraham noted, that India could no longer be categorised by others (i.e. the older members of the international society) as a 'backward' country that was not fit for self-governance. Having built its own nuclear (weapons) programme to entrench its 'national security' just as the other nuclear powers did, India's leadership thought, India had to be viewed as a 'modern' 'nation-state', and treated accordingly (Abraham, 1998). India's was a 'peaceful bomb' in the sense that its primary purpose was not military; yet it was not entirely 'peaceful', 'but something else besides' (Abraham, 2006: 62).

There is yet another puzzle in India's nuclear behaviour. By not testing the bomb for more than two decades after 1974, thereby maintaining an ambiguity about the so-called 'peaceful bomb', India cultivated a 'nuclear ambivalence' (Abraham, 2006) about its stance vis-à-vis other nuclear powers' practices of 'atomic diplomacy' (Alperovitz, 1965). That it was not practising 'atomic diplomacy' could be understood as part of India's leaders' efforts to fashion a distinct 'postcolonial' identity for India, suggested Abraham:

> Producing the postcolonial as an instance of, but distinct from, modernity-as-a-Western-thing, is the product of the third world nationalist desire to produce space marked by a specific set of signs, unambiguously signifying the indigenous-authentic, scientific, and up-to-date.
>
> (Abraham, 2000: 165)

Yet, from 1974 to 1998, the reasons offered in justifying India's nuclear behaviour changed. By 1998, India's leadership no longer seemed interested in portraying India as a postcolonial state, which was 'modern' enough to build its own nuclear weapon and yet postcolonial enough to keep it 'peaceful'. Abraham wrote:

> Previous governments, quite unlike the BJP nationalists ideologically, had ensured that India had converted a latent ability into a viable weapons option a decade before. Crossing the test threshold, however, was symbolically significant as it sought to signal identity with dominant international norms of nuclear meaning. In other words, I argue that framing the decision behind the May 1998 tests was the desire to reduce the multiple meanings of a 'peaceful' nuclear program, to force nuclear ambivalence into a more familiar register...Each nuclear explosion sought to reduce further the range of meanings of the Indian nuclear program, bringing it closer into line with received interpretations of what a 'typical' nuclear program does.
>
> (Abraham, 2006: 54–55)

Inquiring into the international in security   133

Accordingly, carrying out the 1998 tests was presented by the government of the time as acting like a 'typical' nuclear power practising 'atomic diplomacy' by shedding the postcolonial marker of a 'peaceful weapon' (Biswas, 2001).

To recapitulate, new entrants to the international society such as India were mindful of multiple inequalities that characterised their relations with the existing members, who, in previous eras, set and enforced the 'standard of civilisation'. Even as they joined the international society as full members, India's leaders remained concerned about the less-than-equal treatment they received. In response, they sought to remove the grounds for such treatment. Drawing on postcolonial studies scholarship, I suggested that India's nuclear (weapons) programme could be considered as a security response by a new entrant to the international society to remove the grounds for the less-than-equal treatment it received. What we learn from Abraham's account of the Indian 'atomic bomb' is how India's leaders viewed this particular military instrument as a tool for engendering non-military security in a way that was not anticipated by the inventors of the bomb or appreciated by the students of Security Studies.

Others' insecurities as encounters with 'hierarchy in anarchical society'

In this section I offer 'hierarchy in anarchical society' as a concept that captures the hierarchical, as well as the anarchical and societal aspects of others' conception of the international. The discussion begins with the English School account of inter-state relations which emphasises the societal aspects of anarchy while overlooking the hierarchical. I then contrast the English School's self-understanding of the international society as 'benevolent', with the new members' experiences of the international society as 'Janus-faced' (Suzuki, 2005).

In English School accounts, the 'international society' refers to institutionalised practices of European states and empires, and the emergence of understandings between the members that rendered 'societal' the relations of states under anarchy. Hedley Bull (1977) termed this an 'anarchical society', underscoring the relevance, for understanding the international, of both the 'anarchical' (the absence of a world government) and the 'societal' (Bull, 1977, Bull and Watson, 1984, Watson, 1992, Dunne, 1995, 1998, Buzan, 2001, 2004, Linklater and Suganami, 2006). From an English School perspective, the institutionalised practices of the members of the international society are considered as responses to a history of unruly relations between multiple actors in 'Europe'. 'Societal' understandings and practices were developed in time to regulate affairs among Christian actors in Europe so as to minimise violence. In time, as Christianity faded (as the source of understandings regulating inter-state behaviour among members of the European international society) it was replaced by 'civilisation' (Bowden, 2004).

In contrast to some other theories of IR that overlook those 'others' who also helped constitute the international, the students of English School of IR have studied the process of the 'expansion' of international society (Bull and

134   *Inquiring into the international in security*

Watson, 1984), thereby incorporating 'others' into their accounts of world politics (Jabri, 2014). That said, English School scholarship on the 'expansion' of international society does not inquire into the expansion process as viewed from the perspective of others who were not (yet) members (but see Neumann, 1999, 2011). Rather, English School accounts are shaped by existing members' self-understandings of the international society as 'benevolent' (Suzuki, 2005). In contrast, incorporating the understandings of the new members helps to paint a more complex picture about the expansion of international society and the insecurities 'others' experienced in their encounters. A key aspect that shaped those relations was the 'standard of civilisation'.

In English School terms, the 'standard of civilisation' refers to 'the assumptions, tacit and explicit, used to distinguish those that belong to a particular society (by definition the "civilised")' (Gong, 1984b: 172). They were created in regulating relations with 'non-members' (Bull and Watson, 1984, Gong, 1984a, 1984b). In Gerrit Gong's words:

> In the nineteenth century, practices generally accepted by 'civilised' European countries, and therefore by the international system centered in Europe, took an increasingly global and explicitly juridical character as that international system developed. The standard of 'civilisation' that defined nineteenth-century international society provided a purportedly legal way both to demarcate the boundaries of 'civilised' society and to differentiate among 'civilised', 'barbarous', and 'savage' countries internationally.
>
> (Gong, 2002: 78–79)

There was a need for such a formulation, noted Hedley Bull in his preface to Gong's critical analysis of the 'standard of civilisation', for in the European experience, 'non-Europeans' were not always tolerant towards 'European' 'difference' or accepting of them as their equals (Bull, 1984). As such, Bull suggested that 'European' members of the international society had initially adopted the 'standard of civilisation' to maintain their own citizens' security vis-à-vis the non-members. The implication being that if the 'standard of civilisation' was later utilised by some members to justify colonialism, direct and indirect rule, this was not the intended purpose but an unintended consequence. As such, Bull's portrayal of the emergence of the 'standard of civilisation' sustains the English School self-understanding about an international society that was 'benevolent' towards non-members as well as new entrants.

The English School's self-understanding of the international society and its relations with non-members has since been challenged by critical scholarship that pointed to how it was experienced as 'Janus-faced' by those who were not (yet) members. This is because,

> Many non-European states which were incorporated into European International Society in the course of European imperialism did not only witness the norms of 'toleration' and 'coexistence'. They also witnessed the

European International Society which often aggressively intervened in their land in order to bring them closer to 'civilisation'.

(Suzuki, 2005: 147)

Japan's leaders' insecurities, then, were shaped by (and, in turn, shaped) a conception of the international as hierarchical whereby Japan had to climb up the ladder and become a member or risk losing its sovereignty in part or in whole. Accordingly, Shogo Suzuki argued, the Japanese Empire considered membership to the international society not as a 'choice' but a necessity for securing its future (Suzuki, 2014: 80, also see Suzuki, 2005, 2009).

Introducing a 2014 study on non-members' approaches to international order, Suzuki and his co-editors Yongjin Zhang and Joel Quirk suggested that this view of the international society as 'Janus-faced' was not isolated to Japan's leaders, but was shared by many other new or non-members of the international society:

> While it is argued that non-Western polities' acceptance of the sovereign state system constitutes empirical evidence of the internationalisation and global diffusion of European-originated norms in international politics, it is important to acknowledge that many non-European states accepted these 'rules of the game' at gunpoint, and could not exercise much choice over this matter.
>
> (Suzuki et al., 2014: 8)

As will be seen below in the third section, this view of the international also came to be shared by the leaders of the Ottoman Empire in the nineteenth century. Revisiting these historical cases suggests that new members approached the concept of 'civilisation' (which shaped the 'standard') in securitised terms, and viewed their own predicament vis-à-vis the international society as one of 'having little choice' but to change their ways toward meeting the 'standard'.[1]

For example, consider the 'extraterritoriality treaties' that Bull was referring to in tracing the 'benevolent' origin of the 'standard of civilisation'. Notwithstanding their origin in concerns with facilitating trade, by the nineteenth century, treaties governing extraterritoriality came to be justified through resort to a hierarchical division of world's peoples as measured by the 'standard of civilisation'. In time, extraterritoriality treaties further reinforced the hierarchies reproduced by the 'standard'. Citizens of the members of the international society claimed the right to be governed by a different set of rights and obligations than the peoples of the (non-member) countries they were living in. They justified these claims with reference to non-members' failings in terms of the 'standard of civilisation' (as with the 'absence' of citizenship regimes, see Bilgin and Ince, 2015). Such claims, in turn, allowed for direct and indirect intervention into the affairs of non-members. By the late nineteenth century,

> China, Japan and the Ottoman Empire were recognized as sovereign states but not full members of international society. Their authority over their

136 *Inquiring into the international in security*

own people was acknowledged, and generally respected. But Westerners, in those countries, refusing to submit themselves to 'Asiatic barbarism', were placed under the extraterritorial jurisdiction of their own consuls.

(Donnelly, 1998: 4)

Even after the abolition of unequal treaties governing extraterritoriality, the 'standard of civilisation' remained in place (Schwarzenberger, 1955). Students of postcolonial studies have provided ample analyses of the ways in which the 'standard of civilisation' was utilised by some of the existing members to allow for and justify less-than-equal treatment of non-members (Anghie, 1999, 2005, also see Mamdani, 1996, 2001, Grovogui, 1996, 2006). Following World War II and the wave of de-colonisation, newly founded states, while recognised as equal members of the international society, soon found that they were 'yet to be admitted to its more exclusive inner circles and, as a result, [were] subject to updated versions of the European "standard of civilisation"' (Hindess, 2002: 133).

Such updated versions of the 'standard of civilisation' were sustained by a culture of imperialism. In *Culture and Imperialism* Edward W. Said (1993) argued that the culture of imperialism provided the grounds for some to claim the 'right' to 'better' rule, which crystallised in practices shaped by the 'standard of civilisation'. To quote Said:

> Most historians of empire speak of the 'age of empire' as formally beginning around 1878, with the 'scramble for Africa'. A closer look at the cultural actuality reveals a much earlier, more deeply and stubbornly held view about overseas European hegemony...There is first the authority of the European observer − traveler, merchant, scholar, historian, novelist. Then there is the hierarchy of spaces by which the metropolitan center and, gradually, the metropolitan economy are seen as dependent upon an overseas system of territorial control, economic exploitation, and a socio-cultural vision, without these stability and prosperity as home...would not be possible.

(Said, 1995: 36)

The discursive economy described by Said was produced through the twin processes of temporalisation of difference and spatialisation of time.

Temporalisation of difference refers to the 'temporal ordering of humanity' in the minds of the colonisers. Whereas Barry Hindess (2007: 328) traced to classical antiquity the ideas and categories behind the establishment of such 'temporal ordering of humanity', Siba Grovogui (1996) emphasised the significance of the encounter with the Americas. The year 1492 was a critical turning point in 'alterity and the ordering of the universe' in two ways, argued Grovogui (1996: 7): the 'discovery' of America and Americans, and Spain's defeat of African Moors. These two developments emboldened European actors towards envisioning a hierarchical universe on top of which they placed themselves.

Inquiring into the international in security 137

The Christian-inspired 'universe' was justified, then ordered into specific forms of knowledge within a totalizing ecclesiastical system that established hierarchical and exploitative relations between its Christian subjects and the other. This system appropriated the post-discovery Indian, Jew, African – or, more generally, the other – as mere objects of discourse to be 'settled down', stripped of essential communal rights within the European-dominated international order.

(Grovogui, 1996: 8)

Hindess, in turn, underscored the role played by categories and modes of thought already available to European thinkers of the time, namely ideas received from classical antiquity. Hindess wrote:

if the peoples of the New World and of the Old came to be located at different points within the one history, an important part of the reason must surely lie in the interpretative resources provided by the classical tradition. In addition to what appeared to be descriptive accounts of tribal peoples provided by Heredotus, Caesar, and Tacitus, the classics provided early European commentators on the Americas with a variety of broad interpretative schema.

(Hindess, 2007: 333)

This interpretative schema had two main aspects. One aspect was about viewing difference to be 'increasing roughly with distance' and another aspect was 'inversion, in which case others are seen as being what one is not' (see also, Davison, 2014). It was through making use of such an interpretative schema that was inherited from classical antiquity, argued Hindess (2007: 333), that 'America' and 'the Americas' were relegated to the past of 'Europe' and 'Europeans'. While 'the Americas' were labelled as the 'New World' in contrast to Europe's 'Old World', in 'European' thinking it was the 'New World' that was considered as belonging to the past. In time, 'non-Europeans' of the 'Old World' also found themselves relegated to the past.

Temporalising difference went hand in hand with a moralising attitude towards the past thereby resulting in what Hindess (2007) referred to as the emergence of 'derogatory temporalising difference'. Warranting such a moralising attitude towards 'others' was a linkage established between peoples' institutional development on the one hand and moral and intellectual development on the other: 'peoples who are some way behind the West in their institutional development will also be behind its inhabitants in their moral and intellectual capacities' (Hindess, 2007: 335). The culture of imperialism in general and the 'standard of civilisation' in particular were produced through this discursive economy.

To recap, I offer 'hierarchy in anarchical society' as a concept that captures the hierarchical as well as the anarchical and societal aspects of others' conception of the international as reflected in their 'discourses of danger'. As we saw in the

138 *Inquiring into the international in security*

first section, when considering the case of India, the hierarchical character of the society of states is experienced most acutely by those who are 'perched on the bottom rung' of world politics (Enloe, 1997). In offering this concept, I pay heed to John Hobson (2014) and Robert Vitalis's (2005) caution that mainstream IR, for all its stress on the anarchical character of the international, rests on a pre-existing hierarchy which goes unacknowledged (see Introduction). While there have been attempts to render visible the 'hierarchy in anarchy' (Donnelly, 2006) or 'hierarchy under anarchy' (Wendt and Friedheim, 2009) in recognition of 'inequalities' between states, their focus has thus far been on material (or military) inequalities and/or institutionalised relationships of dependency, to the neglect of inequalities that follow relegating one's contemporaries to the past by temporalising difference and spatialising time (Fabian, 1983, Hindess, 2007, Jabri, 2013, Bilgin 2016).

While Jack Donnelly's (2006, also see 1998) analysis does capture the 'standard of civilisation' as an aspect of 'hierarchy in anarchy', his analysis of contemporary world politics does not look at what he regards as 'inequalities without contemporary analogues'. Be that as it may, world politics is shaped by multiple inequalities conditioned by the twin processes of temporalising difference and spatialising time, which shape the way we 'see' the world while rendering less 'visible' their institutionalized effects. A case at hand is how the non- or new nuclear powers view the way nuclear proliferation is managed by the great powers: as a 'nuclear-apartheid'. As Shampa Biswas (2001) noted, this view of the non-proliferation regime points to the 'undemocratic character of international relations' as regards the governance of nuclear weapons. Such a 'racially institutionalized global hierarchy', as viewed by the new or non-nuclear powers, cannot be captured through analyses that focus on inequalities in material power alone but calls for inquiring into the discursive economy that 'determines' who can and cannot 'have' nuclear weapons.[2] Hence the concept I offer: 'hierarchy in anarchical society', which captures those inequalities that were once codified into the 'standard of civilisation' but persisted even after the end of colonialism. This chapter now turns to the case of Turkey's secularisation in the early decades of the Republic (1920s–1930s) to illustrate my point.

Inquiring into the international in security – the case of Turkey's secularisation (1920s–1930s)

The literature presumes that 'we already understand' Turkey's leaders' decision to secularise in the early decades of the twentieth century. Indeed, both the admirers and critics of the decision to secularise Turkey understand the underlying rationale to be 'modernisation'. The former's understanding is shaped by a 'universal' story about what once happened in 'Europe', i.e. secularisation as an essential component of modernisation (Hurd, 2004b).[3] The latter contest the relevance of a 'universal' story for Turkey, but point to 'particular' characteristics of Turkey's domestic politics in explaining why Turkey's leaders put the country on the path to secularisation, i.e. as part of power struggles between

Inquiring into the international in security 139

the 'centre' and the 'periphery'. In doing so, they leave untouched the assumptions behind the 'universal' story, only contesting its relevance for the Turkish context.

In what follows, I suggest that understanding Turkey's decision to secularise requires inquiring into its leaders' conceptions of the international as 'hierarchy in anarchical society' as located in the 'discourses of danger' that have (re)produced the securityness of secularism in Turkey. More specifically, I will offer an understanding of Turkey's decision to secularise as an attempt to address insecurities experienced vis-à-vis the international society.

Securityness of secularism in Turkey[4]

It is not only those who start from 'universal' stories about a relationship between secularisation and modernisation who presume that they 'already understand' Turkey's decision to secularise in the early twentieth century. It is also those who emphasise the 'particular' and underscore Turkey's 'specificities' who presume that they 'already' understand. The latter have maintained that secularism has always been considered as a security referent by Turkey's leaders who sought to safeguard it against those who were suspected of resisting the project of modernisation.[5] Indeed, well until the mid-2000s, secularism was treated as a key referent of 'national security' by Turkey's leaders who wrote *irtica* (obscurantist reactionarism) as a threat into the national security agenda.[6] Be that as it may, this is only part of the story about the securityness of secularism in Turkey. Inquiring into Turkey's leaders' discourses on secularism points to their conceptions of the international as conditioning the decision to secularise in a way that is 'differently different'.

This is not to suggest that secularism in Turkey or elsewhere can be reduced to in/security. Processes of secularisation have followed different trajectories in the United States, Western Europe and India, among others, in response to a variety of dynamics including but not limited to in/security (Bhargava, 1998, 2002, Hurd, 2004a, 2004b, 2008). Rather, the point here is that understanding the decision to secularise Turkey in terms of domestic factors alone misses an important set of dynamics. I locate this latter set of dynamics in the international and suggest that secularism was in part a response to the international society's ambivalence towards Turkey's 'difference' and the insecurities this entailed, as viewed by Turkey's leaders at the time.

That having been said, underscoring the significance of the international to Turkey's decision to secularise need not be viewed as underestimating the agency of Turkey's leaders.[7] On the contrary, when I locate the securityness of secularism (partly but not wholly) in the international, I seek to underscore the need for inquiring into the international as viewed through the lenses of domestic leaders, their conceptions of the international as shaped by (and shaping) their insecurities.

The argument proceeds as follows: I first look at three accounts that prevail in the literature. These accounts invariably focus on the particularities of

140 *Inquiring into the international in security*

Turkey's domestic politics.[8] Next, I highlight the international by looking at the discourses of Turkey's founding leaders and their recourse to the 'discourses of danger' in justifying Turkey's secularisation. Here, I lay out how Turkey's secularism can be read as a response to insecurities shaped by Turkey's leaders' self-understanding of Turkey as placed on the 'bottom rung' of the 'hierarchy in anarchical society' by virtue of the international society's ambivalence towards Turkey's 'difference'.

The 'domestic'

The literature on Turkey does not interrogate the securityness of secularism in Turkey but takes it for granted.[9] Whereas the rationale behind secularism's centrality to Turkey's domestic politics is discussed elaborately (Berkes, 1957, 1964, Cizre-Sakallıoğlu, 1996, Mardin, 1977, Toprak, 1981, 1988), the reason why such centrality is expressed via 'discourses of danger' is never questioned. The presumption being: 'we already understand'; it is about the struggle between those who seek to modernise Turkey and those who resist the project of modernisation. Where scholars disagree is regarding exactly who or what is being safeguarded through secularism, and against what or whom. Three accounts can be identified, namely, the 'separation' account; the 'control' account; and the 'material advancement' account.[10]

The 'separation' account

The 'separation' account considers secularism as both a constitutive principle and an outcome of the project of Republican transformation (Daver, 1955, Kili, 1980, 2003, Ozankaya, 1981, Tachau, 1984, Tanör, 1998, Yavuz, 1990). According to the proponents of this account, secularism was adopted as part of a project of modernisation by Turkey's founding leaders, who sought to separate the affairs of religion from those of the state, thereby pushing out the political and legal manifestations of Islam. The political and societal gains that ensued, according to this account, explain the centrality of secularism to Turkey's politics. Consider the following quote from the political scientist Suna Kili:

> In Atatürk's Turkey, in accordance with the requirements of modernization, religion and religious institutions were removed from areas, such as education and law, which did not fall within the proper sphere of their activity. And in their place, laic concepts and institutions were substituted. Historical experience with the religious groups' opposition to modernization had a profound impact on the formulation of the Atatürkist principle of laicism.
> (Kili, 2003: 244–245)

In Kili's formulation, religion and religious institutions are portrayed as blocking the path to modernisation; they are criticised for having hindered the progress of the Ottoman Empire and for disallowing attempts at reviving such progress,

Inquiring into the international in security 141

thereby rendering the Empire insecure. Other authors concur: the Ottoman experience had proven the futility of attempts to transform without secularisation (Ozankaya, 1981, Tachau, 1984, Yavuz, 1990).

The proponents of the 'separation' account, then, consider the threat to Turkey's security to be a possible revival of the Ottoman past; what is being protected is the Republic of Turkey as a project of modernisation. The security-ness of secularism, in this account, rests on: (1) secularism's having allowed the project of modernisation through separating religiously justified arguments and scientifically justified arguments, and pushing the former outside the realm of politics and education; (2) its having helped to secure the project of modernisa-tion against the future assails of those who might seek to reimpose the *Shari'ah* upon society and politics, thereby putting the gains of modernisation at risk.

The 'control' account

Although scholars disagree as regards the reasons for and the agents of 'control', their arguments converge in explaining the centrality of secularism with reference to the role it has played in disciplining the opposition, thereby keeping on track a particular vision of transformation (Cizre-Sakallıoğlu, 1996, Gülalp, 2005, Keyder, 1987, 2004, Mardin, 1977, Rustow, 1957, Toprak, 1981, 1988). According to political scientist Binnaz Toprak (1981), secularism in Turkey served not to sepa-rate religion and politics (as in the 'Western' model of church–state separation) but to 'control' religion for the purposes of the government in office while casting in an unfavourable light the opposition's resort to religiously justified arguments and/or actions. This was because, Toprak wrote,

> religion in Turkey, especially during the formative years of the Republic, had been the most important centrifugal force with a potential to challenge the state. It is partly for this reason that the separation of religion and state was never attempted in its Western version as Orthodox Islam was put under state control and made subservient to state authority.
>
> (Toprak, 1988: 120)

Since the opposition tapped this 'centrifugal force' and employed religiously justified arguments, suggested Toprak, the state resorted to using secularism to control religion, the ultimate aim being safeguarding the founding leaders' vision for transformation in Turkey. In variations of this account, political scientist Şerif Mardin (1977, 1982) traced the state practice of 'controlling' religion back to Ottoman practices; political economist Çağlar Keyder (1987) synthesised the insights of Toprak's 'control' and Mardin's (1973) 'centre–periphery' arguments and maintained that, following the initiation of secularism in the early Republican period, Turkey's particular conception and practices of secularism have allowed the 'centre' to keep the 'periphery' at bay throughout the Republican era.

The 'control' account, then, identifies those alternative visions of transformation that tapped religion as the threat; what is being safeguarded is the particular

142 *Inquiring into the international in security*

vision of transforming Turkey conceived by Atatürk and his closest associates. The securityness of secularism, accordingly, rests on the latter having allowed: (1) marginalising those who favoured alternative visions; (2) underpinning Atatürk and his closest associates' vision of transforming Turkey by controlling religion as they saw fit.

The 'material advancement' account

The third and lesser-known account was offered by political scientists Andrew Davison and Taha Parla, who rejected both the 'separation' and 'control' accounts. Historicising the self-understandings and justifications of Atatürk and his closest associates, Davison and Parla explained Turkey's secularisation as an attempt to institute 'certain separations in a context of overall control' (Davison, 1998: 163). Against those who propound the 'control' account, Parla and Davison (2004) insisted that the founding leaders' exercise of control involved seeking a degree of separation. However, they also pointed out – in contrast to the proponents of the 'separation' account – that this was not the same as the practice of separation of church and state as found in some other contexts.[11] Atatürk and his closest associates' understanding of secularism, they argued, was a unique mix of 'separation' and 'control' designed to make something else possible: material advancement. There resides the centrality of secularism in Turkey's politics according to Davison and Parla: in the realm of national economic development. It is worth quoting the authors at length:

> In accordance with the RPP's [Republican People's Party] reading of the requirements of contemporary civilisation; and to secure the RPP's hege- mony and definition of national aims in legal, social, educational, cultural and economic matters; and to gain respect for national sovereignty in the internal and external political circumstances in which the national move- ment existed; religion was removed from its previous position of power, separated in this sense, overdefining the theory and practice of legal, social, cultural, and economic spheres wherein it was seen as a fetter, causing arbitrary, confused, primitive, and medieval governance, lethargy, and harmful ills to the people of the Turkish nation.
>
> (Parla and Davison, 2004: 172–173)

A careful hermeneutic analysis of the founding leaders' discourses led Davison and Parla to conclude that they considered it essential to turn to secularism if Turkey were to succeed as a state. The centrality of secularism for Turkey, according to this account, rests in secularism having allowed Turkey's devel- opment at a particular historical period where rapid 'material advancement' was deemed crucial for its survival.

Davison and Parla, then, identify the threat to Turkey's security as the prospect of failing to 'achieve success in the material world' (Davison, 1998: 165, Parla and Davison, 2004: 118–125); what is being safeguarded is the future of the

Republic as an economically successful independent sovereign state. As such, Davison and Parla hinted at the significance of the international political and economic context for shaping the centrality of secularism for Turkey's development (see below). However, their 'material advancement' account did not consider the encounters with the international society as shaping such centrality but focused on the need for 'development'.

To recapitulate, what is common to all three accounts – irrespective of their differences regarding who or what secularism has helped to safeguard, and against what or whom – is their portrayal of the centrality of secularism vis-à-vis actual or imminent domestic threats. The implication being that the centrality of secularism to Turkey's politics (and the securityness of such centrality) was a function of the 'domestic'.

The 'international'

This following section briefly examines the extent to which the literature has considered the international in accounting for the centrality of secularism in Turkey. I will go through the three accounts discussed above to see whether/ how they incorporate the international. Insofar as they overlook the international, I suggest, they fall short of accounting fully for the intimate historical relationship between secularism and security in Turkey. Finally, I will look at Turkey's founding leaders' 'discourses of danger' to show how Turkey's turn to secularism in part was a response to their conceptions of the international as 'hierarchy in international society'.

The 'international' in the literature on Turkey

When they factor in international dynamics – if they do so at all – the proponents of the three accounts introduced above focus on Turkey's diplomatic concerns. While the 'separation' account refers to diplomatic concerns in explaining the rationale for the abolition of the Caliphate, the 'control' account mentions it only in passing. The 'material advancement' account goes further than the other two and points to the founding leaders' search for legitimacy in the international arena for the new Republic. None of the three accounts inquire into Turkey's leaders' conceptions of the international.[12]

According to the proponents of the 'separation' account, the international dimension of the decision to secularise Turkey was secondary to the domestic dimension and was limited to diplomatic concerns about the caliphate and its abolition. The Ottoman sultans had acquired the right to use the title of caliph when they defeated the Mamluk Sultanate in 1517, but did so infrequently, with the exception of Sultan Abdülhamid II during the nineteenth century. The caliphate was abolished by the Republican leaders on 3 March 1924 by an Act of Parliament. In explaining this act, scholars who propound the 'separation' account have maintained that the caliphate had to be abolished because it had become a burden for Turkey's diplomatic relations, particularly with those

144 *Inquiring into the international in security*

colonial powers (such as Great Britain) that ruled over Muslim peoples. Kili referred to (author and public intellectual) Halide Edip Adıvar's 1930 rendering of the early days of the Republic to explain such concerns on the part of the founding leaders. According to Adıvar, who was one of the leading figures of the nationalist struggle,[13] the Caliphate was complicating relations with colonial powers of Europe. In her words, these powers

> either suspected Turkey constantly of scheming against their sovereignty, or else they themselves were involved in intrigue in Turkey in order to get control of the caliphate and use it on behalf of their own ambitions.
>
> (Adıvar cited in Kili, 2003: 356)

Drawing on Adıvar's testament, Kili maintained that the abolition of the Caliphate removed not only the grounds for such interference into Turkey's affairs, but also a cloud of suspicion regarding the ambitions of the founding leaders by making it clear that their ambitions were confined to the boundaries of Turkey.

The proponents of the 'separation' account thus point to one important aspect of the international dimension to Turkey's turn to secularism, the Ottoman legacy. In particular, the legacy of Sultan Abdülhamid II's use of Islam for purposes of legitimacy and empowerment in the international realm[14] carried the potential to complicate the diplomatic relations of the young Republic at a time it sought to re-locate itself as a full member of the international society. While the Ottoman Empire had joined the 'Concert of Europe' after 1856, it was not treated as a full and equal member of the international society, as evinced by the persistence of extraterritoriality agreements and others' interventions in the affairs of the Empire. Turkey's early Republican leaders sought to locate Turkey firmly in the international society, thereby removing the ground for such interventionism. Adıvar's references to international 'intrigues' and the Republic's hard-won 'sovereignty' intimate at the securityness of the decision to abolish the Caliphate.[15]

While the 'separation' account's interest in the international remains limited to Turkey's diplomatic relations, the 'control' account leaves even less room for the international. The centrality of secularism to Turkey's politics and the securityness of such centrality are explained with reference to domestic struggles amongst the founding leaders and their successors. Indeed, the decision to abolish the Caliphate was, at the time, one of the breaking points in the struggle between Mustafa Kemal and his opponents (İnalcık, 2006). From the 'separation' perspective, such domestic factors alone suffice in understanding the securityness of secularism in Turkey. However, as with the Ottoman intelligentsia debating the future of the Empire (see above), such struggles were shaped by Mustafa Kemal and his opponents' conceptions of the international. While references to such debates are available in historical accounts on the late Ottoman Empire and early Republican Turkey (İnalcık, 2006, Ortaylı, 1983), they are seldom tapped by scholars to inquire into Turkey's leaders' conceptions of the international.

Inquiring into the international in security 145

Finally, the 'material advancement' account is singular in terms of the emphasis it puts on the international context in explaining how the turn to secularism was instrumental in the founding leaders' search for international legitimacy for the new Republic. Indeed, Davison and Parla considered Turkey's turn to secularism in the early Republican era not only as a part of the broader project of national economic development, but also as an integral aspect of the overall strategy that made room for the project of 'national economic development' by pursuing abroad a 'political and rhetorical legitimation strategy' for the young Republic (Parla and Davison, 2004: 116–125). That said, neither Davison nor Parla elaborated on these concerns beyond historicising and contextualising Turkey's particular conception and practices of secularism ('certain separations in a context of overall control'; Parla and Davison, 2004: 102–104). Nor did their 'material advancement' account consider the encounters with the international society as shaping the centrality of secularism for Turkey. The explanatory power of the international, in the 'material advancement' account, is noteworthy yet limited.

The 'international' in the discourses of Turkey's leaders

Secularism was written into the Constitution of the Republic of Turkey in 1937. Notwithstanding my characterisation of Turkey's secularisation as a 'decision' made by the leaders, secularism in Turkey is better understood as a 'process' encompassing a series of decisions beginning with the abolition of the Caliphate in 1924, and continuing with the abolition of the *Shari'ah* and the *medrese* system (traditional schools where religion was the basis of instruction) in 1924; Islam being written out of the constitution in 1928; the adoption of a 'Western-style' dress code in 1925, a new civil code (from Switzerland) and the Gregorian calendar in 1926, the Latin alphabet and script in 1928, the metric system in 1931, last names and the observance of Sunday as a holiday in 1934, and a new criminal code (from Italy) in 1936. In what follows, I will look at two of these steps: the adoption of the 'Western' style 'hat' as headgear and the new civil code adopted from Switzerland. Whereas the hat law was about becoming 'similar' in outside appearance, the civil code was more about substance. Taken together, these two steps highlighted two complementary aspects of Turkey's leaders' search for joining the 'contemporary civilisation' by becoming 'similar'. They justified these efforts through recourse to 'discourses of danger' by invoking insecurities generated by previous encounters with the international society and its 'standard of civilisation', referred to, in a text no less significant than Turkey's national anthem, as 'the one-toothed monster called civilisation'.

'The one-toothed monster called civilisation' refers to European great powers of the time. Turkey's national anthem was penned by the poet Mehmet Akif Ersoy during the war of national liberation (1919–1922) and adopted by the Grand National Assembly in 1921. Here are the relevant lines of the 41-verse poem:

146 *Inquiring into the international in security*

> The lands of the West may be armored with walls of steel
> But I have borders guarded by the mighty chest of a believer.
> Recognize your innate strength, my friend! And think: how can this fiery
>   faith ever be killed
> By that battered, one-toothed monster you call civilization?

Rather than rejecting the 'standard of civilisation' that temporalised difference and spatialised time, thereby relegating the Ottomans to the past by virtue of their 'difference', the Republican leaders sought to locate Turkey in this very 'civilisation'. Yet, as will be seen below, the very 'civilisation' they sought to locate Turkey in was represented as a source of in/security.

THE CIVIL CODE

In 1926 a new civil code was adopted by adapting from the Swiss civil code. Consider the justifications offered by the then justice minister Mahmut Esat (Bozkurt) on the occasion of the adoption of the civil code:

> Particularly in those states that are made up of citizens belonging to different religions, it is a must for national sovereignty purposes that the state delinks law and religion – that is, if it is to enforce a single body of law. Because if laws were to be based on religion, a state that recognizes the freedom of conscience would then have to make separate laws for its citizens of different religious creeds. This, in turn, would go against the principle of political, societal and national unity that is warranted by contemporary statehood. It is important to underscore that the state is in interaction with not only its own citizens but also foreigners. In that case there arises the necessity to agree to the imposition of capitulations to regulate their behaviour. This was the most significant aspect of the rationale put forward by our counterparts during the Lausanne Treaty negotiations to make a case for the continuation of the capitulations.
>
> (Bozkurt, 2008: 103–104)

Bozkurt's words underscored Turkey's insecurities vis-à-vis the international society as viewed by the leadership: preventing external interference into the affairs of the state on behalf of non-Muslim citizens, thereby safeguarding Turkey's sovereignty. Bozkurt might have expected his words to resonate with a generation who had, in their formative years, observed the Ottoman Empire's struggle with extraterritoriality treaties, referred to as 'capitulations' in the Ottoman context.

While capitulations were 'granted' at a time when the Ottoman Empire was at the height of its power, during the years of decline, they were utilised towards various ends by the citizens of the members of the international society (Hanioğlu, 2008). Yet, the fact that those who were seeking to live outside the laws of the Empire were not always settlers from international society member

Inquiring into the international in security   147

states but some of the Empire's own non-Muslim 'subjects' added a layer of complexity to inter-communal relations in Ottoman lands. Inter-communal relations in the Empire had already become fragile during the nineteenth century, as the Ottoman leadership's outlook towards its non-Muslim peoples began to undergo a transformation in tandem with the debates regarding the future of the Empire (Braude and Lewis, 1982a, 1982b). During this period, Ottoman leaders made several attempts to resolve the issue of non-Muslim 'subjects' and the protection of their rights, but failed to introduce a lasting solution (Üstel, 2001).

The issue of capitulations and the legal status of non-Muslim peoples in Turkey came up during the peace negotiations in Lausanne (1922–1923) and turned out to be one of the thorniest issues. Particularly distressful for the team representing Turkey had been their European counterparts' reasoning that the capitulations had to remain in place, because 'Turkey was a backward country and still under Islamic law.'[16] The Empire's European counterparts' propaganda efforts during the war of national liberation and the difficulties encountered during the Lausanne peace negotiations had already driven home the lesson that winning the war on the battlefield and the negotiating table was not enough; the grounds for the international society's claim to better rule also had to be removed. The renowned Ottoman historian Halil İnalcık highlighted the twin struggle Turkey's leaders were leading at the negotiating table and in Anatolian village halls. During this period, wrote İnalcık, there were striking similarities

> between Turkish claims to be a fully independent modern nation-state and as such to ask for equal treatment at Lausanne, and Kemal's promises of taking radical measures to modernise Turkey during his Anatolian tour in 1923.[17]

Pointing to both the fragility of formal recognition by the international society, and the potential insecurities that were likely to follow in the eventuality of the withdrawal of such recognition, Mustafa Kemal (Atatürk) set the goal of locating Turkey in the 'contemporary civilisation' (i.e. becoming 'similar') as a solution.

What is significant to underscore here is that 'similarity' was not sought in outward appearance alone. Turkey's leaders set in motion a plan that involved organising a conference on national economy (to affirm Turkey's commitment to liberal economy), convening of a committee for legal reforms (to signal the intention to adopt 'European' law in civil matters), and going on a tour of Anatolia to make the case for Turkey's transformation.

The background to Turkey's leaders' search for 'similarity' with the international society, then, was shaped by their experiences during the final decades of the Ottoman Empire. During that period, the 'right to interfere' on behalf of non-Muslim peoples of the Empire had been justified by the members of international society on the basis of the role religious difference/s played in Ottoman

148 *Inquiring into the international in security*

governance. The founding leaders of the Republic worried about reliving the experiences of the late Ottoman Empire in terms of interventionism by the international society on behalf of the non-Muslim peoples (Deringil, 1998: 112–134). Through secularising the country, Turkey's leaders sought to ensure that the international society would accept that non-Muslim peoples in Turkey were no longer in need of a special legal status to secure their rights and freedoms. Adoption of a new and secular civil code from 'Europe' they thought, would show that the new Republic could guarantee the rights and freedoms of non-Muslims along with the rights and freedoms of the overwhelmingly Muslim majority of the populace. The point being that the decision to adopt the secular civil code was made against a background of insecurities Turkey's leaders experienced in their encounters with the international society during the late Ottoman times, the war of national liberation and the Lausanne peace negotiations. The search for 'similarity' through the adoption and adaptation of the Swiss civil code was a 'differently different' way of responding to Turkey's non-military and non-specific insecurities at the time.

THE 'HAT LAW'

The so-called 'hat law' was proclaimed on 25 November 1925, banning the use of the fez, the traditional male headgear. This change was put into practice as part of the broader effort to adopt what was portrayed as 'Western' style of dressing. The move was designed partly to help unify the society by removing religious symbols as markers of difference within the society (Kili, 2003: 172). During the Ottoman period, different religious groups in the society (ordered within the *Millet* system) could be distinguished by their style of dress and headgear. Adopting a single headgear for men was expected to help to remove a marker of (religious) differences inside Turkey.

Still, the decision was publicly justified through recourse to 'discourses of danger' – not only in terms of the threat of societal fragmentation at home (as the rationale above suggests), but also in terms of survival vis-à-vis the international society, which, in the eyes of Turkey's leaders, was ambivalent about Turkey's 'difference'. As will be seen below, removing the external markers of Turkey's 'difference' as such, and becoming 'similar' were central to Turkey's Republican transformation. In the early years of the Republic, Turkey's leaders came to consider the 'fez' as one obvious symbol that marked their 'difference' from 'contemporary civilisation'. As such, its removal was considered to be of utmost importance.[18]

After the declaration of the Republic, the hat was adopted as a headgear for men as part of a series of reforms regarding the adoption of what was viewed as 'Western' style dressing in Turkey. At the time, Turkey's leaders sought to justify the adoption of the hat as headgear as a move that would symbolise to the world, that Turkey was no longer 'different' from them.

Consider the following quotes from an article published in the government-friendly newspaper *Cumhuriyet* in 1925. The author of the article maintained

Inquiring into the international in security   149

that the 'hat law' gave the following messages to the rest of the world: that the Turk was no longer different but similar to 'them'; that the Turk also 'has the right to live and be happy'; and that 'the Turk is a whole new world, with no difference from yours...The Turk is a person like you, wishing to make use of the fruits of civilisation'. The author maintained that adopting the hat as headgear was helpful in getting these messages across because 'it was easier to show what was outside one's head compared to what was inside' (cited in Mert, 1998: 211, also see Berkes, 1964: 473–474). The point being that the author of this article portrayed the matter of adopting a 'Western' style hat as headgear not as a matter of style, but as a matter of survival vis-à-vis the international society. The points he raised, in turn, were invariably reproduced from the speeches Mustafa Kemal delivered in two different Anatolian locations, Kastamonu and İnebolu, in the summer of 1925, introducing the hat in particular and 'Western' style dressing in general to the public. Needless to say, Mustafa Kemal's speeches, too, invoked insecurities experienced vis-à-vis the international society as the rationale behind the proclamation of the hat law (Nereid, 2011).

One incident that symbolised the securityness of the hat law for Turkey's leaders took place in 1925. Shortly after the passing of the hat law, those who were already sceptical about the new Republic's reforms used this as a pretext to stage an uprising in the Black Sea region of Turkey. While the uprising was immediately suppressed, the government chose to send the cruiser *Hamidiye* to bombard the Black Sea town of Rize, firing blank cartridges. In time, the incident became a staple of popular culture and was turned into a popular song that goes as follows:

> don't fire Hamidiye, don't fire
> we'll wear the hat
> don't fire Hamidiye, don't fire
> we'll pay our taxes

The point being that while it is possible to dismiss the above-quoted portrayal of the hat (as symbolising the Turks' message to the world that they had a 'right to live and be happy') as governed by the whim of one newspaper author, the *Hamidiye* incident showed that Turkey's leaders at the time were prepared to back up their 'discourses of danger' with military force if necessary.

No such hat law governing women's headgear was passed. The method of 'discouraging the veil' was adopted as a way of helping more women to integrate into different aspects of societal life (Çalışlar, 2006). While sporadic instances of local authorities' interferences vis-à-vis women wearing the veil were reported, women's headgear was considered an 'issue' to be resolved in time, by 'making it disadvantageous for any but the old [to wear the veil/headscarf]' (Berkes, 1964: 474).[19]

Yet there was no mistaking the role played by concerns about the international when Atatürk's closest associate and the second President of the Republic,

150 *Inquiring into the international in security*

İsmet İnönü 'encouraged' his wife Mevhibe (İnönü) Hanım to drop the veil (*çarşaf*) when he invited her to accompany him to the peace negotiations in Lausanne. İnönü was the head of the Turkish delegation at the Lausanne peace negotiations (1922–1923). When inviting his wife to be at his side at Lausanne, İnönü expressed his wish for Mevhibe Hanım to set an example for women at home *and* represent the fresh face of the Republic abroad. Decades later, relating those days to her granddaughter, Mevhibe Hanım expressed both her personal trauma about dropping the veil for the first time, and her decisiveness about playing her role for advancing the 'national cause' (Bilgehan, 1994).

That having been said, the politics of women's veil was a complex issue then (as it is now) (see, for example, Göle, 1996). While Mevhibe Hanım was asked to represent abroad the fresh face of a modernising Turkey, Mustafa Kemal's own wife, Latife Hanım wore a headscarf all throughout her short-lived marriage. There is no mistaking the politics of her choice of headgear during her marriage to Mustafa Kemal; she is reported not to have worn the headscarf before her marriage, or after her divorce (Çalışlar, 2006). The point being, the leaders of the Republic were walking a tightrope at home and abroad to pursue the efforts towards transforming Turkey and joining the 'civilisation'. It was important for Mevhibe Hanım to represent abroad the fresh face of Turkey in Lausanne. It was equally important for Latife Hanım to avoid becoming a fodder for the anti-transformation propaganda at home.

What is significant about these particular examples is not that the symbolism of headgear was made use of, but that such symbolism was justified by invoking Turkey's insecurities vis-à-vis the international society. The adoption of the hat law and İnönü's personal request to his wife Mevhibe Hanım were both framed in terms of the survival of the state, and not as mere lifestyle choices. The leaders of the new Republic as a new entrant to the international society sought 'similarity', and justified their efforts through recourse to 'discourses of danger'.

To recapitulate, through inquiring into Turkey's early Republican leaders' conceptions of the international, we understand how the international society (that the English School pointed to as securing international order under anarchy) was considered by Turkey's leaders as a source of in/security. Second, Turkey's leaders' secularisation efforts were designed partly (but not wholly) to address their insecurities vis-à-vis the international society. Becoming similar by meeting the 'standard of civilisation' came across as a way of addressing Turkey's non-specific and non-military insecurities (Bilgin, 2009, 2012).

The threat to the Republic was non-military in that the gains of Turkey's national struggle had been sealed through the Lausanne Treaty in 1923. Yet, while the Lausanne Treaty had reaffirmed Turkey's hard-won sovereignty, independence and territorial integrity, Turkey's leaders were nevertheless concerned about the fragility of such recognition. Accordingly, the threat they sought to respond to was non-specific in that they were not targeting a specific act of a specific counterpart. Rather, their policies were designed to respond to what the future might bring, based on the leaders' remembrances of the past and interpretations of the present (Bilgin, 2009).

Conclusion

Chapter 5 responded to the first question that the book began with: '*How to think about security in a world characterised by a multiplicity of inequalities and differences*'. By reflecting on others' conceptions of the international as we study security, I responded. The method I adopted was to locate others' conceptions of international in their 'discourses of danger' (Campbell, 1992) – 'the international in security'. The first and second sections elaborated on the need for re-thinking that (we presume that) 'we already understand'. Building on Abraham's analysis of India's search for nuclear statehood, I inquired into India's leaders' conceptions of the international through analysing their 'discourses of danger'. I suggested that we understand new entrants' emulation of the existing members of the international society as part of their attempt to address those insecurities shaped by (and shaping) their conception of the international as hierarchical. Here, I offered the concept of 'hierarchy in anarchical society' as capturing all three aspects of the international as experienced by 'others'. The third section illustrated this point by offering a reading of Turkey's secularisation in the early twentieth century as part of an attempt to address non-military and non-specific insecurities that the country's leadership experienced in their encounters with the international society.

Before concluding this chapter, a caveat is in order: The argument here is not to downplay the significance of postcolonial studies scholars' interrogation of the 'relevance' of stories about what once happened in Europe for our considerations on what happened elsewhere. That assumptions about the relevance of such stories need deconstructing is a point made forcefully by Sankaran Krishna (1999), and I follow. Nor is it my aim to underplay the need for interrogating the 'accuracy' (for want of a better word) of our stories about what once happened in 'Europe'. As Sandra Halperin (1997, 2006) argued, those stories constitute misleading foundations for understanding the study of International Relations. Questioning the 'relevance' and 'accuracy' of stories about what once happened in 'Europe' (and elsewhere) is an essential component of addressing the limits of IR.

This chapter highlighted how new entrants' emulation of the existing members could be viewed as a deceptively 'similar' yet altogether 'different' way devised by 'others' in addressing insecurities of the non-military and non-specific kind (Bilgin, 2008c). Over the years, prevalent notions of 'statehood' were adopted by many in response to an international society that rendered as acceptable only certain ways of 'being a state' (Finnemore, 1996: 332). Whereas Japan emulated members of the international society by increasing its military might and acquiring colonies in Asia; Turkey (after the declaration of the Republic) and India (after independence) adopted the 'nation-state' model, sought to build their own citizenship regimes, and pursued strategies of 'development'. In all three cases, there was an attempt by a new or non-member to follow what was viewed as the 'European' example of 'being a state'. The broader point being, new entrants' adoption of models of 'adequate'

152 *Inquiring into the international in security*

statehood and insecurities that followed cannot be understood outside of the context of anti-colonial struggle for some, and the struggle for recognition as an equal member of the international society by the others.

Notes

1 Needless to say, underscoring new entrants' experiences with hierarchy is not meant to overlook their agency vis-à-vis the international society, but to highlight the limits of the agency they exercised against the background of their conception of the international as 'hierarchy in anarchical society'.

2 On race and/in IR, see Chowdhry and Nair (2002), Grovogui (1996, 2001), Krishna (2001), Shilliam (2008).

3 On the 'multiple modernities' literature that contests this story, see Eisenstadt (2000), Göle (2000) (cf. Katzenstein, 2006). For a critique of the 'multiple modernities' literature that nevertheless contests assumptions of secularisation being an essential component of modernisation, see Bhambra (2007). For alternative perspectives on secularisation, see Asad (2003), Bhargava (1998, 2002).

4 This section draws on Bilgin (2008b).

5 I use the term 'secularism' as opposed to the more appropriate 'laicism', while recognising that Turkey's interpretation and practices do not exactly fit either Anglo-Saxon models of secularism or the French laïcité. Even though Turkey's version of secularism was modelled after France (as evinced in the use of the word *laiklik*), the experiences of the past 80 years have deviated from the French ideal type (Asad, 2003, Hurd, 2004b, Taylor, 1998). Although I agree with Davison (2003: 334) on the point that Turkey's self-understanding and practices are better captured with the concept of laicism than with the concept of secularism', I have nevertheless chosen to use 'secularism' in reference to Turkey's *laiklik* to avoid further complicating the narrative.

6 Inquiring into the securityness of secularism is not meant to question whether 'obscurantist reactionarism' constitutes a threat to security in Turkey or elsewhere. Rather, my analysis of Turkey's case uncovers an intimate historical relationship between secularism and security.

7 Indeed, I part ways with the 'multiple modernities' accounts that emphasise the possibility of 'others' experimenting with different ways of being 'modern' (Eisenstadt, 2000, Katzenstein, 2006), and follow Gurminder Bhambra's (2007) call for studying modernity as a product of 'connected histories'. That said, such a stance need not be viewed as negating the agency of domestic leadership.

8 My task here is one of drawing out what often remains unarticulated in the literature, and articulating this in security terms. At one level, there is no need for translation as such, for these writings are suffused with 'discourses of danger'. At another level, there is a need for translation, because the literature discusses threats without explicitly identifying who or what the referent objects are. Accordingly, the differences between the three accounts regarding who or what is being safeguarded, and against whom or what remain unarticulated. Since 2002, Justice and Development Party leadership has adopted a somewhat different stance on the securityness of secularism. For a discussion, see Bilgin (2008a).

9 Those rare studies that scrutinise the securityness of secularism do this within the framework of civil–military relations and focus on the agency of the Military and the General Secretariat of the National Security Council (until the latter was placed firmly under civilian control). See Tank (2005).

10 The first two are adopted, in modified form, from Davison (1998). The third is my characterisation of the alternative explanation offered by Davison and Parla (Davison, 1998, Parla and Davison, 2004).

Inquiring into the international in security   153

11 See Chatterjee (1998) for a similar discussion with reference to India.
12 There is yet another explanation, the 'conspiracy theory' version that explains many of the reforms of the early Republican era, including the decision to secularise, as a 'secret deal' struck between Turkey's leaders and the allied powers as a precondition for signing the Lausanne treaty. Given how the absence of evidence serves as evidence to justify the validity of conspiracy theories, it is impossible to dis/prove such explanations. What is important for purposes here is that the proponents of conspiracy theories as such fail to account for the discursive economy that (presumably) made possible for the allied powers to put pressure on Turkey on this very issue and that Turkey's leaders (presumably) proved susceptible to such pressure. Put differently, such conspiratorial accounts miss the fabric of the international even as they seek to place agency at the international level.
13 On Adivar, see Adak (2003).
14 On this discussion, see Deringil (1998: 16–43).
15 One of Atatürk's closest associates, Falih Rıfkı Atay (1980 [1961]) provides further evidence in this regard.
16 Cited in Davison (1998). On Lausanne negotiations, see Karacan (1943), Heper (1998).
17 See İnalcık (2006).
18 It is useful to note that the 'fez' was not 'authentic' Ottoman headgear but imported from North Africa during the early nineteenth century as part of an earlier modernisation effort by Sultan Mahmut II (Quataert, 1997). At the time, the fez was adopted to remove a marker of religious differences among the men within the Ottoman Empire. Soon, many Muslim and non-Muslim men began to wear the fez. Indeed, the Ottoman Empire was changing so rapidly in the course of a few decades that by the end of the nineteenth century, the fez had become the only wardrobe item that distinguished the Ottoman civil and military officials from their 'European' counterparts.
19 It is worth noting in passing that it was not until the 1970s that students wearing a headscarf sought to enter institutions of higher education in Turkey. At the time they were portrayed by some as a marker of 'resistance' against the project of modernity. The point being that, the fact that the headscarf 'issue' has marked the frontline in domestic battles on secularism since the 1970s need not detract us from understanding the significance of the international in the early twentieth century. The international as viewed by the leaders of the early Republican era, is almost always excluded by present-day discussions on these subjects. As such, our analyses end up missing an important part of the picture on Turkey's secularisation in the early Republican period.

Bibliography

Abraham, I. 1998. *The Making of the Indian Atomic Bomb: Science, Secrecy and the Postcolonial State*, New York, Zed Books.

Abraham, I. 2000. Landscape and Postcolonial Science. *Contributions to Indian Sociology*, 34, 163–187.

Abraham, I. 2006. The Ambivalence of Nuclear Histories. *Osiris*, 6, 49–65.

Abraham, I. (ed.) 2009. *South Asian Cultures of the Bomb: Atomic Publics and the State in India and Pakistan*, Bloomington & Indianapolis, Indiana University Press.

Adak, H. 2003. National Myths and Self-Na(rra)tions. *South Atlantic Quarterly*, 102, 509–527.

Alperovitz, G. 1965. *Atomic Diplomacy: Hiroshima and Potsdam: The Use of the Atomic Bomb and the American Confrontation with Soviet Power*, New York, Simon and Schuster.

154 Inquiring into the international in security

Anghie, A. 1999. Finding the Peripheries: Sovereignty and Colonialism in Nineteenth-Century International Law. *Harvard International Law Journal*, 40, 1–71.

Anghie, A. 2005. *Imperialism, Sovereignty, and the Making of International Law*, Cambridge, Cambridge University Press.

Asad, T. 2003. *Formations of the Secular: Christianity, Islam, Modernity*, Stanford, Stanford University Press.

Atay, F. R. 1980 [1961]. *Çankaya*, Ankara, Bateş.

Berkes, N. 1957. Historical Background of Turkish Secularism. In: Frye, R. N. (ed.) *Islam and the West; Proceedings of the Harvard Summer School Conference on the Middle East*, July 25–27, 1955. 'S-Gravenhage: Mouton & Co.

Berkes, N. 1964. *The Development of Secularism in Turkey*, Montreal, McGill University Press.

Bhambra, G. K. 2007. Multiple Modernities or Global Interconnections: Understanding the Global Post the Colonial. In: Karagiannis, N. & Wagner, P. (eds.) *Varieties of World-Making: Beyond Globalization*, Liverpool, Liverpool University Press, 59–73.

Bhargava, R. 1998. What is Secularism For? In: Bhargava, R. (ed.) *Secularism and its Critics*, Delhi, Oxford University Press.

Bhargava, R. 2002. What is Indian Secularism and What is it for? *India Review*, 1, 1–32.

Bilgehan, G. 1994. *Mevhibe*, Ankara, Bilgi.

Bilgin, P. 2008a. The Politics of Security and Secularism in Turkey: From the Early Republican Era to EU Accession Negotiations. In: Jung, D. & Rauderve, K. (eds.) *Religion, Politics and Turkey's EU Accession*, London, Palgrave.

Bilgin, P. 2008b. The Securityness of Secularism? The Case of Turkey. *Security Dialogue*, 39: 593–614.

Bilgin, P. 2008c. Thinking Past 'Western' IR? *Third World Quarterly*, 29, 5–23.

Bilgin, P. 2009. Securing Turkey through Western-Oriented Foreign Policy. *New Perspectives on Turkey*, 40, 105–125.

Bilgin, P. 2012. Globalization and In/security: Middle Eastern Encounters with International Society and the Case of Turkey. In: Stetter, S. (ed.) *The Middle East and Globalization: Encounters and Horizons*, New York, Palgrave Macmillan.

Bilgin, P. 2016. Temporalizing Security: Securing the Citizen, Insecuring the Immigrant in the Mediterranean. In: Agathangelou, A. M. & Killian, K. D. (eds.) *Time, Temporality and Violence in International Relations: (De) Fatalizing the Present, Forging Radical Alternatives*, London, Routledge.

Bilgin, P. & Ince, B. 2015. Security and Citizenship in the Global South: In/securing Citizens in Early Republican Turkey (1923–1946). *International Relations*, 29, 500–520.

Biswas, S. 2001. 'Nuclear Apartheid' as Political Position: Race as a Postcolonial Resource? *Alternatives: Global, Local, Political*, 26, 485–522.

Bowden, B. 2004. In the Name of Progress and Peace: The 'Standard of Civilization' and the Universalizing Project. *Alternatives: Global, Local, Political*, 29, 43–68.

Bozkurt, M. E. 2008. 'Medeni Kanun Esbabı Mucibe Lâyihası' [Rationale for the Civil Code]. In: N.A. (ed.) *Mahmut Esat Bozkurt Anısına Armağan (1892–1943)*, İstanbul, İstanbul Barosu Yayınları.

Braude, B. & Lewis, B. 1982a. *Christians and Jews in the Ottoman Empire: The Functioning of a Plural Society Vol. I*, New York, Holmes and Meier Publishers.

Braude, B. & Lewis, B. 1982b. *Christians and Jews in the Ottoman Empire: The Functioning of a Plural Society Vol. II*, New York, Holmes and Meier Publishers.

Bull, H. 1977. *The Anarchical Society: A Study of Order in World Politics*, London, Macmillan.

Bull, H. 1984. Foreword. In: Gong, G. W. *The Standard of 'Civilization' in International Society*, Oxford, Clarendon Press.

Bull, H. & Watson, A. (eds.) 1984. *The Expansion of International Society*, Oxford, Clarendon Press.

Buzan, B. 2001. The English School: An Underexploited Resource in IR. *Review of International Studies*, 27, 471–488.

Buzan, B. 2004. *From International to World Society? English School Theory and the Social Structure of Globalisation*, Cambridge, Cambridge University Press.

Çalışlar, I. 2006. *Latife Hanım*, Istanbul, Doğan Kitap.

Campbell, D. 1992. *Writing Security: United States Foreign Policy and the Politics of Identity*, Manchester, Manchester University Press.

Chatterjee, P. 1998. Secularism and Tolerance. In: Bhargava, R. (ed.) *Secularism and its Critics*, Delhi, Oxford University Press.

Chowdhry, G. & Nair, S. 2002. *Power, Postcolonialism, and International Relations: Reading Race, Gender, and Class*, New York, Routledge.

Cizre-Sakallıoğlu, Ü. 1996. Parameters and Strategies of Islam-State Interaction in Republican Turkey. *International Journal of Middle East Studies*, 28, 231–251.

Daver, B. 1955. *Türkiye Cumhutiyeti'nde Layiklik*, Ankara, A.Ü. S.B.F.

Davison, A. 1998. *Secularism and Revivalism in Turkey: A Hermeneutic Reconsideration*, New Haven, Yale University Press.

Davison, A. 2003. Turkey, a 'Secular' State? The Challenge of Description. *South Atlantic Quarterly*, 102, 2–3, 333–350.

Davison, A. 2014. *Border Thinking on the Edges of the West: Crossing Over the Hellespont*, London, Routledge.

Deringil, S. 1998. *The Well-Protected Domains: Ideology and the Legitimation of Power in the Ottoman Empire, 1876–1909*, London & New York, I.B. Tauris.

Donnelly, J. 1998. Human Rights: A New Standard of Civilization? *International Affairs*, 74, 1–24.

Donnelly, J. 2006. Sovereign Inequalities and Hierarchy in Anarchy: American Power and International Society. *European Journal of International Relations*, 12, 139–170.

Dunne, T. 1995. The Social Construction of International Society. *European Journal of International Relations*, 1, 367–389.

Dunne, T. 1998. *Inventing International Society: A History of the English School*, New York, St. Martin's Press.

Eisenstadt, S. N. 2000. The Reconstruction of Religious Arenas in the Framework of 'Multiple Modernities'. *Millennium – Journal of International Studies*, 29, 591–611.

Enloe, C. 1997. Margins, Silences and Bottom Rungs: How to Overcome the Under-estimation of Power in the Study of International Relations. In: Booth, K., Smith, S. & Zalewski, M. (eds.) *International Theory: Positivism and Beyond*, Cambridge, Cambridge University Press.

Fabian, J. 1983. *Time and the Other: How Anthropology Makes its Object*, New York, Columbia University Press.

Finnemore, M. 1996. *National Interests in International Society*, Ithaca, Cornell University Press.

Göle, N. 1996. *The Forbidden Modern: Civilization and Veiling*, Ann Arbor, University of Michigan Press.

Göle, N. 2000. Snapshots of Islamic Modernities. *Daedalus*, 129, 1, 91–117.

Gong, G. W. 1984a. China's Entry into International Society. In: Bull, H. & Watson, A. (eds.) *The Expansion of International Society*, Oxford, Clarendon Press.

156   *Inquiring into the international in security*

Gong, G. W. 1984b. *The Standard of 'Civilization' in International Society*, Oxford, Clarendon Press.

Gong, G. W. 2002. Standards of Civilization Today. In: Mozaffari, M. (ed.) *Globalization and Civilizations*, London, Routledge.

Grovogui, S. N. 1996. *Sovereigns, Quasi-sovereigns and Africans: Race and Self-Determination in International Law*, Minneapolis, University of Minnesota Press.

Grovogui, S. N. 2001. Come to Africa: A Hermeneutics of Race in International Theory. *Alternatives: Global, Local, Political*, 26, 425–448.

Grovogui, S. N. 2006. *Beyond Eurocentrism and Anarchy: Memories of International Order and Institutions*, New York, Palgrave Macmillan.

Gülalp, H. 2005. Enlightenment by Fiat: Secularization and Democracy in Turkey. *Middle Eastern Studies*, 41, 351–372.

Halperin, S. 1997. *In the Mirror of the Third World: Capitalist Development in Modern Europe*, Ithaca, NY, Cornell University Press.

Halperin, S. 2006. International Relations Theory and the Hegemony of Western Conceptions of Modernity. In: Jones, B. G. (ed.) *Decolonizing International Relations*, Lanham, MD, Rowman & Littlefield.

Hanioğlu, M. Ş. 2008. *A Brief History of the Late Ottoman Empire*, Princeton, NJ, Princeton University Press.

Heper, Metin. 1998. *İsmet İnönü: The Making of a Turkish Statesman*, Leiden, Brill.

Hindess, B. 2002. Neo-liberal Citizenship. *Citizenship Studies*, 6, 127–143.

Hindess, B. 2007. The Past is Another Culture. *International Political Sociology*, 1, 325–338.

Hobson, J. M. 2014. The Twin Self-Delusions of IR: Why 'Hierarchy' and Not 'Anarchy' Is the Core Concept of IR. *Millennium – Journal of International Studies*. 42, 3, 557–575.

Hurd, E. S. 2004a. The International Politics of Secularism: U.S. Foreign Policy and the Islamic Republic of Iran. *Alternatives*, 29, 115–138.

Hurd, E. S. 2004b. The Political Authority of Secularism in International Relations. *European Journal of International Relations*, 10, 235–262.

Hurd, E. S. 2008. *The Politics of Secularism in International Relations*, Princeton, NJ, Princeton University Press.

İnalcık, H. 2006. *Turkey and Europe in History*, İstanbul, Eren.

India Review 2003–2004. Special Issue on South Asia and Theories of Nuclear Deterrence. *India Review*, 4.

Jabri, V. 2013. *The Postcolonial Subject: Claiming Politics/Governing Others in Late Modernity*, London, Routledge.

Jabri, V. 2014. Disarming Norms: Postcolonial Agency and the Constitution of the International. *International Theory*, 6, 372–390.

Karacan, Ali Naci. 1943. *Lozan Konferansı ve İsmet Paşa*, İstanbul, Maarif Matbaası.

Katzenstein, P. J. 2006. Multiple Modernities as Limits to Secular Europeanization? In: Byrnes, T. A. & Katzenstein, P. J. (eds.) *Religion in an Expanding Europe*, Cambridge, Cambridge University Press.

Keyder, Ç. 1987. The Political Economy of Turkish Democracy. In: Schick, I. C. & Tonak, E. A. (eds.) *Turkey in Transition: New Perspectives*, Oxford, Oxford University Press.

Keyder, Ç. 2004. The Turkish Bell Jar. *New Left Review*, 28, July–August, 65–84.

Kili, S. 1980. Kemalism in Contemporary Turkey. *International Political Science Review*, 1, 381–404.

Inquiring into the international in security 157

Kili, S. 2003. *The Atiiturk Revolution: A Paradigm of Modernization*, Istanbul, Is Bankasi Yayinlari.

Krishna, S. 1999. *Postcolonial Insecurities: India, Sri Lanka, and the Question of Nationhood*, Minneapolis, MN, University of Minnesota Press.

Krishna, S. 2001. Race, Amnesia, and the Education of International Relations. *Alternatives: Global, Local, Political*, 26, 401–424.

Linklater, A. & Suganami, H. 2006. *The English School of International Relations: A Contemporary Reassessment*, Cambridge, Cambridge University Press.

Mamdani, M. 1996. *Citizen and Subject: Contemporary Africa and the Legacy of Late Colonialism*, Princeton, NJ, Princeton University Press.

Mamdani, M. 2001. Beyond Settler and Native as Political Identities: Overcoming the Political Legacy of Colonialism. *Comparative Study of Society and History*, 43, 4, 651–664.

Mardin, S. 1973. Center-Periphery Relations: A Key to Turkish Politics? *Daedalus*, 102, 169–190.

Mardin, S. 1977. Religion in Modern Turkey. *International Social Science Journal*, 29, 279–297.

Mardin, S. 1982. Turkey: Islam and Westernization. In: Caldarola, C. (ed.) *Religions and Societies: Asia and the Middle East*, Berlin, Mouton Publishers.

Mert, N. 1998. Cumhuriyet, Laiklik ve Din, In: (n.a.) *75 Yılda Düşünceler Tartışmalar*, İstanbul, İş Bankası Yayınları.

Muppidi, H. 1999. Postcoloniality and the Production of International Insecurity: The Persistent Puzzle of US-Indian Relations. In: Weldes, J., Laffey, M., Gusterson, H. & Duvall, R. (eds.) *Cultures of Insecurity: States, Communities, and the Production of Danger*, Minneapolis, University of Minnesota Press

Nereid, C. T. 2011. Kemalism on the Catwalk: The Turkish Hat Law of 1925. *Journal of Social History*, 44, 707–728.

Neumann, I. B. 1999. *Uses of the Other: 'The East' in European Identity Formation*, Minneapolis, Minnesota University Press.

Neumann, I. B. 2011. Entry into International Society Reconceptualised: The Case of Russia. *Review of International Studies*, 37, 463–484.

Ortaylı, I. 1983. *İmparatorluğun En Uzun Yüzyılı (The Longest Century of the Empire)*, İstanbul, Hil Yayınları.

Ozankaya, O. 1981. *Ataturk ve Laiklik: Ataturkcu Dusuncenin Temel Niteligi*, Istanbul, Is Bankasi Yayinlari.

Parla, T. & Davison, A. 2004. *Corporatist Ideology in Kemalist Turkey: Progress or Order?*, Syracuse, NY, Syracuse University Press.

Perkovich, G. 1998. Is India a Major Power? *The Washington Quarterly*, 27, 129–144.

Quataert, D. 1997. Clothing Laws, State, and Society in the Ottoman Empire, 1720–1829. *International Journal of Middle East Studies*, 29, 403–425.

Rustow, D. A. 1957. Politics and Islam in Turkey, 1920–1955. In: Frye, R. N. (ed.) *Islam and the West; Proceedings of the Harvard Summer School Conference on the Middle East, July 25–27, 1955*, 'S-Gravenhage, Mouton & Co.

Said, E. W. 1993. *Culture and Imperialism*, New York, Knopf.

Said, E. W. 1995. Secular Interpretation, the Geographical Element and the Methodology of Imperialism. In: Prakash, G. (ed.) *After Colonialism: Imperial Histories and Postcolonial Displacements*, Princeton, NJ, Princeton University Press.

Schwarzenberger, G. 1955. The Standard of Civilisation in International Law. *Current Legal Problems*, 8, 212–234.

158 *Inquiring into the international in security*

Shilliam, R. 2008. What the Haitian Revolution Might Tell Us about Development, Security, and the Politics of Race. *Comparative Studies in Society and History*, 50, 778–808.

Suzuki, S. 2005. Japan's Socialization into Janus-Faced European International Society. *European Journal of International Relations*, 11, 137–164.

Suzuki, S. 2009. *Civilization and Empire: China and Japan's Encounter with European International Society*, New York, Routledge.

Suzuki, S. 2014. Europe at the Periphery of the Japanese World Order. In: Suzuki, S., Zhang, Y. & Quirk, J. (eds.) *International Orders in the Early Modern World: Before the Rise of the West*, London, Routledge.

Suzuki, S., Zhang, Y. & Quirk, J. 2014. Introduction. In: Suzuki, S., Zhang, Y. & Quirk, J. (eds.) *International Orders in the Early Modern World: Before the Rise of the West*, London, Routledge.

Tachau, F. 1984. *Turkey, the Politics of Authority, Democracy, and Development*, New York, Praeger.

Tank, P. 2005. Political Islam in Turkey: A State of Controlled Secularity. *Turkish Studies*, 6, 3–19.

Tanör, B. 1998. Laikleş(tir)me Kemalistler ve Din, In: (n.a.) *75 Yılda Düşünceler Tartışmalar*, İstanbul, İş Bankası Yayınları.

Taylor, C. 1998. Modes of Secularism. In: Bhargava, R. (ed.) *Secularism and its Critics*, Delhi, Oxford University Press.

Toprak, B. 1981. *Islam and Political Development in Turkey*, Leiden, Brill.

Toprak, B. 1988. The State, Politics, and Religion in Turkey. In: Heper, M. & Evin, A. (eds.) *State, Democracy and the Military: Turkey in the 1980s*, Berlin, Walter de Gruyter.

Üstel, F. 2001. II. Meşrutiyet ve Vatandaşın 'İcad'ı. In: Alkan, M. Ö. (ed.) *Modern Türkiye'de Siyasi Düşünce*, İstanbul, İletişim.

Vitalis, R. 2005. Birth of a Discipline. In: Long, D. & Schmidt, B. C. (eds.) *Imperialism and Internationalism in the Discipline of International Relations*, Albany, State University of New York Press.

Watson, A. 1992. *The Evolution of International Society: A Comparative Historical Analysis*, London & New York, Routledge.

Wendt, A. & Friedheim, D. 2009. Hierarchy under Anarchy: Informal Empire and the East German State. *International Organization*, 49, 689–721.

Yavuz, Ü. 1990. *Atatürk: Imparatorluktan Milli Devlete*, Ankara, Türk Tarih Kurumu.

6 Civilisation, dialogue, in/security

Chapter 6 offers an illustration of what I consider to be at stake in reflecting on others' conceptions of the international as we ponder the question of security in a world characterised by a multiplicity of inequalities and differences. The challenge is not only Huntingtonian (1993, 1996) clash of civilisations scenarios that have their followers and detractors in IR and world politics. The challenge is also those approaches that seek to counter Huntingtonian axioms while building on similar conceptions of (civilisational) 'difference' and 'security'. While the proponents of civilisational dialogue strive to replace clash with dialogue, they still view differences as unchanging pre-givens and as yielding insecurities. What is more, neither civilisational clash scenarios nor civilisational dialogue projects reflect on others' conceptions of the international, presuming that 'we already know'.

As discussed in Chapters 1 and 2, a particular approach to 'difference' has shaped mainstream theorising about IR and security, whereby 'inside' the state is assumed to be characterised by 'sameness' and security, and outside by 'difference' and insecurity (Walker, 1993, Inayatullah and Blaney, 2004). In offering his 'Clash of Civilisations?' scenario, Huntington comes across as having adopted mainstream IR's approach to difference and taken it one step further by the 'remapping of IR into larger units of similarity and difference – civilisations' (Weber, 2010: 161). Subsequently, noted Cynthia Weber (2010: 161), 'both IR and Huntington conclude that sameness reduces instability whereas difference perpetuates instability and that the best way to manage difference is either to assimilate it within the state or expel it from the state'.

In the early twentieth-century practices of states, one prevalent way of dealing with actual or potential conflict was the redrawing of borders and relocation of peoples as practised in the population exchange between Greece and Turkey in 1923 (McGarry, 1998). Similar solutions were proposed to address insecurities in Iraq in the aftermath of the 2003 war (Cooper, 2007). Prevalent understandings of and proposed solutions to both instances of conflict were shaped by a particular understanding of difference/s as pre-given and unchanging, and as yielding insecurities. Huntingtonian scenarios of civilisational clash and their dialogue-oriented critics constitute present-day instances of this understanding. What follows focuses on the Dialogue of Civilisations (DoC) initiatives to illustrate the book's argument regarding the need for drawing upon the insights of both critical security studies

160 *Civilisation, dialogue, in/security*

and postcolonial studies when thinking about security in a world characterised by a multiplicity of inequalities and differences.

Amidst all the war and violent conflict in the world, why be critical of a project for world security? In the search for dialogue, proponents of DoC initiatives have established grounds for communication where none existed; nurtured inter-faith conversations where possible; and, perhaps most importantly, showed that inter-state interaction could aim for more than diplomacy and/or the use of force (Dallmayr, 2002, Esposito and Voll, 2003, Lynch, 2000, Petito, 2007, 2009). Be that as it may, I will suggest that DoC initiatives suffer from the same limits as Huntingtonian scenarios by virtue of resting upon a similar notion of (civilisational) difference as an unchanging pre-given and as yielding insecurities. Indeed, while the proponents of civilisational dialogue strive to replace clash with dialogue, they do not always reflect on how insecurities are (re)produced through attempts at civilisational dialogue that are shaped by particular notions of dialogue (that is not always dialogical in ethics and/or epistemology), civilisation (which is not conceptualised dialogically or studied contrapuntally) and security (undeniably statist and military-focused, devoid of reflections on others' conceptions of the international). I will conclude by outlining how addressing these limits requires fresh approaches to thinking about world security by reflecting on others' conceptions of the international.

Before I begin discussing the limits of the DoC initiatives, a caveat is in order. Critiquing DoC as a project of world security and identifying those insecurities that it is likely to (re)produce is not meant to suggest that it is possible to find another approach that would produce only security and no insecurity! As Didier Bigo argued,

> security is never unlimited, contrary to the claims of politicians and academics seeing security as a public good for all…The definition of what is security in relation to what is insecurity is a political struggle between the actors who have the capacity to declare with some authority whose security is important, whose security can be sacrificed, and why their own violence may be read as a form of protection when the violence of the others is seen as a form of aggression and sign of insecurity.
>
> (Bigo, 2008: 123)

Following Bigo, what I seek to highlight is the choices made by the proponents of DoC initiatives regarding whom they wish to privilege (states) and whom they are willing to sacrifice (non-state referents) – all in the name of world security. In doing so, they, too, overlook others' conceptions of the international and in/security.

Clash of Civilisations scenarios – a challenge to world security?[1]

In his 'Clash of Civilisations?' article from 1993, Huntington argued that the universalism of the West fostered by the globalising forces was bringing it into

Civilisation, dialogue, in/security   161

conflict with non-Western states whose policies were increasingly shaped by their civilisational identity and accordingly were choosing to form coalitions to stand against the West. Hence Huntington's thesis that the future of world politics would likely be characterised by a 'clash of civilisations'. Formulated as such, Huntington's analysis captured the 1990s' epitome of anxiety that followed the apparent 'return of culture and identity' (read: difference) to world politics (Lapid and Kratochwil, 1996).

Huntington also offered a way to reverse this trend. The two-pronged strategy he favoured involved the West holding on to its own in the short term by promoting close cooperation and further integration within its own civilisation, whilst exploiting the differences between other civilisations, thereby preventing the formation of anti-Western coalitions. For the long term, Huntington preferred a rather accommodationist policy and called for developing a more profound understanding of other civilisations so that elements of commonality could be identified (Huntington, 1993, 1996).

At the time Huntington's article came out, civilisation as a 'notion' and as a 'unit of analysis' was all but forgotten in the study of international relations. As Peter Katzenstein (2010) noted, it was largely in response to the influence Huntington's thesis has had on the policy world that IR has turned to the analysis of civilisation. The attractiveness of Huntington's scenario was that it offered a way of making sense of 'new' phenomena (the so-called 'return of culture and identity') within an 'old' framework ('us v. them'). Since then, scholars have questioned the empirical validity of his arguments (Chiozza, 2002, Henderson and Tucker, 2001, Gartzke and Gleditsch, 2006) and the veracity of his essentialist approach to civilisations (Bassin, 2007, O'Hagan, 1995). Yet, notwithstanding its 'scientific' limits, Huntington's scenario has had a life outside the scholarly realm, being picked up by pundits and policymakers around the world.[2]

Dialogue of Civilisations initiatives – searching for world security?

As IR scholars hesitated to adopt civilisation as a category of analysis (due to the aforementioned limits of Huntington's thesis, or for fear of helping reify civilisation as a 'thing', or simply because they found civilisation as too big and vague as a unit of analysis),[3] outside the academia, some other public intellectuals and policymakers worried that the anxieties of some in the face of a world characterised by a multiplicity of differences (as opposed to the 'neat' world order maintained by mutual assured destruction during the Cold War years) would be followed by Huntington's 'clash of civilisations' scenario being received as 'common sense', thereby becoming a self-fulfilling prophecy. In an attempt to address this challenge, they offered Dialogue of Civilisations as a solution.

The first such attempt was made by the then Iranian President Khātamī (1997–2005) who proposed Dialogue of Civilisations as a way of managing 'chaos and anarchy' and seeking 'harmony' in world politics. His efforts culminated in the autumn of 1998 with UN member states declaring the year 2001 as 'UN Year

162 *Civilisation, dialogue, in/security*

of Dialogue among Civilisations'.[4] President Khātamī explained the UN initiative as an attempt to counter the primacy of the clash thesis and minimise its efficacy in shaping policy. 'Dialogue among civilisations is an absolute imperative', President Khātamī said, in reference to the process of globalisation and peoples' increasing awareness of the multiplicity of differences characterising present-day world politics scenarios (Khātamī quoted in Esposito and Voll, 2003: 250).

Khātamī's term in presidency has since come to an end. The current Iranian leadership does not seem as committed to civilisational dialogue.[5] Still, Khātamī's vision for ordering the world through civilisational dialogue is alive albeit in a different guise: The 'Alliance of Civilisations' initiative sponsored jointly by Spain and Turkey under the auspices of the UN and supported by both the European Union and the Vatican.[6]

The Alliance of Civilisations initiative was first presented to the United Nations by Spanish Prime Minister Zapatero. Following UN Secretary General Annan's advice, Spain invited Turkey to co-chair the initiative. Turkey's then prime minister (current president) Recep Tayyip Erdoğan responded positively to the Spanish invitation and assumed co-chairmanship of the Alliance of Civilisations in 2006. This was not the first time that Turkey was involved in civilisational dialogue. In 2002, Turkey's then foreign minister İsmail Cem had hosted a joint meeting of the leaders of the European Union and the Organisation of Islamic Conference (OIC-EU Joint Forum) in İstanbul.[7]

At various instances, the Vatican, former Czech president Vaclav Havel and UNESCO also expressed support for DoC initiatives. Each of the initiatives highlighted here were designed to prevent what their proponents considered to be an impending clash between states belonging to different civilisations. Indeed, DoC initiatives are considered by some to be our best bet in countering the primacy of Huntingtonian scenarios in world politics (Dallmayr, 2002, Esposito and Voll, 2003, Lynch, 2000: 337–350, Petito, 2007, 2009).

In what follows, I raise my contrapuntal awareness and present a critical security studies critique that draws upon the insights of postcolonial studies to argue the following: As an alternative vision of world security, DoC initiatives risk falling short of even addressing the very insecurities they choose to prioritise (i.e. the stability of existing inter-state world order) let alone attending to those experienced by non-state referents (which they decidedly overlook). I make three points in three steps. First, I point to how projects of civilisational dialogue bracket civilisation, thereby leaving intact the Huntingtonian notion of civilisations as autonomously developed entities. These entities are understood as bearers of 'differences' that are viewed as unchanging pre-givens, and as yielding insecurity. Second, I highlight the limits of the notion of dialogue employed by the proponents of DoC and argue that while contributing to opening up space for communication, DoC initiatives have nevertheless failed to tap contrapuntal readings of the history of civilisations. The limits of DoC initiatives in their conceptualisation of these two key concepts, I argue, result in

Civilisation, dialogue, in/security   163

a failure to foster dialogue. Third, I tease out the limits of the notion of security underpinning DoC projects. I argue that the proponents of DoC, in their haste to avert a clash, have defined security narrowly as the absence of war between states belonging to different civilisations. What is problematic here is not only privileging the stability of inter-state order over other non-state referents, but also the limits of insight into others' conceptions of the international.

Civilisation

The proponents of DoC, as they sought to prevent a clash, have bracketed civilisation. In doing so, they offered a correction in terms of highlighting the peaceful 'essence' of civilisations and the potential for peaceful relations between civilisations. Yet at the same time, DoC initiatives failed to do away with the culturalism of the clash scenario or the notion of civilisations as autonomously developed entities.

The notion of civilisation on which the clash thesis rests is culturalist because Huntington attributes civilisations a primordial cultural essence, which, in turn, renders particular societal characteristics and institutional arrangements 'natural' and 'eternal'. Consider the following quote:

> The West differs from other civilisations in the distinctive character of its values and institutions. These include most notably its Christianity, pluralism, individualism, and rule of law, which made it possible for the West to invent modernity, expand throughout the world, and become the envy of other societies. In their ensemble these characteristics are peculiar to the West…They make Western civilisation unique, and Western civilisation is valuable not because it is universal but because it is unique.
>
> (Huntington quoted in Hobson, 2009: 5)

What allows such portrayals of the Western civilisation to prevail is Eurocentrism. Huntington's Eurocentrism is evident in 'his belief that the West developed in its own unique or exceptional institutions, which enabled it to rise to the top entirely of its own accord' (Hobson, 2007: 153). Furthermore, Huntington attributes agency to the Western civilisation in the evolution of what is popularly referred to as the civilised way of life. In contrast to such monological readings of the history of civilisations are contrapuntal readings that reveal centuries of interaction and co-constitution (see below).

The notion of civilisation on which DoC is built is not too different from the clash scenario. First, the DoC notion of civilisation, too, is culturalist in that the major proponents of civilisational dialogue believe in an unchanging cultural essence that could be revived in the peaceful environment dialogue would allow. Cardinal Ratzinger (who later became Pope Benedict XVI) for example, viewed dialogue as taking place between pre-given entities that meet each other to exchange ideas and, if possible, find common ground. In the famous Munich Paper of 2004, Cardinal Ratzinger wrote:

164 *Civilisation, dialogue, in/security*

For Christians, this dialogue would speak of the creation and the Creator. In the Indian world, this would correspond to the concept of 'dharma', the inner law that regulates all Being; in the Chinese tradition, it would correspond to the idea of the structures ordained by heaven.

(quoted in Esposito and Voll, 2003: 254)

A similar outlook was also evident in President Khātamī's characterisation of the ideal process of dialogue as '[absorbing] good qualities of the West while rejecting its negative aspects' (Khātamī as quoted in Esposito and Voll, 2003: 254). President Khātamī's presumption being that whatever is 'good' and/or 'negative' about the West or Islam is in their 'essence' (but not in the processes of centuries of co-constitution). Turkey's then prime minister (now president) Erdoğan exhibited a similar attitude towards dialogue in his address to students leaving for abroad to conduct postgraduate studies. He said: 'The poet who penned the Turkish national anthem [Mehmet Akif Ersoy] said that we should compete with art and science of the West; but unfortunately we adopted the West's immoralities that are contrary to our values.'[8] All three prominent proponents of civilisational dialogue determined what to pick and choose in the process of dialogue based on the assumption that there is a cultural essence to civilisations; that such essence is pre-given and unchanging; and what need reviving through dialogue are techniques and technologies so that such essence can once again be brought to bear on one's own peoples.[9]

Second, as with Huntington, the proponents of DoC assume civilisations to be autonomously developed entities. Even as they acknowledge civilisational interaction, they imagine such give-and-take to be happening at the fringes. Consider the following quote by President Khātamī:

Civilisations rise and fall…Unless they are completely unaware of each other's existence, civilisations ordinarily affect and transform one another… Give-and-take among civilisations is the norm of history…Thus 'new' civilisations are never new in the true sense, for they always feed on the work of previous civilisations, appropriating and digesting all that fits their needs, dispensing with all that does not.

(Khātamī quoted in Esposito and Voll, 2003: 254)

Indeed, proponents of DoC portrayed interaction between civilisations as taking place 'only at their edges' (Hobson, 2009), thereby leaving intact their purportedly unchanging essence.

The DoC approach to the history of civilisations was critiqued by Aziz al-Azmeh, among others, who argued that these approaches

give much too much an impression of closure, sometimes of immobility (Braudel described civilisations as 'glacial'), of homeostasis and of self-reference. They seem to treat meta-historical collectivities as if they were *Gemeinschaften*, without regard to considerations of scale and its complexity.

(Al-Azmeh, 2012: 507)

Civilisation, dialogue, in/security 165

Adopting Fernand Braudel's definition of civilisations as 'glacial' could then be complemented by offering 'contrapuntal readings' of the history of civilisations, to be able to understand self/other dynamics, instances of learning, give-and-take, *and* co-constitution of civilisations.

To recapitulate, DoC initiatives, in their present conception, offer less-than-firm grounds for dialogue by virtue of the limits of the notion of civilisation they employ. This is because, in their haste to replace clash with dialogue, proponents of DoC bracketed civilisation. In doing so, they employed the Huntingtonian understanding of civilisations as autonomously evolved around a pre-given and unchanging cultural essence. In contrast to such essentialism are contrapuntal readings of world history as offered by students of postcolonial studies that view civilisations as mutually constituted and always in motion.[10]

Dialogue

By virtue of the emphasis they put on dialogue, proponents of DoC aspired to offer a radically different vision of world order when compared to the clash thesis. Indeed, As Marc Lynch (2000: 311) highlighted, in contrast to the 'realist assumption that no public sphere existed which would enable meaningful communication between civilisations', as presumed by the clash scenario, DoC initiatives have claimed an 'international public sphere within which communicative action might take place'. Notwithstanding such ambitious and lofty aims of DoC, the promise for fostering dialogue between states belonging to different civilisations has remained unfulfilled (and likely to remain so). This is because DoC initiatives are conditioned by the notion of 'dialogue' that they rest upon, which is less than dialogical.

The notion of dialogue on which DoC projects rest is less than dialogical because the proponents of DoC considered replacing 'clash' with 'dialogue' to be enough of an improvement upon Huntingtonian scenarios. For one thing, dialogue and clash are not the total opposites they are understood to be in everyday terms. It is possible to have a dialogue of sorts in and through violent clashes (as with dialogue and learning that took place during the Crusades). For another, it is possible to maintain a monologue while purportedly engaging in dialogue (as with the Israelis and Palestinians during the peace talks held in Madrid and Washington, DC in the immediate aftermath of the 1990–1991 Iraq war). Accordingly, replacing clash with dialogue would not suffice so long as the notion of dialogue remains less than dialogical.

Xavier Guillaume drew upon Mikhael Bakhtin's works to clarify what is meant by dialogue being less than 'dialogical' (on Bakhtin, also see Neumann, 1999). Guillaume wrote:

> Monological utterances…stand on an unsound ethical and epistemological position. In fact, they tend to subvert the other, and do not allow it a proper conscience that is reflexively identical to them. Within a monological figuration, the other becomes an object of the self's own conscience,

166 *Civilisation, dialogue, in/security*

which can be interpreted and modified at will as a function of the self's own needs as an identity (Guillaume, 2000: 9).

Dialogical utterances, in turn, are defined by the extent to which they take the other into account. Whereas monologism 'denies the existence outside itself of another consciousness with equal rights and equal responsibilities, another I with equal rights', dialogism is characterised by transgradience whereby 'the self alone cannot feel itself within its own realm of existence, since, according to the idea of transgredience (constitutive of dialogism), a person truly is herself only to the extent that she can integrate the regard of the other' (Bakhtin quoted in Guillaume, 2000: 6).

L.H.M. Ling's discussion on the notion of dialogue identifies what is missing from Bakhtin as viewed from the perspective of the other party to the dialogue: Mutual transformation of both sides through dialogue, as opposed to only one side. Ling wrote:

> Bakhtin's notion of addressivity and interactivity gives us a snapshot of the relationship *from* the speaker to addressee, albeit with sensitivity to change and continuity in time and meaning...Not recognising a reciprocal impact effectively erases it.
>
> (Ling, 2014: 69)

Ling suggested that we complement Bakhtin's notion of dialogical dialogue with 'other traditions [that] do not restrict multiplicity or intersubjectivity to one set of dialogics alone' (Ling, 2014: 69).

The kind of dialogue DoC initiatives aspired to is not dialogical in the sense discussed by Guillaume or Ling. On the one hand, forthcoming proponents of DoC have avowedly expressed interest in finding oneself in the other. Consider the following quote by President Khātamī:

> One goal of dialogue among cultures and civilizations is to recognize and understand not only cultures and civilisations of others, but those of 'one's own'. We could know ourselves by taking a step away from ourselves and embarking on a journey away from self and homeland and eventually attaining a more profound appreciation of our true identity. It is only through immersion into another existential dimension that we could attain mediated and acquired knowledge of ourselves in addition to the immediate and direct knowledge of ourselves that we commonly possess. Through seeing others we attain a hitherto impossible knowledge of ourselves.
>
> (Khātamī quoted in Petito, 2007: 111)

On the other hand, by virtue of the notion of civilisation employed, the proponents of DoC evaded the ethics as well as epistemology of dialogism. Indeed, DoC's reading of civilisations could be construed as monological by virtue of its roots in an autochthonous conception of civilisation and the history of civilisations as one of autonomous development. A dialogical reading of the past pursues dialogues between past and present, as opposed to seeking dialogue in the present as if no such dialogue existed in and/or with the past. To quote Guillaume again:

> Dialogism represents the interweaving of utterances that respond to one another, an utterance being characterised by its expression, its context and its relation to other utterances, whether this relation is present and/or past, active or passive.
>
> (Guillaume, 2000: 8)

In contrast to DoC's monological reading of the history of civilisations, which do not recognise past encounters beyond surface interaction, we uncover historical dialogue between civilisations in contrapuntal readings of the history of civilisations. Edward Said wrote:

> A comparative or, better, a contrapuntal perspective is required in order to see a connection between coronation rituals in England and the Indian durbars of the late nineteenth century. That is, we must be able to think through and interpret together experiences that are discrepant, each with its particular agenda and pace of development, its own internal formations, its internal coherence and system of external relationships, all of them coexisting and interacting with others.
>
> (Said, 1993: 32)

To illustrate what is missing from accounts that fail to offer contrapuntal readings, consider Costas Constantinou's account on Ottoman diplomacy, where he contested its characterisation as 'Muslim', calling for recognising the kind of learning that took place between 'Muslims' and 'Christians' in the Ottoman Empire. He asked:

> How is one to classify the practices of highly influential and controversial figures – such as Alexander Mavrocordato, the Grand Dragoman – agents of Ottoman diplomacy who could move with ease across civilisations and religions, whose diplomatic representations could hardly be reduced to acts of single subjectivities, international diplomatists for whom nationality was a career?
>
> (Constantinou, 2000: 217)

Contrapuntal readings of the history of diplomacy, Constantinou's study suggested, would point to the fallacy of identifying 'a (politically loaded) shift of Byzantine diplomatic theory to Venice after the conquest of Constantinople' while overlooking 'the possible shift of "Christian" features to the "Muslim" empire as well' (Constantinou, 2000: 217).

DoC's failure to draw upon contrapuntal readings of the history of civilisations limits the grounds for future dialogue by way of portraying present-day

168 *Civilisation, dialogue, in/security*

differences as pre-given and unchanging. Drawing on contrapuntal readings of the history of civilisations, in turn, would allow recognising the beginnings of these ideas and institutions that are presently viewed as almost exclusively 'Western' inventions. To quote Amartya Sen:

> There is a chain of intellectual relations that link Western mathematics and science to a collection of distinctly non-Western practitioners. For example, the decimal system, which evolved in India in the early centuries of the first millennium, went to Europe at the end of that millennium via the Arabs. A large group of contributors from different non-Western societies – Chinese, Arab, Iranian, Indian, and others – influenced the science, mathematics, and philosophy that played a major part in the European Renaissance and, later, the Enlightenment.
>
> (Sen, 2006: 56)

Hobson made a similar point about the Reformation and underscored that the idea of 'man [as] a free and rational agent' was integral to the works of Islamic scholars and that 'these ideas were also strikingly similar to those that inspired Martin Luther and the Reformation' (Hobson, 2004: 177–178).

Writing values and institutions such as human rights and democracy out of the heritage of civilisations other than 'the West' does not only render invisible others' contributions to the making of (what is popularly referred to as the) 'civilised way of life' but also ends up substantiating the extremists' theses. For, it is based on the presumed absence of such values and institutions outside the West that Huntingtonians have called for strengthening their own vis-à-vis the rest; likewise Muslim extremists have warned against Western plots to export 'alien' values (such as democracy or women's rights as human rights) to the land of Islam. The point being, in the absence of dialogical readings of the past, contemporary proponents of DoC have undermined the otherwise significant potential for fostering further dialogue (also see the discussion on human rights in Chapter 2).

Security

DoC initiatives, given their primary concern with preventing a potential clash between states, come across as prioritising state security to the neglect of other referents. The issue here is not only that they do not prioritise insecurities experienced by non-state referents, but also that they are not concerned with the potential implications such a state-focused approach would likely have for the security of individuals and social groups. What follows briefly highlights three such instances of insecurity.

One instance is that through focusing on the ontology of civilisation and considering individuals and social groups insofar as they are members of this or that civilisation, DoC initiatives risk marginalising other ways of engaging with 'differences'. This is because civilisational dialogue initiatives ultimately locate differences outside civilisations, with little consideration for differences inside.

Civilisation, dialogue, in/security 169

To paraphrase a point Inayatullah and Blaney (2004: 39) made in another context, projects of civilisational dialogue constitute 'a deferral of a genuine recognition, exploration, and engagement of difference' with difference being 'marked and contained' as civilisational difference. In other words, through pursuing world security as peace between states belonging to different civilisations, 'the problem of difference' would be 'deferred'. Such deferral, in turn, could potentially allow for insecurities inside civilisations, including marginalisation of insecurities of those with 'interstitial identities' (Bhabha, 1994).

Second, given prevailing conceptions of civilisations as having a pre-given and unchanging 'essence' (an assumption shared by Samuel Huntington and some of his dialogue-oriented critics) there will not be much room left for inquiring into power/knowledge dynamics in the (re)production of differences inside civilisations. Indeed, betraying their culturalist predilections, DoC initiatives fail to acknowledge that 'identity is not a fact of society' but a 'process of negotiation among people and interest groups' (McSweeney 1999: 73). More significantly, often such negotiations themselves are sources of insecurity, insofar as they take differences in identity as 'pre-given' and unchanging, and as yielding insecurities. This is in contrast to a constructivist notion of security, as adopted by students of critical security studies, who understand that 'the security problem is not there because people have separate identities; it may well be the case that they have separate identities because of the security problem' (McSweeney, 1999: 73).

Third, envisioning a world order structured around civilisational essences could potentially amplify the voices of those who dress their rhetoric in terms of cultural 'essence'. One concrete instance of such insecurity was observed when Pope Benedict XVI embraced DoC initiatives and sought to re-define 'Western' civilisation along religious lines. This is not to reduce the Pope's interest in dialogue to his 'in-house' concerns, but to highlight how engaging in civilisational dialogue allowed Pope Benedict XVI to form alliances with like-minded leaders from other civilisations and justify various policies that overlooked women's insecurities (among others) (Halliday, 2006). In the absence of reflections on others' conceptions of the international as reflected in their 'discourses of danger', DoC initiatives are likely to overlook insecurities experienced by non-state referents.

Highlighting insecurities as experienced by myriad referents should not be taken as underestimating potential contributions civilisational dialogue could make. Indeed, I join Fabio Petito in underscoring the need to

> acknowledge something like a fundamental ethical-political crisis linked to the present liberal Western civilisation and its expansion, and recognize that dialogue of civilisations seems to enshrine the promise of an answer, or rather to start a path toward an answer.
>
> (Petito, 2011: 763)

However, what civilisational dialogue initiatives currently offer in terms of contributing to security is a potential. This is a potential that needs exploring,

170   *Civilisation, dialogue, in/security*

but with a view to what Friedrich Kratochwil (2005: 114) referred to as 'interpretative struggles' that are going on within civilisations, and the insecurities of myriad referents that follow (also see Pieterse, 1992, Narayan, 2000).

That said, it is important to note that the proponents of civilisational dialogue do not prioritise the insecurities experienced by non-state referents for a reason. Their thinking is that given the urgency of preventing a potential clash between states belonging to different civilisations, the current insecurities of non-state referents could be postponed till later. In Fred Dallmayr's articulation:

> Apart from ethical considerations…there is also a concrete pragmatic consideration in its favour: in the long run [Dialogue of Civilisations] offers the only viable alternative to military confrontation with its ever-present danger of nuclear holocaust and global self-destruction.
>
> (Dallmayr, 2002: 21)

Without wanting to underestimate the potential planetary consequences of such a clash, what is also important to remember is, first, that such 'short-termism' may not allow for addressing the medium- to long-term consequences of privileging statist approaches to security.[11] The steps we take here and now allow some future steps to be taken while disallowing some others.

Second, focusing on the short-term as such betrays a non-reflexive approach to security. Non-reflexive approaches to security do not reflect upon insecurities generated as we put various security policies into effect (Burgess, 2011). The point is that DoC initiatives do not reflect on potential insecurities that may follow the adoption of state-focused security policies as such. Cold War policy-making is a scary but useful reminder of potential implications (for individuals, social groups and the environment) of adopting such short-termist, state-focused and non-reflexive notions of security (see Chapter 1).

During the Cold War the threat of a nuclear exchange by the superpowers was put on the top of the security agenda, thereby privileging the stability of a statist conception of world order. Those who sought to push their own insecurities onto the agenda were disciplined into accepting the Cold War hierarchy of insecurities. Those who refused to buy into this hierarchy were labelled 'naïve' at best.[12] In the present-day context, a similar hierarchy is offered by the proponents of DoC who express their awareness of insecurities that are likely to be suffered by non-state referents through ordering the world around the ontology of civilisations. Yet they nevertheless push for civilisational dialogue as the only remedy for preventing a potential civilisational clash. In doing so, they privilege the security of states and marginalise the insecurities of non-state referents.

Conclusion

Recently, DoC intiatives received a boost from an unexpected place, when the Frankfurt School social theorist Jürgen Habermas (2006) identified civilisational

Civilisation, dialogue, in/security   171

dialogue as a remedy to the 'Western' roots of our key concepts including emancipation. On the one hand, the constitutive effects Eurocentrism has had on our central concepts such as emancipation needs addressing (see Chapters 1 and 2). Indeed, dialogues between a myriad actors could potentially help us find the beginnings of our key notions in different 'civilisations'. On the other hand, to achieve such an end, dialogue initiatives would need to embrace dialogue not only as ethics but also epistemology. From a Frankfurt School Critical Theory perspective, the goal, in Susan Buck-Morss's words,

> is not to 'understand' some 'other' discourse, emanating from a 'civilisation' that is intrinsically different from 'our own'. Nor is it merely organizational, to form pragmatic, interest-driven alliances among pre-defined and self-contained groups. Much less is it to accuse a part of the polity of being backward in its political beliefs, or worse, the very key embodiment of evil. Rather, what is needed is to rethink the entire project of politics within the changed condition of a global public sphere – and to do this democratically, as people who speak different political languages, but whose goals are nonetheless the same: global peace, economic justice, legal equality, democratic participation, individual freedom, mutual respect.
>
> (Buck-Morss, 2003: 4–5)

Students of critical security theorising could then adopt a twofold strategy. On the one hand, they could focus on highlighting how emancipation, to quote Ken Booth,

> As an ideal and a rallying cry, in practice, was prominent in many nineteenth-century struggles for independence or for freedom from legal restrictions; notable examples included Jews in Europe, slaves in the United States, blacks in the West Indies, the Irish in the British state, and serfs in Russia.
>
> (Booth, 2007: 111)

This would also allow moving civilisational dialogue initiatives from their current focus on state security. On the other hand, students of critical security studies could inquire into the beginnings of their core ideas as with emancipation in multiple locales (recalling Hayward Alker's advice, see Introduction). As Siba Grovogui wrote when discussing the limits of cosmopolitan approaches to world politics,

> The limits, I argue, are due partly to the absence of methods for indexing and cataloguing comparable and concurrent thought forms bearing on ethics. It is my conviction that cosmopolitans would benefit greatly from intellectual agendas, beliefs, attitudes, values, institutions and idioms which, although not organically linked to theirs, seek to enhance ethical existence.
>
> (Grovogui, 2005: 103)

172 *Civilisation, dialogue, in/security*

Towards this end, approaching dialogue as ethics *and* epistemology carries significant potential.

My drawing on the critique offered by postcolonial studies to join critical security studies' emphasis on emancipatory practices of security may come across as counter-intuitive. This is because postcolonial interrogations of the 'dark side' of liberal cosmopolitanism are sometimes marshalled to warrant communitarian approaches to security – more specifically, when seeking to give primacy to 'culturalist' approaches to security in/of one's own community (as with civilisational dialogue initiatives) against the more emancipatory approaches to security. In those instances, critiquing the particularity of some forms of universalism is conflated with critiquing the universals – as with criticisms regarding the particularity of prevailing notions of 'human rights' being conflated with criticisms of the notion of universal human rights (see Chapter 2). Such conflation is then used as a stepping-stone to make a case for 'lighter' human rights regimes, as with the calls for 'Dialogue of Civilisations'.

In contrast, emancipatory approaches to security could be attuned to counter both the liberal cosmopolitan, the statist communitarian and 'culturalist' communitarian approaches to security (Burke, 2013, 2015, Bilgin, 2015). For, it is important to underscore that the kind of critique offered by postcolonial studies does not warrant security communitarianism (Grovogui, 2005, 2006, 2011), but calls for expanding cosmopolitanism to incorporate others' conceptions of the international and security.

Notes

1 This section and the following draw upon Bilgin (2012, 2014).
2 On the reception Huntington received in Estonia, see Kuus (2002). On the frequent invocation of Huntingtonian assumptions and arguments during the Bosnian conflict, see Hansen (2000).
3 There is also the tradition of macro-history that has looked at civilisations as unit of analysis.
4 Further information on this initiative is available at http://www.un.org/Dialogue. Accessed 19 September 2011.
5 The former president's dialogue-themed addresses have been removed from the website of the Iranian representation to the UN.
6 For the 'Alliance of Civilisations' initiative, see http://www.unaoc.org. Accessed 17 January 2012.
7 See http://www.mfa.gov.tr/brief-summary-of-the-proceedings-of-the-oic-eu-joint-forum.en.mfa. Accessed 19 September 2011.
8 'PM Erdogan: "We Got The Immorality From The West"', http://www.thememriblog.org/turkey/blog_personal/en/4859.htm. Accessed 19 September 2011.
9 This is a process Ahmet Davutoğlu depicted as *ben-idraki* (self-cognition). See Davutoğlu (1997). Davutoğlu's was a (re)discovery of the self through turning inward but not by finding oneself through the other. The latter form is imagined by Presidents Vaclav Havel and Seyyed Mohammed Khātamī, as told by Petito (2007: 103–126).
10 Also see 'relationist' (Jackson, 1999: 142) and 'dialogical' (Hobson, 2009) accounts.
11 A point made by Ken Booth about the nuclear policies of great powers, see Booth (1999a, 1999b).
12 On Cold War insecurity hierarchies, see Booth (1997) and Tickner (1992).

Bibliography

Al-Azmeh, A. 2012. Civilization, Culture and the New Barbarians. In: Mahdavi, M. & Knight, W. A. (eds.) *Towards the Dignity of Difference: Neither End of History nor Clash of Civilisations*, Farnham, Ashgate.

Bassin, M. 2007. Civilisations and their Discontents: Political Geography and Geopolitics in the Huntington Thesis. *Geopolitics*, 12, 351–374.

Bhabha, H. K. 1994. *The Location of Culture*, London, Routledge.

Bigo, D. 2008. International Political Sociology. In: Williams, P. D. D. (ed.) *Security Studies: An Introduction*, London, Routledge.

Bilgin, P. 2012. Civilisation, Dialogue, Security: The Challenge of Post-secularism and the Limits of Civilisational Dialogue. *Review of International Studies*, 38, 1099–1115.

Bilgin, P. 2014. Dialogue of Civilizations: A Critical Security Studies Perspective. *Perceptions*, 19, 9–24.

Bilgin, P. 2015. Arguing against Security Communitarianism. *Critical Studies on Security*, 3, 176–181.

Booth, K. 1997. Security and Self: Reflections of a Fallen Realist. In: Krause, K. & Williams, M. C. (eds.) *Critical Security Studies: Concepts and Cases*, Minneapolis, University of Minnesota Press.

Booth, K. 1999a. Nuclearism, Human Rights and Constructions of Security (Part 1). *The International Journal of Human Rights*, 3, 1–24.

Booth, K. 1999b. Nuclearism, Human Rights and Contructions of Security (Part 2) *International Journal of Human Rights*, 3, 44–61.

Booth, K. 2007. *Theory of World Security*, Cambridge, Cambridge University Press.

Bowden, B. 2009. *Civilization*, New York, Routledge.

Buck-Morss, S. 2003. *Thinking Past Terror: Islamism and Critical Theory on the Left*, New York, Verso.

Burgess, J. P. 2011. *The Ethical Subject of Security: Geopolitical Reason and the Threat against Europe*, New York, Routledge.

Burke, A. 2013. Security Cosmopolitanism. *Critical Studies on Security*, 1, 13–28.

Burke, A. 2015. Security Cosmopolitanism: The Next Phase. *Critical Studies on Security*, 3, 190–212.

Chiozza, G. 2002. Is There a Clash of Civilizations? Evidence from Patterns of International Conflict Involvement, 1946–1997. *Journal of Peace Research*, 39, 711.

Constantinou, C. 2000. Diplomacy, Grotesque Realism, and Ottoman Historiography. *Postcolonial Studies*, 3, 213–226.

Cooper, H. 2007. Biden Plan for 'Soft Partition' of Iraq Gains Momentum. *New York Times*, 30 July.

Dallmayr, F. (ed.) 2002. *Dialogue Among Civilizations: Some Exemplary Voices*, New York, Palgrave Macmillan.

Davutoğlu, A. 1997. Medeniyetlerin Ben-idraki [Self-cognition of Civilizations]. *Divan İlmi Araştırmalar Dergisi*, 2, 1–53.

Esposito, J. L. & Voll, J. O. 2003. Islam and the West: Muslim Voices of Dialogue. In: Hatzopoulos, P. & Petito, F. (eds.) *Religion in International Relations: The Return from Exile*, London, Palgrave Macmillan.

Gartzke, E. & Gleditsch, K. S. 2006. Identity and Conflict: Ties that Bind and Differences that Divide. *European Journal of International Relations*, 12, 53–87.

174 *Civilisation, dialogue, in/security*

Grovogui, S. N. 2005. The New Cosmopolitanisms: Subtexts, Pretexts and Context of Ethics. *International Relations*, 19, 103–113.

Grovogui, S. N. 2006. Mind, Body, and Gut! Elements of a Postcolonial Human Rights Discourse. In: Jones, B. G. (ed.) *Decolonizing International Relations*, London, Routledge.

Grovogui, S. N. 2011. Looking Beyond Spring for the Season: An African Perspective on the World Order after the Arab Revolt. *Globalizations*, 8, 567–572.

Guillaume, X. 2000. Foreign Policy and the Politics of Alterity: A Dialogical Understanding of International Relations. *Millenium – Journal of International Studies*, 31, 1–26.

Habermas, J. 2006. Religion in the Public Sphere. *European Journal of Philosophy*, 14, 1–25.

Halliday, F. 2006. The End of the Vatican. *openDemocracy*. https://www.opendemocra cy.net/globalization/benedict_4156.jsp Accessed 1 September 2007.

Hansen, L. 2000. Past as Preface: Civilizational Politics and the 'Third' Balkan War. *Journal of Peace Research*, 37, 345–362. http://www.jstor.org/stable/425349.

Henderson, E. A. & Tucker, R. 2001. Clear and Present Strangers: The Clash of Civilizations and International Conflict. *International Studies Quarterly*, 45, 317–338.

Hobson, J. M. 2004. *The Eastern Origins of Western Civilization*, Cambridge, Cambridge University Press.

Hobson, J. M. 2007. Deconstructing the Eurocentric Clash of Civilizations: De-Westernizing the West by Acknowledging the Dialogue of Civilizations. In: Hall, M. & Jackson, P. T. (eds.) *Civilizational Identity: The Production and Reproduction of 'Civilizations' in International Relations*, New York, Palgrave Macmillan.

Hobson, J. M. 2009. The Myth of the Clash of Civilizations in Dialogical-Historical Context. In: Bilgin, P. & Williams, P. D. (eds.) *Global Security, in Encyclopedia of Life Support Systems (EOLSS)*, Oxford, UNESCO, EoLSS Publishers.

Huntington, S. P. 1993. The Clash of Civilizations? *Foreign Affairs*, 72, 22–49.

Huntington, S. P. 1996. *The Clash of Civilizations and the Remaking of World Order*, New York, Simon & Schuster.

Inayatullah, N. & Blaney, D. L. 2004. *International Relations and the Problem of Difference*, London, Routledge.

Jackson, P. T. 1999. 'Civilization' on Trial. *Millennium – Journal of International Studies*, 28, 141–153.

Katzenstein, P. J. 2010. A World of Plural and Pluralist Civilizations: Multiple Actors, Traditions, and Practices. In: Katzenstein, P. J. (ed.) *Civilizations in World Politics: Plural and Pluralist Perspectives*, London & New York, Routledge.

Kratochwil, F. 2005. Religion and (Inter-)national Politics: On the Heuristics of Identities, Structures, and Agents. *Alternatives*, 30, 113–140.

Kuus, M. 2002. European Integration in Identity Narratives in Estonia: A Quest for Security. *Journal of Peace Research*, 39, 91–108.

Lapid, Y. & Kratochwil, F. V. 1996. *The Return of Culture and Identity in IR Theory*, Boulder, CO, Lynne Rienner Publishers.

Ling, L. H. M. 2014. *The Dao of World Politics: Towards a Post-Westphalian, Worldist International Relations*, London, Routledge.

Lynch, M. 2000. The Dialogue of Civilisations and International Public Spheres. *Millenium – Journal of International Studies*, 29.

McGarry, J. 1998. 'Demographic Engineering': The State-Directed Movement of Ethnic Groups as a Technique of Conflict Regulation. *Ethnic and Racial Studies*, 21, 613–638.

McSweeney, B. 1999. *Security, Identity and Interests: A Sociology of International Relations*, Cambridge, Cambridge University Press.

Narayan, U. 2000. Essence of Culture and a Sense of History: A Feminist Critique of Cultural Essentialism. In: Narayan, U. & Harding, S. (eds.) *Decentering the Center: Philosophy for a Multicultural, Postcolonial, and Feminist World*, Bloomington, Indiana University Press.

Neumann, I. B. 1999. *Uses of the Other: 'The East' in European Identity Formation*, Minneapolis, Minnesota University Press.

O'Hagan, J. 1995. Civilizational Conflict? Looking for Cultural Enemies. *Third World Quarterly*, 16, 19–38.

Petito, F. 2007. The Global Political Discourse of Dialogue among Civilizations: Mohammad Khatami and Václav Havel. *Global Change, Peace & Security*, 19, 103–126.

Petito, F. 2009. Dialogue of Civilizations as an Alternative Model for World Order. In: Michael, M. S. & Petito, F. (eds.) *Civilizational Dialogue and World Order: The Other Politics of Cultures, Religions, and Civilizations in International Relations*, New York, Palgrave Macmillan.

Petito, F. 2011. In Defence of Dialogue of Civilizations: With a Brief Illustration of the Diverging Agreement between Edward Said and Louis Masignon. *Millennium – Journal of International Studies*, 39, 759–779.

Pieterse, J. N. 1992. *Emancipations, Modern and Postmodern*, London, Sage Publications Limited.

Said, E. W. 1993. *Culture and Imperialism*, New York, Knopf. Distributed by Random House.

Sen, A. K. 2006. *Identity and Violence: The Illusion of Destiny*, New York, W. W. Norton & Co.

Tickner, J. A. 1992. *Gender in International Relations: Feminist Perspectives on Achieving Global Security*, New York, Columbia University Press.

Walker, R. B. J. 1993. *Inside/Outside: International Relations as Political Theory*, Cambridge, Cambridge University Press.

Weber, C. 2010. *International Relations Theory: A Critical Introduction*, London, Taylor & Francis.

Conclusion

Questions of war, peace and security have been central to the study of IR since its beginnings in different parts of the world. Thinking about world security in ways that are cognisant of and attentive to the multiplicity of inequalities and differences of humankind has taken various forms, including peace and conflict studies, alternative defence thinking, Third World security scholarship, and the World Order Models Project, among others. Over the years, these efforts have culminated in a body of security theorising called critical security studies.[1]

What distinguishes critical security studies approaches to world security from their mainstream counterparts is the former's awareness of and self-reflexive engagement with the latter's limits in responding to our question: *How to think about security in a world characterised by a multiplicity of inequalities and differences.* Over the years, critical IR's engagement with the limits of our theorising about IR and security has proved crucial in opening up space for voices heretofore unheard, thereby generating awareness regarding 'our' relative lack of curiosity about how 'others' approach the international.

This is not to suggest that there previously was no awareness of the existence of multiple ways of approaching the world. The World Order Models Project (WOMP), for instance, originated from its founders' awareness that the Cold War search for 'world order' understood as 'better management of the states system' (which they referred to as 'One World') was not sustainable (Mendlovitz and Walker, 1987).[2] This was partly because such a conception of 'order' marginalised the concerns of a majority of humanity, characterised by a multiplicity of inequalities and differences. The WOMP committee considered the search for 'One World' to be unsustainable also because the two superpowers could not agree on the principles on which to base such an order. The risk being, the search for 'One World' would devolve into 'Two Worlds' hanging in the delicate 'balance' of nuclear weapons. Hence the WOMP Committee's appeal for acknowledging our 'Many Worlds'. The project's rapporteur R.B.J. Walker wrote:

> If global structures are inescapable, and if a just world peace must therefore be a struggle for One World, it must also be remembered that both present structures and future aspirations are encountered and articulated on

Conclusion 177

the basis of many different experiences, many different histories. The pursuit of a just world peace and new forms of solidarity must be rooted in an equal respect for the claims of both diversity and unity. One World must also be Many Worlds.

(Walker 1988: 5)

Writing in the early 1990s, Stephen Chan elucidated what the WOMP perspective meant for IR theory, as discussed in Chapter 3. Reminding his readers of Akira Kurosawa's celebrated film *Rashomon*, which tells its story from several protagonists' different perspectives without privileging either one of their stories or questioning their truthfulness, Chan (1993: 442) suggested that the 'Rashomon condition is the true condition which IR faces'. In a joint piece with Vivienne Jabri, Chan clarified implications of the 'Rashomon Paradigm':

a world of inclusions must take into account that not every epistemology is like ours, and that some are very different because of very different ontologies. Communication, debate, and even explanation are possible. Concurrence of imagination and understanding are not always possible.

(Jabri and Chan, 1996: 110)

But then, where does Chan's metaphor of the 'Rashomon condition' leave us, as students of IR, especially against the background of intensive efforts into studying IR scholarship around the world? As discussed in Chapter 3, such efforts have left us puzzled insofar as IR scholarship in other parts of the world seems to adopt those 'standard' concepts of the field, notwithstanding their well-known limits. Where do we go from here?

In this book, I did not venture outside IR and/or Western Europe and North America in search for 'difference'. Rather, I heeded Edward Said's advice to raise my 'contrapuntal awareness' and study the ways in which the ideas and experiences of humankind are 'connected'. Said wrote:

No one can deny the persisting continuities of long traditions, sustained habitations, national languages, and cultural geographies, but there seems no reason except for fear and prejudice to keep insisting on their separation and distinctiveness, as if that was all human life was about. Survival in fact is about the connections between things.

(Said, 1993: 336)

The point being that, 'others' are not 'out there' to be discovered by travelling elsewhere; they are 'in here', which, in turn, calls for self-discovery.

Following Said, I understood my task as studying how 'others' have been left outside prevailing narratives on IR, *and* the ways in which they have always been present through shaping self/other dialectics, trading goods and ideas, learning and responding. There is a contradiction here, as identified by Pal

178   *Conclusion*

Ahluwalia (also see Chapter 3) in discussing the connections between postcolonialism and post-structuralism:

> The post-colonial origin of deconstruction demonstrates the ambivalence of deconstruction, an ambivalence which hinges on a crucial contradiction – the contradiction between the marginality, and indeed provisionality, of the Algerian experience that seeks to challenge the master discourse of the West, and the simultaneous disavowal of that marginality which puts deconstruction at the centre of European thought.
>
> (Ahluwalia, 2005: 145)

Yet, there is no escaping this 'crucial contradiction' (Ahluwalia, 2005: 145). IR's 'constitutive outside' can only be 'excavated' (Inayatullah and Blaney, 2008) by studying 'the connections between things' (Said, 1993: 336). Indeed, if those critical IR approaches that do acknowledge and address the Eurocentric limits of the field still fail to eschew Eurocentrism, this is because of the paucity of 'our' understanding of IR's 'constitutive outside'. In the absence of sustained research into the ways in which the ideas and experiences of humankind are 'connected', challenging the 'big bangs of IR' (De Carvalho et al., 2011) is likely to remain an uphill struggle.

Thus far, students of critical IR have offered precious little as examples of such communication and connections between world peoples. The WOMP Committee's report entitled *One World, Many Worlds* offered a short section entitled 'Connections', but included only a brief recognition of 'historical debts' communities of peoples have incurred, and almost no discussion on whether any prior communication has taken place between peoples in the emergence of 'many worlds' (Walker, 1988). The contributors to the 'worlding IR' literature have focused on exploring different approaches to the international in different parts of the world as found in IR texts as well as unexpected places of everyday practices (Tickner and Blaney, 2012, 2013, Tickner and Wæver, 2009). However, they have so far had relatively little to offer in terms of exploring the communications and connections of humankind.

That said, the study of communications and connections of humankind is flourishing elsewhere in the social sciences. Such knowledge is offered, among others, by the literary critic and public intellectual Edward Said (1978) who highlighted self/other dialectics of 'Westerners' and 'Orientals' that were constitutive of both; by critical political theorist Susan Buck-Morss (2000, 2009) whose research on 'Hegel and Haiti' highlighted the Haitian slave revolution to be one of the sources of inspiration for Hegel's writings on 'master' and 'slave'; by psychologist Alison Gopnik (2009) who traced the inspiration for David Hume's ideas on empiricism back to Buddhist philosophy, as communicated by the global Jesuit intellectual network during the late seventeenth and early eighteenth century; and by postcolonial IR theorists including Siba Grovogui (2006a, 2006b, 2009), Pal Ahluwalia (2005, Ahluwalia and Sullivan, 2001), Robbie Shilliam (2008, 2009), Tarak Barkawi and Mark Laffey (1999, 2002,

Conclusion 179

2006), who have analysed colonial relations as shaping the ideas and institutions of not only the 'colonised' but also the 'colonisers'.

Chapters 1–3 traced our efforts in addressing IR limits, taking stock and identifying those limits that have been addressed and those that remain. I began by explicitly noting that, notwithstanding decades of efforts into addressing the limits of IR, some remain unconvinced that such an exercise is needed. Indeed, they ask: 'what limit?'. Chapter 1 suggested that if we do not see the limits of our theorising about IR and security this is because we presume that 'we already understand' – through analysing 'their' capabilities based on 'our' assumptions regarding 'their' intentions. While this short-hand expression of Cold War approaches to security may come across as caricaturised, its accuracy was affirmed by Peter Katzenstein who wrote:

> In the context of a bipolar, ideological struggle, the Cold War made relatively unproblematic some of the cultural factors affecting national security. Theories that abstracted from these factors offered important insights.
>
> (Katzenstein, 1996a: 1)

Put differently, Katzenstein, who produced some of the most influential scholarship on the cultural dynamics of security (Katzenstein, 1996b, Katzenstein and Okawara, 2001), seemed to suggest that it was only after the end of the Cold War and the demise of bipolarity that the limits of IR in accessing how the 'others' approach the international and security became evident.

One way of responding to those who ask the 'what limit?' question, I suggested, is to raise our 'contrapuntal awareness' and learn how to identify the limits of our theorising about IR and security. Chapter 1 discussed three such limits: ethnocentrism, parochialism and Eurocentrism. In each section of the chapter I considered one such limit, highlighting its implications for our theorising about security. I concluded by noting that the way in which we ask the 'what limit?' question gives away the ways in which those limits have been constitutive of IR.

Chapter 2 considered how critical theorising about IR and security fared in identifying and addressing the limits of our field. I began by focusing on the question, 'who does the theorising?' – initially raised by K.J. Holsti (1985) and elaborated upon by critical IR scholars. I noted that critical approaches to IR and security have tried to respond to this question by seeking to increase the number of differently situated contributions (i.e. by scholars from outside Western Europe and North America). Yet, I argued, the persistence of Eurocentric limits of IR theorising made apparent the need for inquiring into the constitutive effects of such situatedness.

I suggested that the persistence of Eurocentric limits of IR, notwithstanding the role played by critical IR in opening up the field to allow a variety of voices to be heard, could be viewed as a consequence of the methods adopted by students of critical IR who sought to address IR's limits by reflecting on the geo-cultural situatedness of IR scholars – those who 'founded' the discipline

180   *Conclusion*

and those who were apparently 'absent'. What was left out of the discussions was IR's 'constitutive outside', that is, the ways in which the ideas and experiences of 'others' also shaped IR even as they were not (always) visible in debates.

Chapter 3 considered the efforts of those scholars who got frustrated with the persistence of IR's limits and sought to find out about others' approaches to the international by looking beyond IR as studied in North America and Western Europe. Here I focused on two sets of efforts: (1) those studies that looked at IR scholarship around the world to see how 'others' do IR; (2) those studies that inquired into conceptions of the international as found in texts and contexts outside IR and/or North America and Western Europe. Where the latter set of efforts pointed to a rich potential for thinking 'differently' about the international, the former revealed the persistence of 'standard' concepts and theories of IR outside North America and Western Europe.

That being said, Chapter 3 left us at an apparent impasse. For, it seems that notwithstanding decades of efforts, we still do not know how to access others' conceptions of the international. Needless to say, this is not to underestimate the efforts and noteworthy findings of those who turned to texts and contexts outside IR and/or North America and Western Europe. Rather, it is a plea for studying how IR scholarship beyond North America and Western Europe evolved in a world that is already worlded by IR. Hence the point I underscored that 'others' are not 'out there' to be discovered by travelling elsewhere; they are 'in here', to be excavated for the purposes of self-discovery.

Self-discovery through excavation is what Chapters 4–5 aimed for. I suggested that raising our 'contrapuntal awareness' reminds us that worlding is not only about studying the geo-cultural situatedness of IR scholars (worlding-as-situatedness) but also IR's worlding of the world (worlding-as-constitutive). Through worlding IR in its twofold sense, we learn to inquire into others' conceptions of the international.

Chapter 4 argued that if others' IR scholarship seems to adopt 'standard' concepts and theories of IR notwithstanding their well-known limits, we could take this as the beginning of our analysis. More specifically, I proposed that we read others' IR scholarship as responding to a world that is already worlded by IR. Where reflecting on the situatedness of others' IR scholarship reveals it to be 'almost the same but not quite' (to invoke Homi K. Bhabha's turn of phrase), inquiring into the constitutive effects of such situatedness offers insight into how others' insecurities, which were experienced in a world that is already worlded, have shaped (and have been shaped by) their approaches to the international.

Having offered, in Chapter 4, one way of studying others' IR scholarship to gain insight into their insecurities (security in the international), in the next chapter I pointed to one way of studying 'the international in security', by teasing out others' conceptions of the international from their 'discourses of danger' (Campbell, 1992). In offering this answer, I briefly returned to the 'what limit?' question that I considered in Chapter 1 and highlighted how

Conclusion 181

contrapuntal readings of world politics offer insight into others' insecurities that we presume 'we already understand'.

Chapter 5 turned to postcolonial studies to gain insight into the insecurities of those who are caught up in hierarchies that were built and sustained during the age of colonialism and beyond. Looking at postcolonial studies scholarship on the origins and development of India's nuclear (weapons) programme, I showed how studying the 'discourses of danger' as employed by 'others' allows 'us' to go beyond surface understandings of becoming 'almost the same but not quite' as mere imitation, but understand it as a response to non-military and non-specific insecurities the new entrants to the international society have experienced vis-à-vis 'hierarchy in anarchical society'. Here, I offered the concept of 'hierarchy in anarchical society' as reflecting others' approaches to the international – incorporating the hierarchical, as well as the anarchical and societal aspects of the international as reflected in others' 'discourses of danger'. I illustrated this argument by offering a reading of Turkey's secularisation as part of an attempt to address the non-military and non-specific insecurities the country's early twentieth-century leadership experienced in their encounters with the international society.

As I noted in the Introduction, the building blocks of the answer I offered here are already available to us. Students of critical security studies have focused on the constructedness of insecurities, and pointed to the ways in which one's 'basic ideas about what makes the world go round' (Booth, 2007) shape his/her conceptions of security. However, thinking about security in a world characterised by a multiplicity of inequalities and differences also entails reflecting on others' conceptions of the international as shaped by those 'basic ideas'. Learning from and drawing upon postcolonial studies, I suggested, would allow students of critical security studies to study differences as products of processes that need to be read contrapuntally so as to be able to see relationships of learning and give-and-take between peoples in different parts of the world.

Keeping an open mind about others' conceptions of the international calls for 'contrapuntal awareness' on the part of students of critical theorising about IR and security. As Kimberly Hutchings (2012: 214) argued, 'postcolonial thinking reorients the practice of critical theory by challenging it to take its identification with the subaltern seriously'. Inquiring into the international in security entails students of IR raising their 'contrapuntal awareness' to juxtapose the insights of critical security studies and postcolonial studies, and especially to draw upon the latter's 'contrapuntal readings' of world history and politics.

In Chapter 6 I offered an illustration of what I think is at stake in inquiring into the international in security. The challenge to world security, I suggested, is not only Huntingtonian (1993a, 1996) clash of civilisations scenarios (that have their followers and detractors in IR and world politics). The challenge is all those approaches that view differences as unchanging pre-givens and as yielding insecurities. For, they formulate policies that (re)produce insecurities in the attempt to respond to them. I focused on the Dialogue of Civilisations initiatives to illustrate this point.

182　*Conclusion*

'If not civilisations, what' was Huntington's (1993b) challenge to his critics. There is no denying that Huntington's scenario fed the anxieties of many in the post-Cold War world. These anxieties were further reinforced in the aftermath of the 9/11 attacks. In concluding this study, I took Huntington's challenge seriously and considered his scenario by highlighting the limits of the notion of 'difference' it rests upon (as pre-given and unchanging, and as yielding insecurities). I also drew upon postcolonial studies to offer a critique of both Huntington's approach and that of his dialogue-oriented critics. To reiterate: 'If not civilisations, what?' is not our challenge. Our challenge is thinking about security in a world characterised by a multiplicity of inequalities and differences.

Reflecting on others' conceptions of the international in thinking about world security is not an 'add on' to mainstream security studies analyses of 'their' capabilities based on 'our' assumptions regarding 'their' intentions. Rather, it goes to the heart of the discussions about the limits of our theorising about IR and security. Such limits are shared by the proponents of both the civilisational clash scenarios and their dialogue-oriented critics.

Worlding IR in its twofold meaning (as situatedness and constitutive) helps to underscore the point that dialogical engagements on world security need not venture outside IR and/or the 'West' in search for 'difference'. For, such ventures are likely to reify the West/non-West binary and leave unquestioned prevailing understandings of dialogue, civilisation and security. Beginning from studying 'intertwined and overlapping' histories, however, would allow 'excavating' IR's 'constitutive outside', thereby making room for dialogical engagements on world security.

Notes

1　For an attempt at tracing the beginnings of critical security studies, see Bilgin et al. (1998).
2　For a brief history of the World Order Models Project, see http://www.worldpolicy. org/blog/2012/03/07/world-order-models-project. Accessed 8 October 2013.

Bibliography

Ahluwalia, P. 2005. Out of Africa: Post-structuralism's Colonial Roots. *Postcolonial Studies*, 8, 137–154.

Ahluwalia, P. & Sullivan, M. 2001. Beyond International Relations: Edward Said and the World. In: Crawford, R. A. & Jarvis, D. S. (eds.) *International Relations – Still an American Social Science?: Toward Diversity in International Thought*. Albany, NY, State University of New York Press.

Barkawi, T. & Laffey, M. 1999. The Imperial Peace: Democracy, Force and Globalization. *European Journal of International Relations*, 5, 403–434.

Barkawi, T. & Laffey, M. 2002. Retrieving the Imperial: Empire and International Relations. *Millennium – Journal of International Studies*, 31, 109–127.

Barkawi, T. & Laffey, M. 2006. The Postcolonial Moment in Security Studies. *Review of International Studies*, 32, 329–352.

Bilgin, P., Booth, K. & Wyn Jones, R. 1998. Security Studies: The Next Stage? *Nacao e Defesa*, 84, 137–157.

Booth, K. 2007. *Theory of World Security*, Cambridge, Cambridge University Press.

Buck-Morss, S. 2000. Hegel and Haiti. *Critical Inquiry*, 26, 821–865.

Buck-Morss, S. 2009. *Hegel, Haiti, and Universal History*, Pittsburgh, PA, University of Pittsburgh Press.

Campbell, D. 1992. *Writing Security: United States Foreign Policy and the Politics of Identity*, Manchester, Manchester University Press.

Chan, S. 1993. Cultural and Linguistic Reductionisms and a New Historical Sociology for International Relations. *Millennium – Journal of International Studies*, 22, 423–442.

De Carvalho, B., Leira, H. & Hobson, J. M. 2011. The Big Bangs of IR: The Myths that Your Teachers Still Tell You about 1648 and 1919. *Millennium – Journal of International Studies*, 39, 735–758.

Gopnik, A. 2009. Could David Hume Have Known about Buddhism?: Charles François Dolu, the Royal College of La Flèche, and the Global Jesuit Intellectual Network. *Hume Studies*, 35, 5–28.

Grovogui, S. N. 2006a. *Beyond Eurocentrism and Anarchy: Memories of International Order and Institutions*, New York, Palgrave Macmillan.

Grovogui, S. N. 2006b. Mind, Body, and Gut! Elements of a Postcolonial Human Rights Discourse. In: Jones, B. G. (ed.) *Decolonizing International Relations*, London, Routledge.

Grovogui, S. N. 2009. No More, No Less: What Slaves Thought about their Humanity. In: Bhambra, G. K. & Shilliam, R. (eds.) *Silencing Human Rights: Critical Engagements with a Contested Project*. Basingstoke, Palgrave.

Holsti, K. J. 1985. *The Dividing Discipline: Hegemony and Diversity in International Theory*, Boston, Allen & Unwin.

Huntington, S. P. 1993a. The Clash of Civilizations? *Foreign Affairs*, 72, 22–49.

Huntington, S. P. 1993b. If Not Civilizations, What? Paradigms of the Post-Cold War World. *Foreign Affairs*, 72, 186–194.

Huntington, S. P. 1996. *The Clash of Civilizations and the Remaking of World Order*, New York, Simon & Schuster.

Hutchings, K. 2012. Turning Towards the World: Practicing critique in IR. In: Brincat, S., Lima, L. & Nunes, J. (eds.) *Critical Theory in International Relations and Security Studies*, London, Routledge.

Inayatullah, N. & Blaney, D. L. 2008. International Relations from Below. In: Reus-Smit, C. & Snidal, D. (eds.) *Oxford Handbook of International Relations*, Oxford: Oxford University Press.

Jabri, V. & Chan, S. 1996. The Ontologist Always Rings Twice: Two More Stories about Structure and Agency in Reply to Hollis and Smith. *Review of International Studies*, 22, 107–110.

Katzenstein, P. J. 1996a. Alternative Perspectives on National Security In: Katzenstein, P. J. (ed.) *The Culture of National Security: Norms and Identity in World Politics*, New York, Columbia University Press.

Katzenstein, P. J. (ed.) 1996b. *The Culture of National Security: Norms and Identity in World Politics*, New York, Columbia University Press.

Katzenstein, P. J. & Okawara, N. 2001. Japan, Asian-Pacific Security, and the Case for Analytical Eclecticism. *International Security*, 26, 153–185.

Mendlovitz, S. H. & Walker, R. B. J. 1987. *Towards a Just World Peace: Perspectives from Social Movements*, London, Boston, Butterworths.

184 *Conclusion*

Said, E. W. 1978. *Orientalism*, London, Penguin.

Said, E. W. 1993. *Culture and Imperialism*, New York, Knopf.

Shilliam, R. 2008. What the Haitian Revolution Might Tell Us about Development, Security, and the Politics of Race. *Comparative Studies in Society and History*, 50, 778–808.

Shilliam, R. 2009. The Enigmatic Figure of the Non-Western Thinker in International Relations. *Antepodium* [Online]. Available: http://www.victoria.ac.nz/atp/articles/pdf/Shilliam-2009.pdf Accessed 27/01/2014.

Tickner, A. B. & Blaney, D. (eds.) 2012. *Thinking International Relations Differently*, London, Routledge.

Tickner, A. B. & Blaney, D. (eds.) 2013. *Claiming the International*, London: Routledge.

Tickner, A. B. & Wæver, O. (eds.) 2009. *International Relations Scholarship Around the World*, London, Routledge.

Walker, R. B. J. 1988. *One World, Many Worlds: Struggles for a Just World Peace*, Boulder, CO, Lynne Rienner.

Index

Abraham, I. 8, 129–133
Acharya, A. 23, 45, 52, 69, 85, 87–8, 95, 101
Africa 31–32, 56, 86, 94, 96, 136; *see also* South Africa
agency 62, 110, 163; postcolonial 9, 45, 54–5, 57–8, 109, 115, 118, 139, 152–3; women's 65, 67–9
Ahluvalia, P. 42, 56, 110–1, 178
Alker, Hayward 5, 22, 34, 52–3, 171
Alternatives, the journal 70
Amin, S. 26–8
anarchical society 8, 129, 133–9, 150; hierarchy in anarchical society 8, 118, 129, 133–8, 151–2, 181
anarchy 1, 92, 106, 118, 129, 161; *see also* anarchical society
anthropology 17, 45, 66, 94
anti-Eurocentric: critique 4, 57, 65, 71n16; Eurocentrism 30
area studies 21, 65, 130
Asia 52, 67, 87–8, 94, 100, 151
Ayoob, M. 26, 30, 121

Barkawi, T. 4, 24–5, 30–2, 35, 70n3, 178
Beier, M. 92–4
Bhabha, H. 9n3, 107, 113, 118, 122, 180
Bhambra, G. 9n3, 29, 47–8, 54–5, 152n7
Biersteker, T. J. 22, 34n5, 41, 43
Bigo, D. 9n2, 59, 160
Blaney, D. 23–4, 100
Bleiker, R. 90–2, 101n8
Booth, K. 9n2, 18–20, 30, 34n1, 46, 51–53, 66, 71n9, 71n11, 171, 172n11
Bourdieu, P. 56–7, 71n16
Buck-Morss, S. 29, 47, 171, 178
Bull, H. 133–135
Buzan, B. 9n2, 27, 30, 35n11, 60–6, 85, 87–8, 95, 101n12, 108

capitulations 146–7 *see also* extraterritoriality treaties
Chan, S. 69, 86–7, 90–2, 100n1, 100n6, 100n7, 114–16, 177
China 23, 85–7, 100n3, 109, 113–18, 122, 135
civilisation 8, 96, 108, 133, 159–72, clash of 8, 159–72, 181–2; contemporary, in the discourses of Turkey's leaders 142, 145–50; standard of 2, 118, 133–8, 142, 145–6, 150, 159–72
cold war 19–20, 25, 31, 44, 59, 61, 86, 109–10, 118–122, 161, 170, 172n12, 176, 179
colonialism 5, 8, 52, 54, 128, 134, 138, 181; neo- 53; *see also* postcolonialism
connected histories 29, 111, 152n7; *see also* universal history
constitutive outside 4–5, 7, 24, 42, 45, 49, 54, 57, 59–60, 84, 94–5, 98–100, 111, 178, 180, 182
constructivism 70n4
contrapuntal: awareness 5, 6, 17, 32, 53, 57, 69, 162, 177, 179–181; reading 4–5, 10n9, 29, 53, 69, 162–163, 165, 167–168, 181
contrapuntality 5–6, 8, 51, 160, 167, 181
critical IR 5–7, 10n10, 33–34, 41–72, 86–7, 90, 99, 107–108, 129, 171, 176, 178–9; *see also* Frankfurt School, post-structuralism, feminism
critical security studies 1–2, 4–6, 9n2, 41–72, 160–72, 176, 181; *see also* Frankfurt School approaches to security thinking, post-structuralist approaches to security, feminist approaches to security

186 *Index*

culturalism 28, 96, 163, 169, 172
culture 3–6, 8–9, 17, 19–21, 23–24, 26,
  28, 42, 44, 52, 56, 64–66, 68, 86,
  94–95, 97, 99, 108, 136–7, 142, 149,
  161, 163–166, 177, 179; of insecurity 4

Davison, A. 137, 142–3, 145, 152n5,
  152n10
Democracy 24–5, 168
democratic peace 24–5, 35n6
deterrence: theorising 19–22;
  policymaking 34n2, 130
development 29, 121, 131, 137, 142–5,
  151; under- 121
Dialogue of Civilisations 8, 159–172
difference 1–5, 26, 32, 34, 52–6, 64–6,
  68, 71n19, 85–100, 106, 110–15, 118,
  120, 123, 128, 134, 137, 139–140,
  146, 148–9, 151, 159–163, 167–71,
  176–82; temporalising 2, 136–8
differently different 117–18, 120–2, 139,
  146, 148, 151
Dirlik, A. 34, 69–70, 88, 114
Dussel, E. 47, 49–50, 71n7

emancipation 46, 51–52, 58, 171
emancipatory approaches to security 5,
  46–7, 51–3, 58, 172
empire 108, 133, 136
emulation 8; unthinking 106–10, 114, 151
English School, the 8, 22, 28, 70n4, 114,
  133–4, 150
Enloe, C. 1, 2, 64–7, 138, 143
epistemology 5, 8, 22–23, 25–6, 42, 66–67,
  86–89, 91–2, 96, 160, 165–6, 171–2, 177
ethnocentrism 16–22, 28, 32, 41, 52,
  99, 179
ethnography 93–4
Eurocentrism 7, 16, 26–32, 53, 55, 57,
  62, 65, 68–9, 70n4, 84, 108, 129, 163,
  171, 178–9; see also anti-Eurocentric
Europe 26–31, 44–9, 54–7, 60, 62–3,
  85–6, 95, 108, 113–14, 118, 121,
  133–8, 144–8, 151, 162, 168, 171
extraterritoriality treaties 135–6, 144, 146;
  see also capitulations

feminist: IR 9, 33, 64–6, 71n19, 71n20,
  71n21, 110; approaches to security
  66–9; see also postcolonial feminism
Foucault, M. 54–5
Frankfurt School: of IR 46–51, 71n5,
  71n11, 71n18, 171; approaches to
  security 51–3, 71n8, 71n18, 182n1

gender 33, 43, 64–9, 110
geo-cultural 3, 30, 42–5, 47, 57, 85–9,
  92, 96, 99–100, 100n5, 101n9, 110–1,
  175, 180
geo-cultural epistemologies 44, 88,
  100n5, 111
Global Society, the journal 90, 100n7
global South, the 2, 5, 8, 9n4, 93,
  109–110, 119, 121–122
Grovogui, S. 27, 47–53, 136–7, 171–2, 178

Habermas, J. 47, 170
Hall, S. 4–5, 42
Halperin, S. 28–29, 55–6, 108, 151
Hansen, L. 30, 35n11, 67–9, 172n2
Havel, V. 162, 172n9
hierarchy 1–2, 7–8, 23, 68, 92–3, 118,
  128–9, 133, 135–7, 151, 152n1, 170,
  172n12, 181, in anarchy 135–8; see also
  hierarchy in anarchical society
Hobson, J. M. 2, 27, 7, 66, 118, 138, 168,
  172n10
Holsti, K. J. 26, 41, 44, 179
human rights 33, 47–50, 60, 168, 172
Huntington, S. J. 8, 159–72, 181–2
Hutchings, K. 6, 10n10, 46, 57, 72n21, 181

imperial 27, 52, 54, 57, 90, 134, 136–137
Inayatullah, N. 23–4, 42, 169, 178
India 23–4, 63, 129–33, 138–9, 151,
  153n11, 164, 168, 181
inequality 1–2, 4–6, 41, 118, 128, 133,
  138, 151, 159–60, 176, 181–2
insecurity: constructedness of 4; gendered
  66–69; non-specific 8; see also postcolonial insecurities
intellectuals 6, 7n10, 161
International Security, the journal 25
international society 8, 24, 28, 70n4,
  131–152, 181
Iran 33–34, 55, 86, 161–2, 168, 172n5

Jabri V. 45, 50, 54–5, 57–60, 65–6,
  71n20, 100n1, 100n6, 134, 177
Jahn, B. 23–4, 48–9
Japan 28, 85, 91, 135, 151
Jones, C. 90–2, 99

Khātamī, M. 161–2, 164, 166
knowledge 6, 27, 29, 32, 43, 53, 56, 61,
  66–7, 88, 91–3, 95–6, 109–10, 116,
  137, 166, 169, 178; sociology of 3;
  politics of 3; also see sociology of IR
Krishna, S. 10n7, 50, 54, 56–8, 151

Laffey, M. 25, 30–1, 178
Latin America 63, 100n5

MccGwire, M. 20–1
Methods 5, 10n9, 24, 49, 59, 67–8,
  72n22, 93–94, 179
Middle East 16–17, 35n13, 55, 71n10,
  119, 121
Millennium, the journal 64–65, 71–72n20,
  84–86
mimicry 56; *see also* unthinking emulation
modernity 5, 9n3, 48–9, 52–8, 94–6, 118,
  132, 152n7, 153n19, 163
multiple complex inequalities 4
multiple modernities 56, 152n3, 152n7
Murphy, C. 1, 33, 43, 64

Narayan, U. 3, 90, 99
NATO 44, 118–121
non-Western 6–7, 52, 55–7, 65, 87,
  90, 100n7, 135, 161, 168; IR 69,
  86–7, 114; thought 7, 23, 52, 89–90,
  94–8, 100
nuclear: proliferation 138; strategy 20–1,
  172n11; weapons 8, 19, 128–33, 138,
  151, 170, 176, 181

ontology 5, 67, 86–91, 168, 170, 177
Oriental, the 18, 178
Orientalism 52
Ottoman Empire 35n8, 135, 140–8,
  153n18, 167

parochialism 1, 18, 22–6, 32, 34n5, 35n6,
  41, 179
particular v. universal: and India's
  nuclear program 130; and Turkey's
  secularisation 138–42
particularity of IR's approach to the
  international 1–2, 21, 24–5; 28, 31,
  45–6, 50, 70, 91, 106, 108, 112, 130,
  159–60, 172; of Enlightenment ideas
  46–9; of the Third World 27
Pasha, M. K. 1, 87, 95, 111
patriarchal bargain 68–9
patriarchy: *see* patriarchal bargain
Pettmann, J. J. 5, 52–3, 64–6, 72n22, 110
political, the 1, 3, 45, 53–4, 57, 90,
  94–5, 112
politics of theorising 61–3, 66, 71n18
positivism 3, 34n5, 41, 43, 67, 91, 113
postcolonial, the 8–9, 57–59, 118,
  129–130; critics 8–9, 32–4, 41, 47–8,
  50–52, 58, 62, 65; feminism 66; IR

10n7, 56, 168; insecurities 130–1;
  studies 1, 3–8, 9n3, 17, 32–34, 42, 53,
  56, 110–12, 118, 128, 133, 136, 151,
  160, 162, 165, 172, 181;
postcolonialism 5, 42, 56, 118, 178
post-structuralism 42, 111, 178; in IR
  53–59, 71n13; in security studies 59–64
power 1, 8–9, 17–18, 23, 30–31, 43,
  53–54, 57–58, 61–2, 66–8, 89,
  129–130, 143–4; balancing 16–17; and
  knowledge 53, 169;
practice 19, 30, 43, 46, 50–54, 56,
  59–60, 62, 64, 67, 70, 90, 92–98, 113,
  133, 141; colonial 4, 29, 90; gendered
  43; representational 42; theory and
  50–51, 180–181; of everyday life 7,
  43, 92–95

race: in IR 152n2; in world order
  57–8, 138
referents of security ;31, 61, 139,
  152n8, 168–70; non-state 50, 162,
  168–170
reflexive; 51, 109, 165; non- 170;
  self- 43, 53, 176

Said, E. W.2–6, 9n3, 10n8, 27–9, 57,
  71n16, 96, 110–12, 136, 167, 177–8
secular: criticism 111; interpretation 6;
  thinkers 52
secularisation 152n3; in Turkey 8, 129,
  138–53,
securitisation theory 59–64, 71n18
security: national 31, 67, 89, 106–7, 110,
  119–20, 131–2, 139, 179; world 1–4,
  8, 25, 50–1, 160–2, 169, 176, 181–2;
  Third World 71n11
Shilliam, R. 27, 47–8, 94–9, 178
similarity: production of 99, 121, 128,
  145, 147–50; in IR theorizing 2, 7,
  106, 113, 116, 118, 122–3, 151
Smith, K. 94–6
Smith, S. 22, 41, 43, 100n1, 100n6
sociology 17, 44, 54, 116; of IR 3, 65,
  109, 111, 113; of science 4, 66, 88
South Africa 10, 71, 85, 96, 112–3
Soviet Union 19–21, 115, 131
Spivak, G. 9n3, 57, 65, 93, 112, 123n8
standard of civilisation 2, 118, 133–8,
  145–6, 150
standard: concepts and theories of IR 1–2,
  7, 26, 32, 84, 96, 98–9, 106–8, 114,
  117–22, 128–9, 131, 177, 180;
  textbooks 95

188 *Index*

state of nature 23–24
state: Third World 26, 32, 115, 134–5; -centric 31, 67, 71n12, 107, 110, 119–20, 131, 170
statehood 29, 31, 97, 120–1, 132–3, 136, 151–2
strategic essentialism 50, 57–8
subaltern, the 181; realism 26
Suzuki, S. 8, 28, 133–5

temporality: see temporalising difference
the international 1–5, 16, 23, 32, 45–6, 52–3, 55–6, 58–60, 64–6, 69, 70n4, 84, 87–100, 100n5, 106–23, 130, 133, 135, 137–9, 143–52, 153n12, 153n19, 159–60, 163, 169, 172, 176, 178–82
theory and practice 43, 50–1; in strategy 19; *see also* constitutive theory
Third World 9, 26, 29–32, 93–7, 112, 115, 119, 121: scholarship 93–5
Thomas, C. 26, 31–2
Three World Theory, China's 115–7
Tickner, A. B. 2, 10n6, 63, 72n22, 85–9, 92–5, 99, 100n5, 100n10
Tickner, J. A. 64, 67, 70n2, 172n12
travelling theory 2–3
Turkey 24, 63, 71n18, 109, 113, 117–122, 123n2, 138–52, 159, 162, 169, 181

ubuntu 94–6
United States 22, 30–1, 34n3, 34n5, 45, 53, 85, 109, 114–16, 119, 121–2, 131, 139, 171
universal history 29; *see also* connected histories
universalism 22, 45, 47–8, 50, 130, 160, 172; IR's claim of 2, 7, 20, 22, 86–7, 106–8, 110, 122, 138–9
universals 46–53, 172

Vale, P. 26, 85, 112–13
violence 58, 91, 133, 160; epistemic 112

Wæver, O. 3–4, 9n2, 10n6, 35n10, 44, 59–63, 69, 71n18, 72n22, 85, 87–9, 99, 100n5, 111
Walker, R. B. J. 2–3, 9n2, 43, 59, 70n1, 71n13, 113, 176–8
war 21, 25, 30–3, 39–41, 109, 114–17, 160, 163; Iraq 159, 165, 176; limited 20; Vietnam 18
Western 6, 9–10n4, 24, 47–50, 54–5, 87, 94–9, 132, 141, 163, 168–16 171
World Order Models Ppoject (WOMP) 71n11, 176–8
worlding 3, 7, 30, 65, 72n22, 110–13; IR 1–3, 7, 30, 32, 42, 47, 54, 58–9, 64, 72n22, 88, 99–100, 106–8, 110, 123, 178, 180–2
Wyn Jones R. 51, 71n11

Printed in the United States
By Bookmasters